New Yorkers

New Yorkers

A City and Its People in Our Time

Craig Taylor

W. W. NORTON & COMPANY
Independent Publishers Since 1923

For information about permission to reproduce selections from this book, write to
Permissions, W. W. Norton & Company, Inc., 500 Fifth Avenue, New York, NY 10110

For information about special discounts for bulk purchases, please contact
W. W. Norton Special Sales at specialsales@wwnorton.com or 800-233-4830

Manufacturing by LSC Communications, Harrisonburg
Production manager: Beth Steidle

Library of Congress Cataloging-in-Publication Data

Names: Taylor, Craig, 1976– author.
Title: New Yorkers : a city and its people in our time / Craig Taylor.
Description: First edition. | New York, NY : W. W. Norton & Company, [2021] |
Includes index.
Identifiers: LCCN 2020051546 | ISBN 9780393242324 (hardcover) |
ISBN 9780393242331 (epub)
Subjects: LCSH: City and town life—New York (State)—New York—Anecdotes. |
New York (N.Y.)—Social life and customs—21st century—Anecdotes. | New York (N.Y.)—
History—21st century—Anecdotes. | New York (N.Y.)—Biography—Anecdotes.
Classification: LCC F128.36 .T39 2021 | DDC 974.7—dc23
LC record available at https://lccn.loc.gov/2020051546

W. W. Norton & Company, Inc., 500 Fifth Avenue, New York, N.Y. 10110
www.wwnorton.com

W. W. Norton & Company Ltd., 15 Carlisle Street, London W1D 3BS

1 2 3 4 5 6 7 8 9 0

For my father, who made the journey.

What a strange, what a fantastic city . . . there was something here that one experienced nowhere else on earth. Something one loved intensely. What was it? Crossing the streets—standing on the street corners with the crowds: what was it that induced this special climate of the nerves . . . a peculiar sense of intimacy, friendliness, being here with all these people and in this strange place . . . They touched your heart with tenderness and you felt yourself a part of the real flight and flutter—searching their faces, speculating about their dooms and destinies.

—ISABEL BOLTON, *DO I WAKE OR SLEEP*

Contents

PART TWO

Introduction

One night, on a Manhattan-bound F train, a man pushed his way past me. He stumbled, grabbed at a pole for balance, grabbed at it again, succeeded, stood for a few moments, and finally sat. He placed one hand on a yellow plastic seat, stared at it, and said, "More pain." The man lifted his head and addressed a stranger standing nearby: "More pain," he said. When the doors opened at East Broadway I stepped out before More Pain Man was pushed onto the platform by the stranger, who followed him for a few steps and kept repeating the words "I don't want to fight you" before his friends pulled him back onto the F. The train left the station. Now alone, More Pain Man stood on the platform. It was late. The station was empty, so the acoustics were perfect when he yelled out those same words—a description of what he had already received or a demand for the future, I wasn't sure.

More life, I'd been told when I arrived in New York, and more *of* life. You will hold the inside doorknob of your apartment—I was told—and you will think to yourself, *Get ready to enter the oceanic power*. It's no use arguing with it. It's no use doing anything but relenting, letting it hit you, moving with that force. In New York you will always get more.

New York meant more of everything. More joy, more sorrow, more pleasure, more pain. More experience, more possibilities to find love, more wealth, and a poverty with more of a sharp, punitive edge. Even if, statistically, New York was now smaller than Baoding and Tianjin and Hyderabad and many others, it still overwhelmed in its old familiar ways. More awe as the skyline rose, more moments of incredulity as light flooded down the canyon of an avenue, and more disgust at what looked to be grease smeared on the back of an Elmo costume in Times Square. More Elmos. More actual height could be found in the skyscrapers of Kuala Lumpur. Still, it just felt like the city held *more*: more elevators, more LED lights, more nail salons, more rats, more bridges.

Over the course of my years in New York, I felt that pain, but also enveloping love, and I got caught up in more diversion than expected. I was awed by what was endlessly offered up. I loved the concentrate; I loved the proximity to strangers, how every day you were inches from weirdness, greatness, and everything in between. It was the greatest ongoing flicker of human life I'd ever encountered. Something or someone came at you in each moment, and what you got, in interactions with the city, was a consistent assault on the senses. Your senses were worked and exercised and reworked every day. I loved the endless sense of "and-this"-ness: this man, and this woman, and this look, and this detail, and this necklace on that cyclist, and this and this—a richness that sank down beneath you 'till it hit the serpentinite and schist, the Fordham gneiss and Inwood marble and Hartland formation. Until that point, there was always more. And then you crossed to the next block and started the process all over again. *This and this and this.*

ALL OF IT WAS NEW to me when I moved to New York in January 2014 to start reporting *New Yorkers*. I had spent the previous decade researching, reporting, and writing two books about other places. They were based on my experiences interviewing a wide array of people to get a feel for their lives, their work, and the places they made. For the first one, *Return to Akenfield*, I had spent a couple months in an English village with hunters, farmers, apple pickers, priests, publicans, teachers and shopkeepers, commuters and retirees, and a gnarled old rag-rug maker, all in an effort to capture rural life a generation after Ronald Blythe's classic 1969 book, *Akenfield*. As a follow-up I spent five years walking the streets and squares of London, interviewing Londoners. The book that resulted, *Londoners*, presented a contemporary portrait of the city from more than eighty voices, street sweepers to investment bankers, a manicurist to a dominatrix.

Neither of those books were about places I'd grown up knowing;

I had moved to London from a seaside village in western Canada. But not knowing a place, not being of a place, left a space for others to step forward to explain. I imagined there would be no lack of candor. I only knew that I wanted to craft a book about New York in the twenty-first century, filled with the voices and sounds and places and people of New York, the life of the city *right now*. A book that would capture the richness of its conversation, the complaints and quiet admissions of a city in flux; and one that would weave together the voices of an enormously diverse city: people from every borough, the rich and the poor, young and old, immigrant voices and native, those emboldened by the city as well as those who'd felt its sharp edge.

It takes one proof of address to get a New York Public Library card. Mine allowed me to keep going back to James Baldwin and Joseph Mitchell and Vivian Gornick and Jacob Riis, Marianne Moore and Edith Wharton and Langston Hughes, Jane Jacobs, Frank O'Hara, Bernard Malamud, Oscar Hijuelos, and Ralph Ellison. I had my own copy of Robert Caro's *The Power Broker* and was told that some people couldn't travel with such an enormous book on the subway, so they cut it into thirds. The first incision should be made at page 359, the second at page 828. I kept mine whole.

I was also surrounded by the excellent writing about New York City that comes out every month, every week, every day, every few minutes in the stack of remaining hometown newspapers and magazines, in the *New York Times* Metro section, as well as the eruption of superb reporting online and on the radio and the commentary that unfurled on the social media feeds of observant New Yorkers. All of this work is vital, intimidating, often entertaining, but I wanted to find something more direct, and to create a kind of oral portrait of the city grounded in the flow of New Yorkers' speech.

I took my cue from writers who had walked the streets and done the legwork. From Riis's reports from the filth and degradation of tenement blocks in *How the Other Half Lives*, and from E. B. White's *Here Is New York* a half century later, in which he wrote about "strangers who have pulled up stakes somewhere and come to town, seeking sanctuary or fulfillment or some greater or lesser grail." These seekers teemed through New York in the hot summer of 1948 when White wrote the piece; they still fill the sidewalks. It was these sidewalks that seemed to usher forth conversation. I liked books where you could almost see New York conversation rising from the pavement. I started walking the city, and then I started walking with other people, and got to feel the incantatory power of New York sidewalks. In one of my many guides, *The Odd Woman and the City*, Vivian Gornick endlessly walks the streets of New York with her mother because they visit best by walking. "Walking brings out the best in us." And then there was the lesson from Joseph Mitchell, whose extraordinary work simply says, in that quiet, persistent voice: *Go out into the city and listen.*

I'd enter all these redolent New Yorks of Gay Talese or Sharifa Rhodes-Pitts, feel the frustration of not having gotten here earlier, and mourn my inability to experience the same city. It was overwhelming, even dispiriting, but then I'd say fuck it—even the greats had not gotten *this* New York. This afternoon in Brownsville or Bensonhurst, this person, this moment in their life, this enthusiasm, this incarnation of a grievance, these words. I took it as my task to capture this particular moment of New York.

And what a strange and wonderful moment. When I arrived, totems of New York for decades (Times Square, the taxicab, "Don't Honk" signs) were being transformed, and there were monumental physical changes to New York City's infrastructure—the High Line, the World Trade Center site, the new arena and development in downtown Brooklyn, the East Side subway, the revitalization of the waterfront throughout the city. And then there were the more subtle but no less dramatic demographic changes, as gentrification accelerated and the ethnic composition of the city changed. When I moved to New York, it had recently become a majority nonwhite city.

I wanted to create a book that reflected these physical and demographic changes. But I also wondered how the psyche of New York itself was changing, and particularly how it had been affected by the dramatic convulsions in its recent history: the terrorist attacks of 2001, the blackout of 2003, Hurricane Sandy in 2012, the police killing of Eric Garner in 2014 ... and then the pandemic, quarantine, and Black Lives Matter protests of 2020 hit. In New York that March, as I scrambled to talk with many of my sources, the city seemed very dark indeed. On a bus in Flushing, I watched a man retrieve his hand from a strap and douse his palm with sanitizer, most of which slithered onto his shoes. More cleanliness. More fear. Each day there were more sirens, and they seemed to grow longer and louder. Every day the ballet of the sidewalks changed. Some people had started reciting Psalm 23 while washing their hands; others sang "Blitzkrieg Bop." Interviewees working in hospitals described a new jitteriness. Black SUVs started slinking out of town, but the FreshDirect delivery guys couldn't escape. "What if Yankee Stadium becomes a hospital?" someone asked. A woman working at Best Buy said people were "loading up on as much screen as they could."

When the restaurants closed, the variety of explanations posted to the doors was another example of the profusion of voice in New York—handwritten or printed on corporate letterhead; ironic, defiant, or just sad beyond belief. A doctor told me he'd seen patients who were hallucinating as a symptom, as if we all weren't hallucinating, as if the sight of a hospital ship off Manhattan wasn't from an alternate reality abutting our own. I feared for my list of interviewees. Before long I received an email from one of them with the subject line: *Something for the book.* He was in the hospital with the coronavirus, he said. "Stay tuned," he wrote.

OVER THE COURSE OF six years I spoke to more than 180 New Yorkers. Some spoke to me briefly; others kept the conversation going for years. I ended up filling 71 notebooks and just under 400 hours of tape. I spent what seemed like days on the subway. I cadged rides and caught the odd taxi when I was late, sweaty, confused. I tried to find logic in the streets of Queens. I apologized profusely for miscalculating how long it took to get to the Rockaways. Mainly I walked and walked and walked. Near the end of the project I snapped my right Achilles tendon and wondered if it had been from overuse.

I was drawn to talkers of all sorts. Who would be better at revealing the churn of the city's past, the variety of its present, and the unknown of its future, than those working to make the city run? I steered clear of commentators, pundits, personalities, functionaries, PR flacks, and city hall reps—the kind of people the writer Iain Sinclair once described as "those ironed faces schooled in saying nothing at great length."

Everyone wanted to show me how many people they knew, whom they'd collected, who would talk. "You know who would talk?" they'd say, pushing another name on me. They wanted to demonstrate the richness of their New York, they wanted to show their broad and varied city, how many social lines could be easily crossed, or how deep into their own social strata they could dig. "I was just thinking," said one woman, emerging from a reverie, "of all the wonderful people I know. It's not a bad way to spend some time."

I chased leads, I talked to strangers, I hung around, I wandered across the boroughs. I set up countless meetings with people in the nonphotogenic New York: in Champs Bar in Penn Station, at the throbbing McDonald's on Southern Boulevard in the South Bronx, outside the Chuck E. Cheese at Barclays Center in Brooklyn. I'd enter into a conversation in the M&M's store in Times Square, the TGI Fridays near Wall Street, Starbucks everywhere. This type of nowhere New York seemed to be always expanding to meet me.

Often, the blander the place we'd meet, the more interesting the person and the stories they'd tell. I'd start with pleasantries in a chain café, and soon both more of the person and more of the city would be revealed. We'd progress to deeper conversation at Elias Corner in Astoria, or revelation with a rich pasta sauce at Manducati's in Long Island City. Even in the blandest spaces, unexpected language would fly from someone's mouth. Sometimes the backdrops brought the individuals more vividly into focus. In New York, I was told by an ex-cabbie, the people are the texture. I kept coming back to that line. I learned to believe it.

I was led into experiences. I held a rope connected to a giant balloon and walked down Fifth Avenue in the Macy's Thanksgiving Day Parade. I ate a sandwich at a table covered with multivitamins and composition books in a redecorated room at the Chelsea Hotel, talked to a woman whose son was in trouble while she packed condoms into a safe-sex kit at a safe injection site in Washington Heights. "I'm going to take you on a series of tours," a personal injury lawyer from Queens said, and I spent hours in the passenger seat of his minivan. "Here's the name of the church in Fort Greene," I was told. "Be outside at 9." I said yes to it all. *Yep, I can find that car dealership in the Rockaways; I'll see you there.* Stuff happened in one day that couldn't have happened in the same day anywhere else.

I told the New Yorkers I talked to: *You get to say what you want, it's your view of the city I want.* At a party a woman asked me, "So, are you looking for boldface names?" The person next to her said, "No, he's looking for the lightly italicized." Every day that seemed more apt. I loved listening to people explain what they do—the lightly italicized ways a city makes and remakes itself every day.

THE NEW YORKERS I spoke to did their self-mythologizing on the go. They watched their life, related their life, made sure it was already a story, almost before the moment was done. I was in New York to listen to people, but in New York, listening is more like feeling sound surge past. You grab and corral what is spoken. I encountered the opposite of reticence: assertion, self-possession, volume. In New York, it takes very little to bring on the onrush, and I'd marvel at the velocity with which people spoke, the mere speck of time it took for interviewees to get into the personal.

I'd put down a little Edirol recorder and let it go, sometimes for hours. Conversations were set down and logged and the audio was typed up. Those transcriptions contained the interviews, but unlike in London, there were many interjections, dutifully picked up by the mic. This city barged into conversations, people slid in because they couldn't sit nearby in silence. "I was just listening to what you said about radio stations in New York," one woman said from the next table over in a café. She couldn't help herself. "Just call me Girl in Café," she said. "I want to be known as Girl in Café."

In many cases the interviewee peered back at the interviewer. "So, what about you?" the Orthodox lice consultant asked me as she went about her work. "Tell us about yourself." New Yorkers challenged me in ways Londoners never did. Race was not an afterthought or a submerged current; it was right there. "How is your white skin feeling today?" I was asked. "Who are you to ask me that question?" and "How do you expect to understand this as a white man?" and "No offense but *¿Cómo puedo transmitir lo que es esta ciudad a alguien que no es de El Salvador?*"

From the start I wondered who even gets to be called a New Yorker. I figured it was the decision of the interviewees to make, not mine. Some had just arrived; others knew no other place. "One belongs to New York instantly," was the opinion of Tom Wolfe, "one belongs to it as much in five minutes as in five years." Sure. But some shrugged off the term. Others felt the label would never apply to them. Maybe their children would call themselves New Yorkers, or Americans. Some thought they'd lost their right to it, or they were uninterested. They just wanted to get on with their work.

London had insinuated like damp; New York hit. It celebrated hitters. One of my first interviews took place at Jimmy's Corner in midtown, a bar whose walls are covered with photos of the best. In my new apartment building, the faded clippings taped to the side of the boiler were Gary Carter, Darryl Strawberry, Reggie Jackson, Alex Rodriguez with an X across his face. On the streets outside, New York unapologetically hit: wind to face, garbage to nose.

SOME 75 NEW YORKERS appear in *New Yorkers*. I was surprised by how many of them told me they could teach me something. Sometimes the lesson was practical: how to recycle cans, how to steal a car, how to walk the crowded sidewalks without bumping into anyone.

But often it was something profound: how to be compassionate, how to live artfully, how to live an uncompromising life. The advice may have been particular to this city, but a New York life well lived was an accomplishment like no other.

Many of them told me I'd missed the real New York—by a couple years, or by a decade, or by several decades. "New York was better before," they'd say, or "You should have known Avenue C when it was . . ." (and he'd waggle his hand), or "You should have known Jackson Heights when it was . . ." (and he'd give the thumbs up). "This is good," one woman said and gestured to the noodles spread on her plate, "but Flushing isn't what Flushing was." The place with the good pupusas in the Bronx? Of course it was gone by the time I arrived; it's always gone.

"It's just a playground for the rich." Nearly everyone I spoke to said something similar, like a forlorn chorus resounding across the boroughs, as if a nurse in Inwood and an old Irish man in the Rockaways made a pact to speak the same phrase with the same amount of venom. It's just a playground for the rich—until you take the private elevator and step into the scented apartment and the well-moisturized man says, "You know, it's not even that great a playground for *us* these days."

The New Yorkers I spoke to thought their city was actually slipping. It was happening within their lifespans. They were witnessing deforestation of their shops, the killing off of diverse species. One mentioned "air people," those you used to see walking the streets of Manhattan whose presence made you think: *What do they live on, air?*

Some people needed to expunge their personal list of what was gone, to get it out there and acknowledged, to say the names of the missing and the dead out of reverence and respect. It was instructional; it was about status, too. *You will never know this city like I know it, never love it like I love it, never have seen and lived through these spaces, like flowers, that dazzled and were gone.* "I knew this place before it was nail salons." That was repeated a couple times, to show me what was what.

Change cut. Change reshaped. Change pushed people farther out.

"This stop," one guy said in Forest Hills, "is where you get on the E at 5 a.m. and all the guys working in kitchens in midtown are bundled up and sleeping." And then I was told that change was the only continuing attribute: "Don't listen to them. Part of loving New York is just mourning the hell out of it. The mourning is the love."

In this way they were engaging in an age-old trait of the true New Yorker, a heartfelt mix of mourning and celebration. As Colson Whitehead has written, "No matter how long you have been here, you are a New Yorker the first time you say, *That used to be Munsey's*, or *That used to be the Tic Toc Lounge*. That before the internet café plugged itself in, you got your shoes resoled in the mom-and-pop operation that used to be there. You are a New Yorker when what was there before is more real and solid than what is here now." (That internet café? It's now a nail salon.)

But the people I talked to were also full of vigor, gall, and drive. New Yorkers were often defined by their desire. *I'm going to get it, or at least I'm going to try.* It was a place so powerful I saw a man fresh from prison upstate asking for the city's forgiveness. *Let me back in, New York. Let me return to who I was. Let me experience more of you again.*

For a while I lived near Grand Street, close enough to the Williamsburg Bridge to hear its oceanic rush. I often ran into the rabbi who lived on the second floor and his kids, who rolled their tzitzit in their fingers as the slowest elevator in New York rose. They pressed their faces up against the window when I walked toward the front door. In the autumn one year my father visited from Canada. One afternoon, my downstairs neighbor negotiated her walker into the elevator just as my father and I were about to ascend to the ninth floor. She looked him over, inquired about his health, where he was from, what he did before he retired. When the elevator hit the fourth floor, she said, "I've had the nicest time talking with you. Would you mind if I carried on up to the ninth?" She did, she stared at him, and one day the next week, while I was retrieving mail from my mailbox, I heard the approach of her walker and the clink of the segments of her long necklace. "Craig," she said, "I had the most wonderful time speaking to your father the other day. Now, tell me, is he single?"

It seemed fitting that a city that always had more to offer seemed so often to leave its people hungry for more.

New York seemed to work its residents hard, to mold their bodies, their decisions, their careers. I saw the evidence of the force in the marks it left, beating some with a poverty-hating mercilessness that shouldn't have existed in the US, transforming some into imperious figures. Some felt the ghosts of an older city press against them. I met people who wanted those ghosts, who courted those ghosts, who loved the idea of a city not only their own but inherited and pulsing with the past.

I kept running into people who were acutely aware of their role in propping up the city, adding to a now that had no choice but to be polyphonic and rich, adding to the history, leaving a mark. One man ran a fabrication company in Long Island City and worked with a library of all the different stones of the city. I saw that library—it stretched across the wall; brownstones and grays and dusty whites— and when I was up on the eighth floor of a building site on the Upper East Side with him, looking past the flapping tarps onto the streets below, he told me about a cornice piece he'd once replaced. The terra-cotta at the time of installation had been soft, and when he removed the piece he saw nestled in the corner all the thumbprints of those who had first installed it; the ridges of the fingerprints were still legible. He thought, for a moment, about all the fingers that had left those prints. Then he took the cornice away, measured its length, and added the new piece.

You worked with the stuff of the New York you got. You worked with the materials of your present, and then you left, or you died, or you moved to Florida, or your visa ran out. You worked with the electrics, or the sewage, or on Broadway, or with New York's dog population, or you worked to ensure its elevators ran smoothly, or you worked in the courtrooms, with the city's elderly, you opened its doors. You pressed hard. You left an impression.

IN THE END, though I thought I could simply interview people to get a sense of what New York is like now, it was of course more complicated than that. It wasn't easy to turn off the encounter when I turned off my recorder. It wasn't easy to stop caring, and unlike London, people didn't quickly let go. If I was taking something from them—that was the implication—they were going to ask for something in return.

One year I ate Christmas dinner with Elliott Carter, a man who'd grown up in Brownsville, had been homeless, and now made a living—a sort of living, anyway—by recycling. I'd gotten to know Elliott well, and for years we'd met up for Cubanos on Avenue C. Sometimes we'd go return cans at a Duane Reade near 14th Street, or I'd eat lunch with him up in the Bronx. Once, during my father's visit, Elliott had dropped off ribs he made with his mother's recipe. I was around to see him hard at work. He was around when I was packing up to leave the city. Like the city itself, there was always more to Elliott. He was inexhaustible, he was the complete New Yorker, he was always leaning back to say, "The thing about New York is . . ." And I got the sense that we could go on for another three years, another decade, eating Cubanos, looking out at the sidewalk, spearing plantain slices, and he'd dredge something up from within him. *The thing about New York is . . .*

"You are part of this too," he said to me once. "You are a part of this thing now."

"Not an important part," I said.

He waved me away.

"You're in this city now too. You're a voice."

We were walking toward the bodega near my apartment that was kept under eternal scaffolding with a clamped car marooned out front. Two elderly men were propped against the car in their sweaty Yankees jerseys. I told Elliott I was leaving New York. My visa was running out.

I left, but Elliott was still in it: there would always be more cans, certainly more pain, more hassle, more fear from the virus, more crowds, more uncertainty, but sometimes he conveyed to me what he knew was more transcendence, the look of the Bronx in the morning, Battery Park at twilight. You just keep going.

I left a lot of stuff behind. Elliott took a rice cooker off my hands. Now I text him when I want to know the temperature of the city and how that old machine is doing.

"Still cooking," Elliott says. "Still cooking."

THE
BRONX

MANHATTAN

QUEENS

BROOKLYN

STATEN
ISLAND

0 miles   5   10

New
Yorkers

OVERTURE

A Sense of the City

FRANK SENIOR A singer

My seeing-eye dog and I, we'll walk from 125th Street down to Houston Street. The sound of children in the park tells me what time of day it is. Maybe it's afternoon—you can hear that in kids' voices. Morning you can hear the horns, the hustle. Nighttime, you don't hear trucks as much. The traffic is lighter. Now, if you just drop me out of the sky, maybe I wouldn't know if it's rush hour in the morning or in the evening, but I know it'd be one of those. Then you go by the feel of the sun.

When I'm walking, construction is the hardest thing. 'Cause you can't hear, you gotta fight your way. I don't even know what I pass, the cane is hitting everything. And I'm walking much slower, you have to concentrate that much more with the cane so when you're trying to concentrate and you hear jackhammers and trucks and banging and you smell the construction, your concentration's gone. With the dog, I don't have to worry about that stuff. We just breeze by.

When I pick my dogs, when they match me up, I always make sure they give me a dog that can move fast. I need speed. Don't give me a dog that can't go any faster than a stroll. I want to move. We get on Fifth Avenue and we just move, man. She loves going in and out of the people. You feel yourself going around the people. She's shooting up in the corner—*boom*. The light changes and she's gone. The people are just stepping off the curb. I'm hearing them behind me saying, "Oh, that's a pretty dog you've got there." I'm already by them. I'm moving faster than New York.

If I'm walking with the cane, I'm very slow. So that's when I can feel New York going by me. When I go to another city, I feel like I could slow down. I like it because I don't feel like I'm competing. In New York I'm just in it.

AS WE WALK I hear the different kinds of neighborhoods; Black people turning into white people, Spanish people turning into Black

New Yorkers

people, you know. And then you got the sounds of the languages, the vendors, the different ways that the different cultures sell their stuff.

I used to be able to pick out if someone was biracial. They just had a texture in the voice, and a clarity in the voice, and a thickness in the voice that would say, *This is both.* Now it's harder to do because everybody's mixed now. The New York voice has changed, because everybody's so mixed, mixed races, mixed cultures.

When it was more New York–ish here, you could hear the different parts of where you're from. Brooklyn had that thing, the Bronx was close but it was a different kind of an A-sound, you know. Black people had their own flavor. Now I couldn't tell a Bronx guy from Manhattan or Brooklyn.

You can smell gas leaking from buildings. You can smell tenement—the smell of mold. But then you can go to Central Park and smell the flowers, smell the grass, the dew. If you go to Smoke on 105th Street, you can smell the instruments in there. Horns have like . . . I don't know how you say . . . a dry saliva smell. A trumpet smells different than a sax. The trumpet you smell more. A guitar has a smell, like the strings, the wood.

I used to perform at this place, Roth's Steakhouse up on 93rd and Columbus, I was there seven years. Each set would be different. The first set you'd hear the plates, and people chewing, and talking amongst themselves as the music was playing. The second set would be bright, loud, everybody's drinking now. It got more crowded. Now I'm singing stuff that's more *up.* Then the third set it was just freestyle. From set to set, the smells would change. The people, especially when they came in, they were fresh. They take off their coats, they sit down. They'd be sipping on their little drink. They'd be eating now, the food smells is starting to get on them. Now they're feeling no pain. Their vibe and the smell would change because the liquor changes the chemistry of the perfume. The sweating of the body changes the chemistry of the perfume. It's more of a subtle smell. Now you don't smell it as much, but you know it's there.

In Hell's Kitchen, you'd pass all the railroad apartments and tenement buildings and people sitting on the stoop playing checkers or dominoes. You could hear dominoes, you could hear the checkers. And then you could hear who's playing them. Because Spanish people love dominoes. You hear them talking Spanish but banging the dominoes, *boom boom boom*. You hear them slamming the checkers. They'd be all over the stoop, they'd be sitting on a car.

I used to go up to the Empire State all the time. On the top, you're dealing with wide-open sound. It's got a peacefulness about it.

I always go to the pier down by the seaport, to sit by the river and listen to the boats, listen to the water. It's so beautiful, but you go on a cruise somewhere on real beautiful water, water that's real, and you realize how dirty this smells. You're like, *Oh shit*. It's atrocious.

I've been living in the city all my life. When Times Square was, you know, the dump. When you got off the bus at Port Authority, it smelled like sex. I used to say: *This is what tourists have to come in to?* I would freak out. It just smelled nasty—sex, groin, and hair and underarm. You name it, that's what it smelled like, that's how bad Times Square was. It was horrible. I didn't know it 'till I'd go away and come back. Then you'd say, *Wow, this city stinks*.

Everybody has a body chemistry, and everybody tries to bring it out with the various oils, colognes, perfumes, pheromones. I don't remember names but I know what I'm smelling. I love vanilla, I love wood-aged colognes. And in the summer all the sunscreens going at you. I met this girl who has no smell. She doesn't wear any cologne or perfumes. So when she walked by me, I said, "I don't get it. I don't feel you." She goes, "Because I don't wear anything." It was an unbelievable feeling to walk next to someone who had nothing on.

She was almost a ghost.

WEIRD THING HAPPENED to me the other day. I was standing on Madison and 23rd. I came up to the corner and the dog kind of like—I felt her head move someone over a bit so we could fit in. So I said to the person, "Oh damn," just to say something, 'cause I knew we hit him a little bit. "This is 23rd?" I mean I knew it was, but I was just letting him know I knew we made contact. And he goes to me, "What are you, blind or something?" I started to say, "Fuck you," but said, "Yo, man, what do you think I got the dog for?" He goes, "Oh, you got a dog? I'm blind too." He said, "I was going to ask you to help me cross the street." I said, "I can do that. I can help you across the street, man."

He grabbed my arm, held it tight, and we went across.

ITAMAR KUBOVY A dance producer

In New York, you're in a million situations a day where you have to adjust your body to the reality of the situation. And in and of itself that's choreographic. You're improvising some kind of physical choreography, and it becomes more forced because there's not a lot of room. So getting into an elevator, getting into a subway, making your way through a subway turnstile, negotiating who's gonna go through the exit—that weird moment where you're like, "No, me, no, you," and then you think about race, age, color, privilege, money.

There are these weird little political dances about how to quickly negotiate your way through. A big source of choreographic inspiration comes from constraint—literally, physical constraints. If you have to pass through a narrow space, you're going to twist your body to do that for a completely practical reason. You just want to keep going, you know, or you want to rip-tide across a group of people walking down the sidewalk, and you've got to have some sort of a rip-tiding strategy. You can't just barrel through. You kind of have to be like, "Excuse me, excuse me." Or move away. Or "There's a spot. I'm gonna just dart there and wait, and then I'm going to wait for my next spot."

So that all becomes almost inevitable, and I think part of what's interesting in the city is that the theatricality of New York is an inevitable thing. It's not like someone decided to do it because they had like a funny character. It's theatrical 'cause there's no other way to solve the problem other than to declare what you are, and what you need, and what space you're going need to do it.

And then to hope that you're able to actually get that.

Yesterday I was at a coffee shop on the Lower East Side getting a cup of coffee, and one of the guys who worked there was one of those barista-ish, fancy, "it takes them way too long to make your cup of coffee because it's good" kind of thing. He was dancing back there, and I don't just mean a grace. In fact it was quite awkward, but everything he did—he reached, lunged, and then put the cup down. *Click, click, click,* and turned around. Everything became this kind of routinized dance for him that was both a performance for the clientele but also a performance for himself. He was making his own space. He was decorating his own space. And you sensed that the person that was most being served by his dancing was him. Like that's what kept him engaged.

I sat there with a friend and I was like, "Look at this guy." Every move . . . from the rinsing of the thing, to the *this* of the thing, to the *that* of the thing. It was almost worth going to watch this guy do this weird dance, 'cause it's just such an odd kind of way of making a cup of coffee.

There are constantly situations that force this. Density is always the one reason. Elevators become a very big choreographic endeavor. Busy sidewalks are obviously ones.

When you have a certain responsibility for space that you need to preserve in order to get something done, you very often need to change your approach to the choreography. If you need to carry something somewhere, or you need to transport something somewhere, or even you need to take a child somewhere, or you need to take three children somewhere. Suddenly your whole sense of yourself as a body expands in some imaginary way to envelop the added responsibility of what you have.

And this poses a whole new set of considerations about what the most effective way to move around this city is going to be. You not only have this kind of personal choreography, but there's also a molecular choreography. Sometimes we're part of a larger thing, that needs to address its movement now as a larger organism.

You want to stay close to the people that you trust, and you want to stay away from the people that you don't.

And that has a whole influence on what that flow is like.

We think often of the challenges from a choreographic point of view as being really dependent on what it is that you're trying to move, more than on the sort of constitution of the person who is moving. Because in a way the river washes you along, and you can be a better swimmer or a worse swimmer, but the speed of the river is the speed of the river.

One of the things about New York's anonymity, and cruelty, and in a way, beauty, is that it won't ever stop for you. It won't ever stop. You can come, you can go, nothing matters to the city. That's one of the great things about it. When things matter a lot to you, sometimes it's nice to be in a world that doesn't care. It's relieving.

COOK MONSTA DA ILLEST A rapper

To mix Spanish music with English music, start a whole new genre, that's what I want to do. I want to be in history, man.

All the friends that I was running into as a young boy, everybody did music. Everybody wants to do music, everybody sings, everybody raps, but not everybody's good. Even if they're a bad rapper, you got to respect the hustle. There's a lot of bad rappers out there who are persistent, they work harder than most rappers do now. They're not going to make it, no. You understand what I'm saying. But they still work. So you have to respect it.

Everybody's somebody's favorite artist.

In my music I'm talking about my neighborhood. I'm talking about New York. I'm talking about life. Everybody can relate to something, whether you're rich, poor, hungry, stomach full, good shoes, bad shoes, good car, no car, everybody can relate to something that I say and that's what I try to rap about. Life, on life's terms. Pain. The struggle. I know what it is to starve. I know what it is to be homeless. I know what it is to sleep on a roof, a bus, a train. I'm not going to say what else I know about, you know what I'm saying?

This is New York, man, this is the home of the spit game. The lingo is crazy out here, right bro? The language, how we speak is different, you know what I'm saying? Uptown, downtown, what's good flee, what's good mo', what's popping boy, what's rocking, huh?

It's crazy, I mean, New York, New York, man, dollar slices. Dollar slices, you heard? Twenty-four hours, they take a two-hour break, clean up, close down, the other people come up and open up, dollar slices all day, all night, 24/7 all around transportation. Prostitutes, liquor stores, loosie spots. If you don't got money to get a motherfucking pack of cigarettes, you go outside and get three cigarettes, two cigarettes, you know what I'm saying? Bootleg liquor spots, weed spots, crack spots, dope spots, hoe spots, other spots.

This city is where all the major films, all the major artists, all the major book writers, all the major song writers, all the major painters, all the main chefs, all the main maids, servants, butlers and drivers, escorts, bus drivers, train workers, store owners, all types of business owners, this is where everybody wants to have something at. This is the most productive city in the world. Maybe some cities in other countries make more money than New York City, but the life, the lifestyle, that we show you, that we give you.

There's a ghetto everywhere. There's a hood everywhere. There's drugs everywhere, we just do it a different way. We make everything look different. We make eating look different. You see how he grabbed that spoon? You see how he grabbed that fork and that knife? You see how he poured that salt and that pepper? Why he put ketchup on everything, hot sauce. Come on man, we make it look good, baby, everything.

There's nothing like it, I'll tell you that.

It's the way we say it, it's the way we express ourself. It's so much different shit going on out here, that everybody got to create their own wave, and once you create a wave, wave like Max B said, Wavy, and all that shit. The way I'm saying it now, you could put it as in ling, once you create your own ling and you run with it, then you have a whole bunch of other followers running with whatever you run with and with what you created. New York City, it's the capital of the world.

It's the way we talk, it's the way we walk, it's just the lifestyle. We got to be loud, man. We grew up next to train stations, we can't fucking hear shit. We grew up next to train stations, buses passing, all types of cars, bikes, bikes with motors on them, fucking motor scooters. Mopeds, who you know doesn't wheelie on a moped? I know somebody that does. This is New York.

All you got to worry about is having a roof over your head, food in your stomach, and clothes on your back. Something to watch on the TV, something to listen to on the radio, that's about it. Now all the other shit, it comes within time, that's what you save money for.

You just make sure your living necessities is taken care of. You can pay another extra month on top of your rent? Do it. That will give you some free time to play around and have fun and then buy expensive shit, or live an expensive lifestyle. If you don't have an expensive income, don't live an expensive lifestyle because it's not going to work out for you, especially in New York City. This city will drain you out of your last dollar. With no remorse, it ain't no "I'm sorry." It's just "Bye, thank you for this money, have a good time. Come back. Holler at me when you get your next paycheck, or when you get your next dollar. I'd be glad to take it."

JOY KANG A doctor

I grew up in Queens but I wanted to get out from New York City. I was like, *There's something greater than this, something better than what New York City can offer.* New York City is rich in terms of culture and a lot of different things, but I wanted to go away.

So I moved to Florida. I was so disappointed. Everything was so far away. It was beautiful but the houses were ugly-looking... I hated Florida.

Then I did my residency in Illinois. I lived in an area where the entire city was two blocks. The fanciest restaurant was in a strip mall. I was surrounded by cornfields. Everything revolved around food; it was like, *Let's hang out and eat.* Six months of the year it was so cold you could see ice literally being created when you poured water on the street. It was bone-cold coldness.

I moved to California, where I trained in HIV medicine. People were extremely friendly there. Everything was like, *Oh, let's have lunch!* But I wanted to know *when* and *where*; they were like, *Whenever, yeah, wherever!* It was just like that.

So I came back to New York.

I don't see myself as a true New Yorker. In California, when I was thinking about coming back, I was like, *Am I a New Yorker?* If you google it—like, "How New Yorker are you?"—there's this website that has a little online survey. I did it with my friend, who actually was from New York. She wanted to stay in California, and I wanted to come back to New York. We both did it. She was 30 percent New Yorker; I was 70 percent New Yorker.

I was like, "But I don't think like a New Yorker anymore!" New Yorkers are go-getters, right? I'm not like that. When you think of a New Yorker, you think of someone who's angry all the time, aggressive, will do anything to get what you need or what you want. I don't see myself as that. I think, perhaps, in a more polite and diplomatic way, I am, but not... Well, I no longer walk fast. I used to walk so fast. I can, but I just... It's not natural anymore. Sometimes I have to consciously think, *Oh, I'm in New York, I've got to walk fast.*

People say you've got to have thick skin in New York City; if somebody spits at you, you move forward. I have those moments too. If you know who you are, if you're confident of who you are, then you'll be okay, regardless of what other people say. Of course, you've got to still do what you've got to do. That's the hard balance. I'm learning that, and I want to continue to help my patients and also my students and other people that come along the way in my life.

My perspective has changed. Instead of taking it as it is, I began to observe, and I analyze. Why is that person this way? Why are they acting that way? Why are they so busy? Even at work, I wonder, *Why do you need to do that to prove that you are good at what you do?* Why can't we just focus on three things and be good at them? Well, everybody else is doing a million things, so we've got to do a million and fifty things. I still strive for excellence, please don't doubt that. But it's no longer a competition for me.

I used to think New York City was such a dirty place, but now I find it tearfully beautiful. I sometimes actually cry when I'm walking or when I'm looking at the skyline. I don't think I ever appreciated that. I'll be driving by, say, Amsterdam Avenue on the Upper West Side, and it's quiet on Sunday evening. You see these lights, and you see apartments, and not many people are walking. It's just beautiful.

My family now lives in Jersey, so I purposely come back in the evening on the George Washington Bridge. The lower deck, not the top deck, 'cause I'm average height. If you're tall, you could actually see the view better, but my height, I cannot see it, so I go on the lower deck. I purposely drive slowly, and I enjoy the view. I tell myself, "Oh, my gosh. I love New York." There are times I really get teary. Even the dirtiness itself, I think it tells a story—of someone throwing away. Why did that person litter like that?

If you go to Central Park, to the ice-skating rink in the park, you can go and observe. There are Caucasian, Black, Hispanic, Asian, mixed-race people. . . . Everybody's so nice to each other, picking up each other. It's overpriced, but, you know, everybody mingling together in this tiny place enjoying the ice and the scenery. . . . I mean, it's not like Paris, but it's still beautiful to me.

My whole family is from Washington Heights. My father's family is Puerto Rican and my mother's family is Irish Catholic. My mom makes Irish soda bread and, on Saint Patrick's Day, corned beef and cabbage. My paternal grandmother had a narrow kitchen always full of Sazón Goya packets. She would use all different kinds of classic Goya seasonings. This is not farm-to-table Puerto Rican food. She had all the pots and pans in the oven, always a frying pan on the stove with an inch of oil that she would reuse. To me, New York food is really Puerto Rican food.

Pastelitos de carne or pastelitos de queso y guayaba, so she would do white cheese and guava paste. Or she would do a picadillo, like a minced meat. Usually white rice, but sometimes arroz con gandules, but that was specifically for Christmas or holidays—which is the yellow rice, it has the fish and peas and all of that. Tostones and maduros, of course, and she would do both because there were taste preferences in the families. She would do these beautiful home-cooked meals, but she also would have so many packages of cookies and Hostess cakes, Twinkies and honey rolls, in plastic, like you get at bodegas.

Nothing feels quite the same way New York feels in terms of the food that is everywhere. But you can't have all of the best next door, right? It's not possible to live in one neighborhood that has amazing everything. You have to travel. And part of it, I think, is the trip, the journey to get there.

The best bagel place is in Manhattan, up on 108th and Broadway—Absolute Bagel. Everyone always rivals it with Ess-a-Bagel, but the texture is different. A really good bagel has a unique texture that you can't get unless you have the process right; they're bready and fluffy and chewy in all the right ways. It's such a special chew. It satisfies in the same way a *really* thick rice noodle satisfies. I have the fortune of living really close to Ugly Baby, which does incredible northern Thai food. But I also go to Jackson Heights and Elmhurst in Queens for rice noodles, because that area is incredible—you have a Thai community, a Chinese community, Colombian, Ecuadorian, and all Central and South America. Mexican too, if you go a little farther up to Corona. Indian. Tibet, actually. There's all these momos around there too, which are delicious.

There's a lot of Ecuadorian street carts there that do the big choclos, the big corn. The Ecuadorian street carts are not to be confused with the trucks; they're like a hot dog cart retrofitted to serve Ecuadorian food. Ecuadorians have the big pieces of corn; they grill it or have it fried up, with really strange little crispy bits that are delicious.

In the subway there are the churros carts but not traditional churros, the big ones that are doughy and filled with something. The ladies who have the carts will do atole, almost a porridge, a to-go thing in the morning because you can drink it, but it's substantive, and in the summer the mango con chile y limon.

The person I talk to the most about all this is my partner, Ernesto. He and I disagree on a lot of things when it comes to food. He's a Costa Rican and he's lived in lots of different neighborhoods in the city. We have this big argument about pupusas—they are delicious, Salvadoran, usually with cheese or beans or something in the masa, and you griddle it. Ernesto is obsessed with pupusas. He lived in Washington Heights, so he has a place up there that he loves, but we also go down to Red Hook in the summer. There's a food cart, El Olomega, that does them only on the weekends, and they're my favorites personally. But he works in Industry City and there's a place down there that has them. I stand by El Olomega. It has the best flavor in the actual masa, the best texture. There's the pupusa, but then you always get the tomato sauce to go with it and the curtido, like slaw, so I evaluate a place on not only its pupusa but also on the quality of that tomato sauce and the curtido. If one of those pieces is not good, it ruins the experience.

I've got a little bit of a New York bravado. You own your point, right? You own your opinion. Even if there's a little seed deep down inside where you're like, *I know that maybe they're right too* . . . No, you don't ever let that in. That is a distinctly New York thing, just full trust in that you're right. Defending food preferences and food choices, what is the best and what's not, requires the same level of confidence.

I am right about the pupusa. Ernesto is wrong. He can have his opinion, but I'm not going to change mine. I'm not going to concede my position on this.

GUS POWELL A photographer

Taking a photograph is like pointing a finger at something and saying, *This is interesting.* I learned so many different things from Joel Meyerowitz, but one thing that really stuck with me was this idea that whenever you pick up a camera, point it at something and press that button, you're saying, *Yes.* You're saying, *I believe in this. There's something significant. I embrace it.*

As you evolve, you point your finger at subtler and subtler things. In the beginning, it's the Empire State Building that's interesting, or the pretty girl, or the man that falls down. Your sensibilities change and I think what I try to do now is to point my finger at things that aren't even there, use the camera to make an observation, or to give importance to something that everybody else would let pass by. That's embracing the quotidian poetry of New York.

AT A CERTAIN POINT, I had begun taking pictures on the street but I didn't necessarily know what I was doing with them. Then I had this poetry friend from college who sent me Frank O'Hara's *Lunch Poems,* which were all written in midtown on O'Hara's lunch hour. They weren't necessarily documentary in the sense of describing exactly what happened. They were very intimate and personal about him feeling something. He made those poems when he was at the Museum of Modern Art. I was then working at *The New Yorker* on 42nd Street, midtown. It was kind of the same space, but with thirty or forty years between.

That small book became this passport for me. I kept it on me and would walk around with it. I started making pictures on my lunch hour. Some days I had fifteen minutes and some days I could sneak away for two hours, but it meant that it was this one pocket of time when I had to try and feel something and see something. Sometimes that was as small a thing as just: what does it look like to take these five people who have nothing to do with each other and try to organize them into a picture that has meaning in some way, so that those five people are now forever set together, endlessly having to deal with each other in the photograph?

I have this one picture of a woman who's essentially passed out lying down on the steps of the New York Public Library. It's the middle of the day. She's a tourist. She's asleep. You can go up and take pictures of her and it's like shooting fish in a barrel, but what does that do? If you have the confidence or the interest to know that she's not going to go anywhere, you put her anywhere in the frame. Your viewer will find her. The same way you found her as you walked down the street. They will find her. What can you add to it? Then you push her to the side of the frame and then you see this other guy walking out of the door and he's in a suit and he has some dignity and he's looking for somebody. Then you have him. Then other people are crisscrossing in the foreground. All of the sudden, you have these three elements in play and then you use the camera to stop it all. That way of catching one fish to then catch another to then catch another.

NEW YORK IS an incredibly generous place. I'm inherently an optimist. The sidewalks are generous, the light is generous, the people are generous. This is why you can get things done here. There's so many opportunities as a photographer. You go other places and it's like squeezing water from a stone. Whereas here, it just keeps coming and coming and coming. Some days there ends up being this proprietary moment when you feel like New York, it's all for you. You'll even walk past another photographer and you can tell the way they're holding the camera and the way they're looking at the world and they'll just nod like, *Yeah. This is all for us. This is like Disneyland.*

We all use our cell phones now. If you see somebody using a pay phone, you know they're really in fucking trouble. The stakes are higher. Whereas in the past, we all went up to a pay phone. You put in a quarter or you dropped a dime and you made a call. I remember seeing pay phones that I had certain conversations at and if you walk past them, you remember those conversations. I remember one time going up to a pay phone on Canal Street. This woman was on it and she was crying and then she got off. I went up to use it and I picked up the receiver and it smelled like her chewing gum. It was the whole residue of her tears, her chewing gum, all of it. It was like, this is a confession booth where there's someone on the other side. There it is. I still see that spot and the phone booth, it's gone.

New York is a stream and you find your spots in the pools where there's a little shade and there's a little light and there's something that stays.

MY CAMERA IS usually set at twelve feet away, which is this perfect amount of space where I see you but I'm not necessarily interested. It's also head to toe. I have a couple of pictures that I've named *Fifth Avenue Frieze* or *Sixth Avenue Frieze* because at one point, I realized that this idea of the architectural shard, we have these things from antiquity where it's just a shard of a frieze that was a significant story. We don't know the story anymore. Maybe we do because it's a Greek myth or whatever, but there's all these people head to toe in silhouette and they're telling the story of a battle or a myth or this or that. Then I feel like that's what I've tried to do with photographs sometimes—take six or seven people, show them head to toe, and say this is like this little frieze. It's this little narrative moment that says something.

My pictures are rarely about a single person. They're usually about a collection of people and finding a moment. So sometimes when people ask me, "Are you taking my picture?" I'll say, "I took your picture but it wasn't about you. It was about him and her and this and a tree and all these things combined. If I wanted *your* picture, I would ask you but I wanted all of this and I'm here and you're here." Sometimes they still are angry and other times, they're just like, "Whatever, okay, fine."

I had this moment with this guy handing out flyers near Saks Fifth Avenue.

"Did you take my picture?"

I was like, "Well, yeah, you're in the picture but I'm like you. I'm out here trying to take advantage of all of the stuff that's passing." Because the guy said, "You owe me. You owe me for taking my picture." I said, "If I owe you, I owe *all* these people. I owe everyone." You know what? I do. But I owe everyone. The guy looked at me like I was weird and backed off. Then it was maybe two weeks later and I was photographing on the same corner, he came up to me.

"I was thinking about what you said." He goes, "I owe all these people too."

That's New York, right? Yes, I am taking that person's picture and that person, but my interest is in the plasma of New York. I try to make pictures where you have multiple people that have nothing to do with each other, that just crisscross in a transitory moment, but often because you can't really look at seven people, you look at the negative space. You look at the space between people as a singular object and you find a moment when all of that feels right. There's a charge between them and you can't see it all but there's intuitive moments when you feel the gravity and you can see this one singular larger object. That, for me, is the plasma that we share. That is the negative space between multiple people. And that's what I'm looking for.

Part One

1

Nonstop Hustle

I moved here four months ago from Little Rock, Arkansas. What did I know of New York growing up? Not much. I heard that when you go there, it's like there are great opportunities for you if you want to become an actor, a singer, or a model. You can link up with a lot of people and you'll be able to try to work your way up to the top.

Me personally, my reason for being here is I want to be able to be my own musician, 'cause I love to sing and I want to be able to work with other singers or other artists out there.

It took me two days to get here. I rode the Greyhound. I went past places I never been before. Cincinnati, Ohio; Nashville, Tennessee; New Jersey. Ultimately it was like five states I passed. In Ohio, it stops by a stadium. You stretch your legs and then you go right back. I had got me a little munch and crunch, went to the convenience stores. They also had some stuff inside the Greyhound station so I got me something to eat and got back on the bus.

I sat next to some people who'd never been to New York before, some people who was going to other states and whatnot. It was like a little road show, meeting new people on the bus. They was like, "You must be going for a good purpose," and I was like, "Yeah, I'm trying to become a singer." They said, "Yeah, that'll work out for you," and *du, du, du*. And I was starting to believe them. I'm like, "Okay, okay. I think this is going to be a good decision for me."

They told me to be careful because New York can chew you up, eat you alive. They told me to watch out for the scammers, 'cause there are mad scammers in New York. For example, there's this thing they do. They ask you for your credit card and what they do, they say if you give them $45, they are going to end up giving you $500, all they need is your bank card. And then once they get your PIN number and everything, they find a way to hack into the bank system or whatever you call it and they end up getting the money. It's crazy. So many people fall for it. When I came across it, I'm like, "You must think I'm stupid.

I'm not stupid at all." There's like five people since I been here tried to get me to do that.

That's another thing that people said when I was on the Greyhound bus too. They was like, "Don't put yourself in a bad predicament 'cause it's hard to get out of it, especially while you staying in New York." That's why so many people do things that they don't wanna do—to at least have a place to stay. I'll try to get my butt a job.

WHEN I STEPPED OFF the bus in New York, it was unbelievable. It looked just like it did on TV. I'm like, *Oh my God.* I was so surprised. It was beautiful. To this day, being in my four-month period of being here, it's like still unbelievable. Every time I wake up in the morning, I always say to myself, "Wow, I'm actually here in New York." 'Cause I always dreamed of being here and I'm actually here and I'm actually you know trying to make it. I feel like I'm in a movie.

In the subway, everybody have a story to tell. Even if they not even saying anything, you can just see the story. Like I see a story of sadness. A woman she's sitting down on the bus or the train crying. Or just listening to the sad music and everything. And you can obviously tell that she's going through something really bad in her life. She feel like she can't do it on her own.

After two weeks of me staying in New York I ended up finding me a job. I was working at Macy's Herald Square. I helped the customers and I tried to make the front look good and everything. Every time people step from the elevator, they see the front and if the front not looking right, then there's a problem. So I have to zone the area and then if they needed help I would help them out with the different clothing lines that they have available there at Macy's.

I was working there for a seasonal position, so just to have experience. Now, since I have the experience and I've been working there for like three months, now I'm in the process of working there full-time. I want to work there full-time and also work another job. 'Cause believe it or not, you need two jobs to stay in New York. I don't care what nobody say. This rent up here in New York, 1,000 some dollars for a month. Come on now. I don't see how they keep . . . They shop, they do this, they buy clothes. It's like every week, every day, they be shopping. They just have to go in there to just get one outfit to wear for the bar or to go to the club or whatnot. But, they really crazy about Macy's, oh my goodness. They love them some Macy's. New York people love them some Macy's.

I like Macy's too, I just didn't know they had good clothes like that. Everybody in New York is about fashion. Everybody have their own way, their own unique style. It's very interesting. I've never been in a city where everybody have their own unique style and they own way of life. Everybody's like free-spirited. It's like they go for it.

And they will hustle. Trust me when I tell you, they will hustle to get that money. They singing in subways, singing outside, sing inside the store. They'll try to do anything to try to get them some money. Since I've been here that's what I've been seeing. Yeah, it's a nonstop hustle.

ANDREA PAWLAK The owner of a dog-walking business

I know every animal that gets walked during the day. I know about every single visit, every single one of them. I know every single dog we have. Every one of them. And we have about two hundred. I need to be able to kind of dictate what to do or what not to do. Essentially, I guess I'm the alpha dog.

A doorman recently said to me, "You know, don't take it personally, but you guys just walk dogs." But we literally are helping these people live better lives. And we help these dogs to not get given up. Because a lot of these people work so damn much. "I'm going to work fifteen hours. My dog is still in a crate, oh my God, I have to work, or I can't go to this meeting, or I can't have this date."

One client that I have, I think he's in his twenties, he lives in a penthouse. He's one of those kids who's made tons of money and doesn't know what to do with it. He has like seven couches because he can't figure out which one to keep. You know? At one point apparently one

New Yorkers

of the dog walkers that he had before brought up some issues with him, so he fired them. So now he hired us.

I'm just like, "Hey, dude, this is what you have to do." I'm not going to fluff it for him. But you know, I'm constantly getting calls like, "Hey, get my dogs, I'm going on three dates." He tells me all his personal stuff. I know all about his dating world now, and I just walk his dog. "Does this woman know she's number three for the night?" He's like The Bachelor but can't deal with the responsibility.

I GET A CHEESE DANISH every single day because I have no time for anything else in the morning. I usually do the morning walks because I don't want to burn out my dog walkers so I burn myself out. And while I'm doing this I'm sending schedules for everyone to make sure. Because sometimes so much has changed since a few hours before. I have to make sure I send everybody their schedules before I even get to my first dog. To make sure that everybody is on time, to make sure that everybody has everything.

Every appointment that they go to visit a dog, they have to send me a photograph and an update on what happened. There's not one appointment that goes by without me knowing about what happened to it. The photographs are really really good. At this point I think I've downloaded like fifteen thousand. We see our photographs on people's Christmas cards. All day long, we send photographs and an update. "She took a quick walk out, peed, had a nap, pooped, had a snack while I freshened her water, all is well." But then we created this monster: a few people are expecting these things now in the middle of their work.

Or I get, "Hey, Andrea, what happened to Peanut? Is he okay?" And then, "What do you think of Peanut?" and "What do you think we should do about *blalalalala* . . ." And now I'm finding out from this one woman who's pregnant, she's like, "Andrea, what do we do? We're pregnant!" I don't know!

I just hired a guy who's a comic, who's going to be really really funny. I can only imagine the stuff he's going to be writing, because he's so funny and observant. Sometimes he speaks in the dog's voice, he is very good at becoming the dog. He does it really well. And it's what makes people want to work with him.

But I think people love me as their alpha dog, they trust me with everything. While I'm walking a dog, with one hand, I'm texting with my other hand. I'm responding to new inquiries, and I'm also invoicing while I'm on the subway. Because, you know, I'm always behind on invoicing.

So the day essentially turns into about four hours of really intense "Are you there yet? Are you not there yet? You're not there yet?" It never ends.

It's not just traffic you've got to watch for, and not just people that hate dogs. It's the other dogs. It is like gang warfare. You'll see somebody who will walk maybe seven Frenchies. Or there's one guy who walks all brown dogs together. You have to worry about other dog walkers because now we have these packs of dogs walking on the streets. You have to dodge them or else you have these brawls. Dogs are pack animals, that's how they protect themselves. So now we have one dog that's just going bonkers and then they all go crazy. It's wiped me out a few times.

We have so much stress. I mean just to live here. You miss one step and it's over. You know? Skip a couple months of rent and you'll go to court, you'll never get a lease again. It's done. Maybe it's not *fearful* as much as like, *always trying to get a step ahead* mode.

Maybe I just don't want to end up being homeless. Because, I don't know, people give up in the city here. They think once you're out, you're out.

ZACK ARKIN A former cab driver

In order to make it, you've got to connect with people. You gotta be creative, and you gotta go outside the box. If nothing works, you have one second to do something. You've got that one chance. Say it. Do it.

Show up on time, do the job, know what you want to do, ask if you need help, go the extra mile, don't gossip, keep your hand out of your pockets. It's a New York thing.

Driving a cab. I used my skill, which was connecting with people in the cab. I would drive Sunday morning. And I'd go up to Harlem on the way up to the churches. In the summertime, hot sweltering heat, I knew my friend was up in the barrio, in Spanish Harlem.

Being in a cab gave us power because you had mobility. You shot through cultures, neighborhoods. You shot through levels. You had a virtual reality.

That's why art is fascinating with the textures. In New York, *people* are the textures.

Every breath that you take you have to realize that you have an opportunity. And so if you let New York swallow you, you're going to be sorry. It's up to you. You have to help people. But they're going to help you. There's a balance of life, you know. And it always comes back. Never worry about getting repaid. And don't get caught up in the money. Don't get caught up over living in a particular place. You may be living where it is.

Have fun. Who cares if you're on fucking Fifth Avenue in Trump Tower or you're in a fucking tenement. You go meet a girlfriend and you fall in love. People can find love. It's hard. It's a thing that you can't buy. You can't buy New York. You've got to live it. You have to live New York every second. Otherwise, you don't get it. Go out to the burbs.

The thing about New York is the eyeballs. You have to make contact with people in New York. If you don't, they're going to put one over on you. Why do people get robbed in New York? They turn away. Do you notice that? Don't ever turn away from someone. New Yorkers eyeball you, make you stay in the eye.

For me it was, *What am I all about?* Look in the mirror, what do you want, you know. For me, working was the thing that kept me going. If I didn't work, I was depressed.

You redefine yourself through work. You can have a business, you can do whatever you want to do. If you don't do it, it's because you didn't want to do it. You didn't want to put your money into it. You're not into it. So don't tell me you can't make it in New York, because you didn't *want* to make it in New York. There's no other bottom line.

DEJON SANTOS A street bookseller and author

Thousands of people tell me, "Oh, you the author?" See, that's why I publish my picture on the back cover. Once they see that it gives them more of a reason to buy it. It gives them more incentive.

One lady, she was behind me in her car, and she heard me say I'm the author. She got out of the car and said, "Why are you telling people you the author? I know you're not the author."

I'm like, "I'm just doing this to try and make a little money," this and that. She was like, "Well, if you was the author, I'd buy all your books." I ain't say anything, I just went like this: *Look at that picture.* She looked, looked at me, and looked down. She ain't say a word.

WHEN I FIRST STARTED selling books, it was authors everywhere. Jamaica Avenue, you'd see about ten authors. Everybody had their bookstands set up selling their books.

Either they call it urban fiction or street literature or hood books. But I don't label my books that no more. I call it crime fiction. I don't want myself in a box, like for only one group of people. I don't do that 'cause you paint yourself into a certain corner.

It was authors here, authors there, people selling.

Downtown Brooklyn, you know, Fulton. There's booksellers that are still down there, but they're not authors, they're like regular people who sell books. Right now in New York City, I know almost all the authors that sell their own books. It's about seven.

A lot of people don't have enough confidence to come out and sell a book, because of the *this*, the *that*, the e-books. So they're not confident. I'm here to tell people, that's not the case. First of all, you're not selling your book, you're selling yourself first. It's all about presentation and how you carry yourself, though. See, when I talk to people, they look at me and say, "Okay, let me see what this guy got to talk about." Then I talk about the book, they laugh, crack a couple jokes. I'll be like, "Yo, read this part." And once they read the part, they're like, "Oh my God, I gotta get it." Even though the book is 2005, it still sells.

I'm constantly spending $2,000 a month on books. I spend a lot of money on books because I know I'ma sell them. I know I'm gonna sell them on the street.

The number one trait you have to have, in my personal opinion: you gotta look a hundred percent presentable, especially when you're dealing with the public. Because people judge you by your appearance and how you look and how you carry yourself. So when I go out there, I'm always making sure I'm super clean, nose is clean, I get a haircut like twice a week, smell good, nice outfit. If I have a small stain, I'm changing my shirt. I'm changing my shirt, 'cause if you stand and talk to somebody, they look at everything. They look at everything. So, you can't say, "Oh, I'm a author, my books are selling," and you're wearing Too $hort hoodies looking like you're homeless. So, presentation is number one.

Second, you gotta establish a rapport with the customer. Some people come at me like, "I don't read these type of books; all those books are the same," and I try to tell them, "So, how is it some books sell five hundred thousand copies, and some books sell maybe five hundred copies? Why is that?" Same thing with R&B albums. You know, when you say R&B albums, they're all the same? No. Some sell ten million copies and some don't sell at all.

So, you can't put everything in one basket. I try to use logic and reason. I love talking to people, I love meeting people, I love having fun, I love selling my books. And one of the greater joys I get in selling my books: when somebody coming to me I don't know, "I heard about your book, I read your book! It was so good. When is part two?" Just like my first book, *Ice Cream for Freaks*, and everybody been waiting for part two. These books sold so well, they waiting for part two for so long.

But a lot of people ask me, "Can you get it on Kindle?" No. You can only get it from me.

Currently I got seven copies left of this book right here. Seven copies left.

If you're a reader, you're a reader no matter where you're from. The Brownsville section of Brooklyn is one of my top selling places also, even though it's considered one of the poorest neighborhoods in New York City. They love my books out there. And not only that, even before I started going to Brownsville, I got Brownsville in my first book.

Of course I do! Now, as you know, in New York City, every borough has a motto. Okay, like Bed-Stuy. You know Bed-Stuy's motto? Bed-Stuy's motto is "Do or die." That's been around for a lot of years. And "Flatbush, 'cause they always rush" . . . Queens, they call Queens "Quiet Queens." Manhattan, they call Manhattan . . . "Moneymakin' Manhattan." So, every borough has their little catchphrases. Now, Brownsville has their own little catchphrase that's been around since the '60s. Now, the motto is: "Brownsville never ran. Never will." See, what I do as a author, I add a little extra twist, so I put, "Brownsville never ran. Never will. Walk slow so the Guinness don't spill."

So, I tell people, I say, "Are you from Brownsville?"

They say, "Yeah, I'm from Brownsville."

I say, "No you not!"

They say, "Yes I am."

I go, "Okay." Right? "Are you from Brownsville? I'm gonna give this book to you for free."

"Man, for real?"

It's like, "Yeah. But only one condition: if you tell me the Brownsville motto."

They like, "I know the motto. 'Brownsville never ran. Never will.' "

I said, "95 percent right. You missing one more part."

"What? What?"

I said, "I'll give you a chance. Call somebody."

These people get on the phone, call their uncles, cousin, "What's the motto?" I'm trying, I have to put it on speaker phone—see I make everything fun. And the guy'll be like, "I don't know the motto, I'm missing a part of it."

I show people the book. "Brownsville never ran. Never will. Walk slow so the Guinness don't spill." Now, "Walk slow so the Guinness don't spill," that's entirely made up, on my part. But the people on the street, they don't even know that. They think, "For real? I never knew that." But they laugh, they joke. They say, "I love this book. I want it." And they end up buying it. So it's all about establishing communication with people, making them laugh.

This book did sell well 'cause the title's so unusual. *Ice Cream for Freaks.* Is it a sex book? What is that? So, it piques their curiosity and makes them want to read the book even more, though. So, when you read it, you find out why it's called *Ice Cream for Freaks.* They say, "Oh, now I know why." And the way I write, I leave people on the edge. So, part two been in the making for a long time.

Summertime, they will talk to you two hours. I don't mind it. At one time I was talking so much I had to go to a specialist for my throat. The throat doctor, what do they call them? He thought I had throat cancer.

He stuck a special tube into my nose that went down to my throat, which had a miniature camera on it that was attached to, like, a screen TV. I saw my voice box and everything. I'm like, "That's my voice box?" "Yeah, yeah." And the tube is in. But he told me I didn't have throat cancer.

Overuse. 'Cause I would talk so much, 'cause that's how I get money. I talk to people, so I was talking too much, though. So, average, the most I sold books, I'ma keep it real, was three days a week.

It's not only the physical part, it's the mental part, because sometimes I would talk to somebody for like a hour and a half. You know what they were telling me? "Are you gonna be here tomorrow?" Or, "I'm going to the bank. Sign a book." But I don't never do that. I never sign a book 'till I see the money in hand. "Sign a book. Wait, no, I'll be back in one minute." I never see them again. You know what I'm saying? So, those people frustrate me, but only for five minutes, because when the next person comes, I completely forget about that person and focus on this person.

I INVEST THOUSANDS and thousands in myself, all this money. I didn't go and try to get a publisher. I just did it myself and I made the money back, like I said this book right here, I did everything myself, I did the cover myself.

I'ma tell you, you will not see this nowhere, 'cause it shows quality, it shows that you believe in your work, it shows that you care about the product. I noticed that the cover, it was getting scratched up too easy. So what happened was I ordered the new cover. Laminated. Extra gloss. Because I don't want my customers to have books that are . . . scratchy. I want my covers to last. I was looking at my books. I was taking a cloth and trying to wipe it, and it still had that little scratch.

I'm one of the surviving few authors that's out there. I'ma tell you I know all the authors in New York, though. It may be, oh, there's another author, he be on 165th Street, I know him. Only thing about him is he don't travel, he don't go to Brooklyn, he don't go to Bronx, he don't go nowhere. I try to tell authors, you gotta travel to get experience, go to different places.

The technology is changing so, so much. Is there any Blockbusters around or are they completely gone? That's what I'm saying, they went out of business. And Polaroids? Polaroids still there? Some people be like, "Oh, I can get it on Kindle. I can get it on this, I can get it on that," right? So I tell people this: they say in five years from now you can get a steak meal, you get a T-bone steak, mashed potatoes with gravy, a salad, and a side dish, all that comes in a pill.

So, which one? Do you rather take that pill and get all the nutrients from that meal, or have the actual meal? People like, *I want the actual meal*, so I try to connect it to my books. So, you rather go on the internet and scroll down, or you have a physical book you can sit down, open, fold the page, come back.

It's like slowly they fading out, though. There are people that still want to have the physical book in their hand. I'm a true testament to that saying. I go out there, I can make $500 just tomorrow. I'ma make $500 tomorrow.

SHAYNA BROWN A lice consultant

At her home, she is picking the nits from the head of a child while the parents stand nearby.

This is a nine-year-old that I did the other day. *[She holds up a paper towel full of marks.]* Isn't that great? There's lots here. She must have had it for sure six to eight weeks, to get this bad a case. But she came back and had nothing. It makes you feel so good, to know that you're helping people to get this out in one try. It's a shame you weren't here when I was combing her hair. There was enough for like ten people.

I'm an EMT, I'm a nurse, I'm allowed to do this. I'm doing it for over thirty-five years, and I trained all my daughters. I have seven daughters. Now they all do it with me now. And this is the way I do it. You'll watch, this is a real demonstration. So, what I do is I just take my Pantene conditioner, pour it on the dry hair . . .

[She demonstrates on the child.]

The lice have changed. In the thirty-five years that I'm doing this, they've changed. Lice have gotten smaller. They're very very close to the scalp, and it's very easy to miss them. Lice used to be about an inch and a half to two inches away from the scalp, and now, you saw that nit that I showed you? It was literally on the scalp. I could have missed it. And it just doesn't pay to miss something if you want to make sure that the family's clean.

I work in about fifteen public schools in Brooklyn, Manhattan . . . well, all over. Battery Park I did on Thursday. They had it bad. When we first started there, before they had an awareness in place, we would take out like fifty kids. This time we were there we had only ten kids out of two thousand. And it's all because we come like four times a year and there's an awareness of lice, people start hearing about it, thinking about it . . .

But in public schools that don't do anything—and there are many of them where they choose to just ignore it—most of the time it's a principal who just doesn't want to be bothered. The Board of Ed doesn't want to have anything to do with this. The Board of Ed says their new policy is that if a child has nits you cannot send them home.

I had a boy in middle school, who walked in here with dark red hair and he walked out with strawberry blond hair. Because every time I put the comb in his head like this, there were lots of bugs.

[She points to the girl whose hair she's been working on.] She did not have a lot. But she had a hard case, 'cause her hair is so thick. So far I don't see anything on her, which is a good thing. I'm trying not to take out any hair from you, sweetheart.

In the public schools boys get it just as much as the girls do. It makes no difference. Men don't get it as often. They have a higher acid content in their blood. Little boys get it all the time. I love when people walk in and they say, "Don't sit on her couch." Excuse me, guys, you're walking in with the lice.

My daughters are excellent at this. They have golden hands. They're incredible. They really are so good at it.

[To one of her daughters: "Can you get me another paper towel and another Pantene?"]

Always Pantene, 'cause it's the thickest conditioner on the market. The other ones just roll right down their hair. This one, you put it on, you blob it on, and it stays there. It doesn't roll down, you know? So, that's why we use it.

[She begins working on the husband, who asks, "Do I take my payos out?"]

No, let me first do the head. If I don't see anything on the head, I'm not so worried about you. I doubt you got it.

[She cleans.]

New Yorkers

What I do when I comb is, I comb with the comb flush with the scalp. The nits are so close to the scalp that unless you comb on the scalp, you're not gonna get everything out.

His beard is not gonna be an issue unless he has it. If the scalp doesn't have it, I'm not worried about the beard. It doesn't go to the beard. The beard is a different kind of hair. It only goes on the head, and it's purely a human problem. It doesn't go on animals.

[The husband says, "I'm just waiting for you to say, 'OK, you're through.'"]

You don't have anything. We'll throw you in for free. Bonus. You're good.

["Thank you."]

Why have they changed? I guess survival. You know, years ago they used to be bigger, they used to be further away from the scalp. I used to be able to see them better. And now the shampoos don't work on them, and they've gotten resistant to all the different lice shampoos.

It doesn't work anymore. You know, people that used to come, years ago, thirty-five years ago, used to go home, use Nix, use RID, use, you know, the Permethrin, and it used to kill them. And there's another chemical that we used to use, the Ovide, which has the . . . I don't know how to pronounce it, the Malathion, and that still does work, but it's extremely expensive and it's usually not covered under insurance. One little bottle is like $10 or $15 for a few ounces. And that smell is horrible, really vile. Why put poison on a kid's head if you don't need to?

So, years ago, you used to just use your lice shampoos and, you know, that's it. You were done with it. And now, it just doesn't work. So . . . We go through a lot of conditioner. I go to Costco and buy about two dozen of them.

My girls all come here and sometimes we'll have a whole row of my girls, me and my three daughters, you know, doing big families, or doing more than one family at a time. Like, if I go to a school, there's some schools that I go to that they insist: whoever I find in the school comes home with me.

But this way they know that their kid is clean. And people come back for follow-up re-checks, which I include in my price for them. They come back, 'cause it takes about three to five days for all the nits to be visible, in order to be able to see them all. So I can't one hundred percent guarantee the work until they come back for the follow-up.

It takes three to five days for all the nits to be visible. When they first cement them on the hair, they're a clear, pearly-white color, and as the bug grows inside it turns the nit dark. All of her nits were all dark and ready to hatch.

It transfers from head to head. On the train, on the bus. Sitting next to someone on the subway. A lot of girls, today, in the high schools, they have lots of sleepovers. And did you ever see the way girls take pictures with each other, with their heads right next to each other?

In New York everyone's on top of everybody else. Even the schools. When I first started out, at one of the public schools, there were twenty kids in the class there. Now they have thirty-four kids in the class. There's so many more people moving into New York. There's more lice because people are much more on top of each other. When I was in the country, my closest neighbor was a mile away, you know what I mean? I mean, you're not gonna get it from your chickens.

And a few years from now I'll probably have my daughters doing it and I'll just, you know, stay home, because you have to really have good eyes in the school not to miss it.

Even though this is how I make my livelihood, I feel so good about helping them. To make a good experience out of a lousy one. No pun intended, of course.

JOSEPH LEWIS A private cook

It started with this lady from around the area; I guess she had a crush on me, I don't know. She was an older lady, just somebody in the neighborhood. You meet some people in life, you may not know their name but you say hello every time you see them. She was just like, "You should come and cook some breakfast one day, because I'm really sick." No problem. I came in and cooked.

We never arranged any money or anything. She just asked me to cook, I was bored and had nothing else to do, I figured why not? That was the start of my private cooking thing.

From that point, I was just like, I want to do more private cooking because I like that feeling. I started getting girls saying like, "Oh, hey, can you cook?"

I started cooking for people in the projects, baby showers, and I said I'm going to do this until I can get a net for myself and a name. A friend of mine was like, "Oh, I know this guy, they got this kitchen thing, I'm sending your resume." I get to go into the apartments and it's more of a wealthy clientele. They have the money to afford these meals, do you understand? And then on the side I do the affordable ones.

I used to promote, and I just took the promoting into cooking. I would look at whoever's birthday was coming up and instead of me sending them a promotional paragraph, I would say, hey, your birthday is coming up, I'm a chef, I'll cook a meal for you half off, come inside your house, give you something different. At first people were a little hesitant, some people were like, *hey, that's great.* I was charging like 40 bucks, 50 bucks, I didn't know what to charge or what I was capable of. Not for nothing. Even though it's affordable in poverty, these aren't people that are going to sit here and stroke your ego. I felt like these were harder than my bigger clients. Because the wealthy client would just not say anything and pay for somebody else to come in there and finish. But somebody that works hard for that 40, 50 dollars, they are going to let you know, "My man, step this up."

It started off as really simple things. If you had a baby shower I would probably come in and do my Cajun sautéed shrimp. I would check for the restaurants. If they were big on Italian restaurants in this area, I knew I couldn't compete in that Italian lane so I would just try to do soul food or whatever I could afford.

This one girl, she was from Bed-Stuy area and there was a baby shower. It was a last-minute thing. A friend of mine was like, "Bro, come over here and cook for us please." *Where are you guys at?* They said Chauncey Street, and I just remembered Chauncey Street is really the hood. So I'm like, "Alright, I'm coming." I went over there. I was more intimidated by the crowd than the actual food.

I saw they had a bag of shrimps, French fries, it was things in my lane. Like fry them or sauté real quick. I was just like, *What can I do that won't get me beat up?* You have to think about these things. They're about to pay you to cook for their mother, father, grandmother, whoever is in. And they are going to let you know.

I did a sauté shrimp. I just kept braising the shrimp. If it's juicy and cooked, they can't say anything. I fried some onion rings, French fries, wild rice. The only thing that was "wild" about it was the cilantro and the seasoning on it. You can just make up names and it will work. I was like, "Yeah, this is Chauncey Shrimp," and they were like, "Oh, this is great."

There was one guy, who was their uncle. The whole time he just gave me this look like, *If you mess it up, I'm following you home, brother.* Even when it was time to eat, he just sat there cracking his knuckles. I was just like, *Oh my God, I'm going to bring this guy the plate.*

"Here you go, I want you to tell me what you think." His daughter came over and grabbed one and she ate it and was moving away and then she stopped. "Oh my God, this is really good." I said, "Thank you," and he said, "No, I don't want that shit." That's what he told me. He pushed it away. I was just like, "Not a problem, is there anything I can help you with, you want me to fix you some fries? Juice or whatever?"

"Get me some Henny, and then we'll move from there."

I was thinking, *How come I gotta get Henny?* But I had $20 in my pocket, so I said to my friend, "Can you go get a bottle of Henny for me?" He went and got a little $10 bottle, and I was like, "Look, man, eat this, and I'll let you drink this." He ate the food, drank the Hennessey, and I hadn't heard from him or seen him the rest of the night. I was getting ready to leave and he was the first person at the door as I was leaving. He was like, "Yo, come here, man. You think you're slick, right?"

"What did I do?"

"So, you just going to get me drunk so I can give you a good response?" I was like, *no, that wasn't it. I was just trying to get everybody happy in here*, and he's like, "F that," and he just kept saying that for about five minutes. He's the guy that's supposed to pay me as well. I'm nervous, I don't know how this is about to turn out. I'm thinking we're about to fight. All kinds of things are running through my head, so I was like, "Don't even worry about it, brother. I thought that I did what I was supposed to do. My apologies." He's like, "You young bucks these days are so frail, man. I was just joking, brother."

I was like, "Aha *ha*." He said, "That's good, bro. That's good, keep up that good work. I like to see brothers like y'all." Jeez. I went home and I called my mother. "I almost thought I was going to get shot tonight." My mother is really religious. "You have to pray. Go with God. Nothing, nobody will do anything to you." I was like, "You are right. You are right."

I made 60 bucks. I was happy because it was the first time I cooked for more than ten people.

I COOKED FOR this guy and his friends in the Bronx, man, and it was such a weird experience. They were like, somewhat hippies in a sense, and they believed in chakras and energy and shit like that. To each his own, but the way the whole house was set up, they didn't really want lights.

"Can you cook in the dim, brother?" And I was just like, "Whatever, man." So, I had my cell phone light over everything I was chopping up. It made me realize this is part of why I do it, you know what I'm saying? To see the different people.

It was almost like a temple. Candles everywhere, then they had these little lava lamps set up, and this disco globe light that went through the whole house, almost like it was scanning the house. And they had these stones, they were called nakshatras, and they'd go in there and meditate before they eat and it was just, whoa.

At the end of it I was just like, "Do you want me to turn the light on to, you know, plate it and serve you?"

"No man, no light."

There was no chairs, they were just sitting on these humongous pillows, the table was really low. And I came and I handed them the food. And they did some little chant, and they was like, "We know this is gonna be good." "Oh, okay. Thank you." I'm just smiling, so I cleaned up.

"Brother, do you want to sit in for one of our sessions?"

And I said, "No, I'm fine, man. Next time."

LAST WEEK I COOKED for these wealthy individuals that live in a predominantly Russian Jewish area. I have this thing, a late-night menu I call What's In Your Fridge? Whatever's in your fridge I just make a meal out of it. So, the guy calls me, "Alright, man, it's four of us, we're drunk, just come over here and make something good. I'll be home in like a hour, can you meet me?"

"Yeah, I'll be there."

I got my whole uniform on. I get inside the house and it's literally just boxes of cereal all in the fridge. Milk, Oodles of Noodles, Hot Pockets. I said, "Bro, I gotta go to the store or something." I said, "What do you want me to do with this?"

"You don't know how to make anything out of these noodles?"

I said, "I could try, man." And I ended up taking a Hot Pocket and splitting it in half, taking the meat out of it, chopping it up and putting inside the Ramen noodles, and I gave him that. I figured, this guy's drunk, he doesn't care what he's eating. I don't know if he was so hammered, he just didn't even have the strength to stand up and cook or what. I was asking him like, "How'd you guys get home?" He said, "Bro, can you believe I drove from the city?" I said, "You're a wild man, bro, and I could tell from this fridge you get wilder."

"You know it, man."

When he saw me cut the Hot Pocket open, he's like, "What are you doing?" He was so stressed out, like I was really messing up.

"You don't have any meat. I need some type of protein. I'm gonna take the pepperonis out of here, slice them up, and put it in the noodles."

He was like, "Bro, do that, I gotta see this now."

He sat down right there and watched me, and I had the cilantro and I put it on there, he was like, "This is like not . . . this wasn't in my fridge, man."

I said, "Yeah, you're drunk, boy." All I did was heat up the pasta in the bowl, that was it. He was just amazed, like I had made the best meal in the world.

Thank God for poverty, you know what I'm saying? Poverty is what helped me make that Hot Pocket meal the best it could be. Seriously. And that's really where that menu itself came from, being poor.

'Cause when you're poor you get tired of eating noodles the same way, you try different things. Let me put a little lettuce in it, let me put a little crushed-up cereal and Vienna sausages, and so on and so on, you understand. Being poor taught me how to survive. That's why I can go in somebody's fridge and see what they've overlooked and create a meal out of it.

I HAD THIS CLIENT. He had his whole family there. When I walked into his home, I was amazed because it was beautiful. I looked at him. I was like, "How you doing? Let me introduce myself. I'll be your chef for the evening." He just gave me this look of concern, like, "Who is this guy?" Instantly I felt it, but I didn't say anything else.

I could feel the tension already. I'm setting up and I'm getting ready to cook. He's asking me questions. Other clients have asked me questions like, you know, *how'd you start this, where have you been working?* His questions didn't seem generous. They were almost like he was interrogating me. As we're talking, he's going to his phone. I'm paying attention to him. I could see his movements. He's googling to see if we're actually a real company and if my name is on the boards or wherever. I was just listening and looking. I'm trying to remain professional, but inside of me is like, this is really awkward.

His wife comes home and the son comes in. I thought, *Alright, the family's here now, things are about to smoothen out.* I see where it all stemmed from because she comes in and she goes, "Oh, okay. Yeah, so how long you going to be with this?"

"I shouldn't be any longer than fifteen minutes."

The son comes in. He's a little softer. He asks me, "What's the menu?" I said, "It's braised lamb, mixed vegetables."

"That sounds great, man."

He sits down. When he sits down, I'm trying to focus on the positive energy in the room now. So I'm talking to him.

The wife comes and sits down. She goes, "Yeah, so let me tell you about my day." She completely cuts me off. She goes to explaining to the family. Now the husband comes to sit down, the wife is there, the son is there. They have this marble table, it's really big. They're talking and I'm cooking right in front of them because the stove is connected to it as well. So now it's really awkward. They're talking and she's like, "Yeah, so the white guy tells the Black guy . . . Sorry, the white guy tells the Spanish guy, get that N-word out of here right now. He's a stupid N-word."

I looked up and in my head I was just like, *Oh, man.* I understand everybody may not be comfortable with a certain race. I'm in your home and I respect that one hundred percent, but please respect the business cordiality of the situation like we're meeting off of a business route. Let's respect that mutually and let's please keep the distasteful names out of each other's mouths because if I have negative opinions about you, I'm not gonna speak them about you. You know what I'm saying? I'm gonna keep them to myself. You being older than me, I would assume you should know that. She's still going. I felt that when I looked up, to let them know I recognized the conversation, they would switch it up. But she just kept going in.

Some of the N-words became harder. I'm trying to, you know, finish their food, but it's just so much going on and it's already awful—the vibe. Now I see the husband. He's looking at all my tattoos. I can see him and feel his eyes going up and down my arms. I was just like, *I got to get out of this house.* So, I'm presenting and plating the meal, telling them what it is. I go to shake his hand, saying, "Thank you for the beautiful evening. You guys have a nice night." He doesn't shake my hand. He just looks down at it. He goes, "Yeah, thanks, guy." As he's getting ready to show me the door, the little daughter comes in. She goes, "Hi, chef." I go, "Hi, how are you?" He goes, "Yeah, this way, buddy." You know like, *Don't talk to the kid.*

So I called my team captain. "I had an interesting client, man." And I explained it to him. He was asking me the location and what's the problem. I told him. He was like, "Man, that's crazy. Tell the company."

"I don't want to tell the company. I don't want to seem like the guy that's nagging. It's not something I haven't been through before. I'm just informing you because you're my team captain. I'm doing my chain of command. If you want to tell them, go right ahead, but it won't come from me."

Then I got my report back. You know, 'cause every client could write. "Chef was full of tattoos. I felt like he was gonna rob the place. I didn't want to leave my daughter in the house with him, safely." You know. And it depressed me, like, *Damn, how is this acceptable?* You can't please everybody.

As the years progress, they find a way to still stick that knife in you, man. It definitely did make me feel like I have to get some tougher skin and realize you really can't cater to everybody. You can get caught up with the good clients and the decent clients. You forget about the negativity that's out there. It just was somewhat of a reality check, like I guess I got too comfortable.

SOCIETY HAS A WAY of beating you up, man. New York was a humongous obstacle course to get people to trust me. Even now. You know how many clients I've lost once I meet them for the payment and they see me, and they're like, "Oh, I just . . . you know, from the phone you sound like a . . ." They don't want to say I sound like a white guy on the phone, but they just say *Thanks, but no thanks.* Right on the spot.

I had a guy, maybe a month ago, he wanted to do a housewarming for ten people. I charged him for everything that he wanted: filet mignon bites, cheesecake bites, expensive stuff. So I said $1,100. That's a great price considering all the things he wanted. And he's like, "Oh, man, that's perfect, could you come and meet me here on 23rd Street, and I'll give you the money."

"Alright, cool, I'll be there shortly." I drove there. I called him out by name. He's like, "Yeah, where do I know you from?" I said, "Chef Joseph." He goes, "You're not Chef Joseph." And he gave me that look like I was pulling his leg. And I was just like, "No, it's me."

Sometimes it works to my advantage, because they're so in denial, they don't expect me to be able to cook, and then I end up wowing them with the food. But for the most part, they're just not ready to deal with it or accept it. I used to be shocked and hurt, but I'm aware of it. I cook with my emotions, with my feelings. So, if you're being racist, it deprives me from achieving the goal for this actual meal. Because when I'm cooking I'm locking everything out. I'm allowing the food to talk to me. I just want to get in the zone, but I can't get in the zone if you're on edge and you're making comments . . .

So, I just understand now like, there's some people in this world that you're not gonna be able to change. They're not gonna be happy, they just won't understand because they don't want to. And you just have to leave those people in their own light.

Sometimes I want to just slam the knife down and say, "If I cut myself and I cut you we bleed the exact same color, you know?"

Wherever poverty is, you're gonna see more cops. They'd do these random searches in the train station and I would tell them off the bat, before they even pulled me, "I'm a chef, here's my card. This is what I do." They're looking at it, still pulling me to the side. They're looking at all the knives, touching them. And they're looking at me while they're touching. I even had some cops say, "You know I could give you time for this, right? You not supposed to carry around a blade over the size of your palm." I'm showing him my license for it. Now I'm pleading with the guy not to arrest me. It's like, wow.

What do you do? What do you do? The equipment you have that you're using to try to get out of this situation, they're willing to take from you. They take my knives, where am I?

2

Stressed Out

DEBORAH KARLSSON A therapist

My clients are not that heavily into trauma. It's all anxiety about work, about potential, about whether this really is the person I should be with and whether New York is really where I should be. New York is a focus in the sessions, like, *Is it impossible to date in New York? Are all the men in New York jerks? Is there no job that will pay me a living wage in New York?* I don't know about this for the other cities, but for sure in New York, the city plays a big role. New York itself almost becomes like a presence.

It takes a certain kind of drive to get to New York. A lot of people will look at New York and say, "This is insane." My father, when he first saw my apartment, was just horrified, like this is not human. He loves coming here for two or three days, but the idea that he would actually as an adult choose to live in this kind of situation? That takes a certain kind of person.

This is the best place you could be dating: you have the opportunity to meet anyone, any night, from anywhere around the world. But the city breeds these men that have made a lot of money when they're young, that aren't mature or don't really know what they want, and have the pick of all of these fantastic women. What's going to make them settle down with one?

I see a lot of single women that are looking to have a partner, a boyfriend, or a husband. For many of them, they want a really wonderful career and they want a really wonderful relationship, so the bar is very high. So it might take them a little bit longer, but that struggle and that pursuit will be so much more worthwhile. Because then I see those people that kind of knocked it down in college and are going through horrible divorces in their thirties.

I have this girl who's a stylist, like top-level, has worked with everyone that you can imagine and is so good at what she does. I can even tell by what she wears to our sessions that she has so much going for her. She's funny and beautiful. But instead of taking all of that and feeling a real high out of that, she just looks at her dating life and gets frustrated and depressed. She talks in a way that doesn't match up with what she has going for her. I think a lot of women lose sight of that. They equate success with having a marriage. Is the end game to be happy or is the end game to just kind of be married?

They blame New York. It must be the city. Trust me, the city is involved in almost every session I have. It's constantly in the room in a way that I'm not sure any other city would be, certainly not in the United States. And always talk of moving, moving, moving. All of my clients bring it up at one point or another. You know, "What if I could get the hell out of here, where else could I go?" To be someplace else. It doesn't have to be so expensive, it doesn't have to be such a rat race, whatever. That's what I feel my clients are really going for, they want to feel some sense of relief from this and that is a very viable, relieving fantasy to have.

One woman I see came to New York with pretty much nothing and has created a very interesting life for herself. Married a very nice guy, they have a young daughter and they're realizing that the kind of life that they want for her, support-wise, family-wise, money-wise, is not here, and so they might move out West. That has been a stress in their marriage for the past year. It's feeling like a huge failure for her to leave.

There's a certain kind of a heartbreak, but then you have to say, well, is it really a failure? You created this fantastic life for yourself, you've achieved things that you probably would have never imagined, you're leaving with this accomplishment, with this professional life. Is it really such a heartbreak or a defeat, or is it maybe for everything there is a season and you have a family and it's kind of time to acknowledge that and put that as a focus first versus living in New York.

If you're coming to New York, you are ambitious and you want it all. So you're not just going to be happy with being so fabulous at your job, you're going to want a marriage, you're going to want children, you're going to be sending them to the best private schools for whatever insane amount of money. When you look at it like that, no one will win that game, no one. Why are you even thinking about your life in twenty-two years? We are not there yet. Just start by appreciating what you've created for yourself in this city, which is an accomplishment in itself.

ARTHUR KENT A dentist

My dad owned my dental lab and unfortunately he passed away about sixteen years ago, but I still have patients that have crowns that he made. We'll be doing an exam and I'll think, *My dad made that thirty years ago.* So there's a connection. And every now and then, one will fail and I'll take it out and it'll be in my hand and I'm like, *Wow, this was in my dad's hand.* It gets a little spiritual for me.

I respect everyone's time. New Yorkers' time is the most important commodity they have and I respect that. I'm not one of these guys that books every twenty minutes. I used to work with a gentleman in the city and he booked, I think, quarter-hour appointments even knowing that some of the appointments were an hour and a half long and patients would sit in the waiting room for hours. It would make me nervous, because to me that's showing a disrespect for those people's time.

In New York, you get a lot of grinding. You get cracked teeth, TMJ issues, joint issues. Grinding is one of the worst things that you can do to your teeth because the forces that your jaw exerts are stronger than any other force in your body and you'll get cracked teeth. It'll cause root canal on virgin teeth sometimes, on crowns.

You saw a lot of people having TMJ issues after 9/11, clenching their teeth because everyone's stressed out of their mind. During the financial meltdown you'd see these brokers coming in and they're like, "Why are the insides of my cheeks getting all yellow?" It was from fatty deposits. It's just a way of their body dealing with stress. When the garment center was imploding, because everything went overseas, you'd see these garment center guys coming in with cracked teeth. Or they're biting on pencils or ice. In 2007, '08 that was huge, huge. People grinding their teeth, just clenching and grinding their teeth.

You were seeing cracked teeth. You were seeing ground-down teeth. You were seeing things called apthuous ulcers, which is when you're run down you're gonna get sometimes an ulceration in your gums which hurts like hell. You've got to stay away from certain spicy foods and that kind of thing. You'd see neglect. You'd see people not wanting to come in because they don't know how they're going to pay. There was a slowdown in dentistry.

A lot of people lost their jobs and with that they lost their insurance. And even though we don't accept insurance they get reimbursed a certain amount of money. At the end of the day there's no out-of-pocket expense; now they don't have that insurance. They're canceling the appointment or putting the appointment off. Instead of coming in four times a year they'll come in twice. Or, instead of coming twice they'll come once. When they come back—if they come back—there's so much more that's gone on in their mouths because of neglect.

When I first started, I had a patient who was a phenomenally successful finance guy. He was in his twenties and was probably worth a couple hundred million dollars already at that point. I think he was a bond trader. This guy's teeth were ground to like pegs. I said, "You've got to learn how to relax." He said to me, "You don't get as successful as I am if you relax."

DYANNE ROSADO A Wall Street HR executive

When I started, it was the era of suits, like in *Working Girl*. I had suits with shoulder pads and gold buttons and stockings and pumps or heels, and those little silky chemises that you wear under a suit. It wasn't casual; it was still business dress. But by the end of my time at Chase, in the summer you could do business casual on Fridays. And then my real personality would come out: sundresses and sandals and things like that. But I remember sending a woman home because she wore a skort—you know, a skirt in the front and shorts in the back. Now it's: *Go crazy.* A year and a half ago, the place where I now work relaxed its business dress policy, because we still had pretty formal attire. And the first day that we published the policy, people emailed to confirm that they could wear sneakers and asked if they could wear shorts to the office. So it's twenty-five years later, people are still confused about what to wear to the office in a financial services business setting.

Most of my characters, the real characters, are New Yorkers, guys who grew up in New York and made it up the ranks. They're strong personalities, and these guys work hard. They know the city really well. There is something very rich about being in New York and having that iconic backdrop of Wall Street. I don't know if anywhere else you'd have someone say to an intern, you know, *Go with our chauffeur and go get us pizzas from L and B in Brooklyn, because it's the best pizza in New York,* you know? Or, *We all want Cuban coffees, go to Hoboken and make sure they come back hot.* It's like the city lends itself to these great big personalities. It's New York.

It's just human beings who have a little too much time, a little too much money, a little too much ego. And they're in a place, a playground, it's New York City. They can pretty much find anything, and other people who can keep up with them. There's some things that you laugh at and you say, this is part of the way we work. But other things you say, *No, we can't do this. This is not right.* You have to be the moral compass sometimes.

Before I came to my current job, I was head of HR for an interdealer broker on Wall Street. These are the guys that you see in the movies, like it's a trading desk and you have ten guys and they're yelling prices. And that's the best example of the need for camaraderie. Those folks are on contracts and they commit to be in their role for three years and they get equity. They get cash signing bonuses, and they get really high commission rates that translate into what you and I would understand as a salary. But they work together. They yell and scream and fight, but at the end of the day, they help each other close the transaction and that's what makes them successful.

I went from Brown Brothers Harriman, which is a white-shoe firm, old-school, the oldest partnership on Wall Street, to this crazy trading floor where my door opened and all these guys were there. At first I didn't understand it 'cause they're yelling and constantly bickering or chiding each other. But they need each other, and I came to understand that what they're doing is communicating. The really good ones are best friends with each other, or they have come up through the ranks together. And now they're at the mortgage-backed desk together, or they follow each other from firm to firm. And when they do their contracts and they start their desks, they bring their teams over because they understand each other and they trust each other to move fast and get the deals.

I've been in a lot of environments where I'm the only woman or one of a few women. After 9/11, I had a senior partner for the group that we were in come to get me very early one morning. He said, "Come walk with me, bring a pencil and a pad." I was like, "Okay, where are we going?" Literally counting butts in seats. He was taking attendance, who was there, who wasn't, at 8:58 a.m. Once you sort of strip away the ridiculousness of it, this guy's a PhD, a JD, who's running a multimillion-dollar practice, and he's walking around taking attendance.

He did that because he felt like the team had to come together and get out and generate business and work with their clients because we were in the deficit after 9/11. There was a lot less consulting and business being done around the team. So he was worried that we were going to have to lay people off. So it made sense after you took it away. But there are times when I think to myself, *I have a master's degree from Columbia. What am I doing? Are you kidding me?*

Then there was the old-school Brooklyn guy who was managing director of another firm I worked for. I remember being in a meeting when he was reprimanding someone. It was a guy who was on one of these big fat contracts and the guy wasn't generating revenue to cover his costs, cover his nut. That's what they call it. *You had to cover your nut.*

So we're paying you $20,000 a month. You have to at least be making 25. Because we need some for the house and whatever you're taking home.

This guy was failing and he didn't want to improve. He didn't want to take guidance or coaching or make any adjustment. And he started coughing and says, "Can I have some water?" to the managing director. And he goes, "No." The guy's coughing and I'm thinking, *Oh my God, as the HR person, should I get him some water?* I'm there taking notes. And then the guy turns to me and says, "Dyanne, can I get some water?" And I look up and the managing director slams his fist down on the desk and says, "No water!" I just kept taking notes.

It's funny because these are really powerful people in their industry, but they have a hard time firing others. On the trading floor for a while, my nickname was the Black Crow and they would *caw-caw* when I walked by. I had someone tell me, "You must have really bad karma for what you do." I had someone else once come into my office and say, "You just fired the company Santa Claus for our Christmas party." Another said, "This is why the banks failed in 2008, because there are people like you without heart." I'm like, *Okay, thank you. You still have to give me your laptop and your badge.*

But then I've also had people say to me, "I'm glad you're the one firing me and not somebody else, because you made this a lot easier." Or, once someone said, "Look, I don't care about my severance. I have a son who had leukemia five years ago; I just want medical insurance." I said, "Yeah, let's figure this out. Let's do that together and make sure that we'll cover the cost of your COBRA for the 36 months that you can have COBRA."

You just try to do your job, and you try to do it with as much humanity as possible.

BEN TURSHEN A meditation teacher

So, what we experience in New York, it's a sensory experience. People talk about stress and they think, "Oh, my job's stressful" or "My relationship with my partner is really stressful" or "I hate riding on subways." Those things are demands and we have a certain capacity to adapt and interact with demands. And once we get overloaded we start having stress response, so it's not that those things are stressful inherently. If we have enough capacity, they're not. But we have a limited capacity and the city is demanding. You got to get from here to there and people are in your way and it's not all up to you. In fact, very little of it is.

Our bodies haven't evolved to live in a place like this. Our bodies are still evolved to live at the end of the last Ice Age. The sensory experience that we have in one day is more than a person 250 years ago would experience in their lifetime. So, it's a total overload. And now we have our devices, where it's a constant flow of information and connectivity, which does wonderful things for business and interaction, but it's also in overload. The body stores it and it's running all of these programs in the background, going, "Hey, if you see this, if you smell this, if you taste this, if you feel this, you should respond and react this way."

What meditation does is increase our ability to adapt and actually defrags all that programmed old information that's now irrelevant and redundant. It's a hygienic experience, but it allows us to go out into the world with less history and more adaptability.

And then we find New York a more palatable experience. It takes more than our morning commute to get us totally unraveled. And the meditation I teach, it's designed to be done twice a day, because you need that second round of it to keep you going through the evening, because you're getting hit with all that stimulus all day, so the meditation that you did in the morning wears off by the afternoon, so you want to re-up it.

Eight million of us in New York City aren't going to learn how to meditate, but if we get enough of us doing it, it would have an impact. Because it's affecting the collective consciousness, really. You walk down the street and you're a little anxious and nervous and terrified. That's affecting everybody who's in your event horizon and they start to get a little anxious and nervous and terrified. You start walking around calm and relaxed and happy and blissful and someone sees that smile on your face for no reason and they go, "Alright, not so bad."

MY MEDITATION STUDIO is right on Fifth Avenue and that's purposeful. I face Fifth Avenue. I've got to teach people to meditate in New York City with all that street noise and all the honking and all of that.

When I was looking around at spaces, the guy who was showing me around, we'd get to certain buildings and they're like, "What do you want to do here?"

"Meditation studio." He's like, "It's really loud, but we can double-pane the windows."

"No, no, no. I need to teach them how to meditate in New York City."

That street noise is really good.

I have to teach them how to meditate in a loud environment and really understanding what those sounds are and the experience of sound is actually you having a thought of it. You treat it similar to any other sound that you had, any other thought that you would have in meditation. You can be thinking what's for dinner or the movie you want to see this weekend, and it's the same as you noticing those sounds, same as you noticing the sensations in the body. I have to teach people how to meditate when they're in pain, when they're sick, when they're in loud environments. My studio's great. I love the location and the light that's in there, but also the noise. I actually want the noise, but I think that's an overwhelming experience for a lot of people. You walk outside, they're doing construction and there's traffic and the honking, so I think meditation just gives you more capacity before you feel overwhelmed.

The expectations for someone living in New York City are relatively high. That can absolutely feel overwhelming. The city's designed for you to get caught up in that, because it's expensive to live here, so if you want to increase your quality of life, you want to make more money so you can go from the 200-square-foot apartment to the 300-square-foot apartment and have a room to sit down and eat a meal not on top of your bed.

What's the relative percentage of the things that we experience on a daily basis that we can actually control? It's a fraction of one percent, but we want to try to control all of it. We want it all to happen a certain way, and we have this big expectation. If it doesn't happen the way we expect, then we're upset and angry.

You start meditating, you start just letting go, letting go, letting go. The whole idea is just letting go, letting go, letting go, and then you start doing that with your eyes open and the whole thing's just easier. It's just easier to be there.

I was riding the subway with someone last night. We were coming down from my meditation studio and I get the 6 train at 33rd Street and I take it down to Brooklyn Bridge. The 6 train runs local the whole way. At 14th Street, the 4/5 comes down the same track and you can transfer right across. I was riding the subway with one of my students who lives down here and it was a crowded train. We each had a seat and I have a rule for this for myself. If I see the train across the platform, I'll go across. If I don't see it, I'm not going to wait.

We didn't see it, and I just said, "I've timed this out, actually. It's a three-minute difference," and so we agreed to stay seated and the express train rolls up. She pops up and she's like, "Let's go get it," and there's a bunch of people. I'm like, "We're okay."

You have to let those things go. Really, you're going to see everybody running across the platform for three minutes. It's a three-minute difference.

NEW YORK CITY IS absolutely stunning if you just open your eyes and look. That's one of the things that stress does. It really constrains our vision. We're kind of in this survival mode, where literally, our vision changes. When you're overwhelmed, you start to get myopic focus. We usually have about 140 degrees of peripheral vision, and we lose it. We just see straight out. We stop seeing out of the sides of our eyeballs.

Even the people who just work in New York City or commute in from Westchester, they get into Grand Central and they make a bee-line right to the subway or their office. They're not looking up at the ceiling. We tend to get annoyed at these tourists who are looking around and checking all this stuff out. You don't have to sit there and take a million photographs. Just look at it for a moment. Take that in. I think that's an important thing for New Yorkers to do. I think not only does it build acceptance of this place, but it also builds admiration.

The dynamism of it, the movement of it, it's just … Look at any time-lapse photography of Grand Central Station or Times Square, and all that movement is incredible. It's movement that we see in nature, but it's here too, and when you're just a little water molecule moving in a wave, you don't know that you're part of a wave.

You're just getting knocked around, so it can feel like that. You don't know that you're part of something bigger. But when you pull back the lens and you get that perspective of, "Hey, this is all moving, it's all dynamic," and you're not getting knocked around, there's absolute beauty in that too.

MY PARENTS LIVED IN this awesome duplex on 14th Street in the Meatpacking District. Back in the early '80s, when I grew up there, there was still meatpacking. There were no hotels, there was no fancy boutique shops, there was no nightclubs, there was no nice restaurants. None of that. There was the Old Homestead, the steakhouse that's still there, and a little diner called Florent. Those were the only two reasons you ever came out of our apartment building and made a left. You never went west. You always went towards Eighth Avenue. You never went towards Ninth Avenue. There was nothing of interest there, everything possible that you wanted to avoid: meatpackers and drug dealers and drug addicts.

I remember the smell of it. You could smell the blood and all of that stuff coming out of the cobblestones, which was disgusting. It was gross. New York City in the '80s wasn't as bad as it was in the '70s, but it was still bad. New York in the '90s is where it really transitioned from being a pretty dangerous place. It was still pretty gnarly and raw back then.

When my parents bought the brownstone that I grew up in it was an SRO, which is Single Room Occupancy. There's still some SROs that exist in Manhattan, but—very rare. There used to be a lot more of them. That's the way a lot of people lived. It was very affordable because all you had was a room, a shared bathroom in the hallway, and a pay phone in the hallway. People didn't have leases, they paid weekly rent. It was like a hotel or a hostel.

My parents bought the building from the former owner who, prior to the sale, was able to either evict or not renew leases for something like 95 percent of the building. Then three of the tenants who lived in that building took the former owner to housing court and said, "Hey, we have rights. We're protected under the landlord/tenant laws here. You can't evict us."

They settled, joining my parents to the case, by building out three studios on the ground floor of this brownstone. Then my parents converted the brownstone to a co-op, which was the popular thing to do in the '80s, and sold the top two floors as floor-through apartments. We lived in the duplex on the first and second floor, which was awesome, and my parents had these three tenants on the ground floor who paid zero rent, pretty much.

There were two men who lived in the studios. They're small studios, like 250 square feet. One of them was an artist and I think he was a bookkeeper or something like that. The other one was also an artist who happened to work security at museums. The woman who lived in between, she was an acupuncturist. We sold our duplex in 1993, but my parents still had these three tenants on 14th Street because they didn't sell those apartments to the owner. He didn't want them. There was no reason. You're losing money on them, if anything.

3

Building Stories

When my wife and I got married we were looking for a place to live. We were living in a studio apartment, and I was looking around the city. It was a time when there was a lot of development going on and the city was funding a lot of stuff. I found this building on 14th Street, on the West Side, between Eighth and Ninth Avenue, just a block up from the Meatpacking District, at a time when it literally *was* the meatpacking district.

We bought the building for $260,000, which was less than what we were seeing apartments going for. I was excited to do a project. My wife wasn't so excited about it, but I was. It was a building that used to be a rooming house. When we bought it, the guy who owned it had already in one way or the other gotten rid of something like fifteen tenants, and there were three tenants left in the building. They were organized by one of the tenants, and they really weren't leaving.

It was at a time when the city was trying to convert what were rooming houses into, not luxury apartments, but class-A apartments, meaning full apartments with kitchens and baths. So we ended up doing a somewhat convoluted thing. We turned the building into a co-op and created three apartments upstairs. Because it wasn't vacant. We had those tenants. We created little studio apartments on the ground floor for them.

The other reason that we bought that building was that I had already lived in the Village, and shopped at Jefferson Market, which used to be a great market. I just loved it, so my only rule of where I was looking was to be able to walk to Jefferson Market to get the groceries. It was really a local grocer. They had a great butcher, they had great fish, they had great produce. It was the only one around then, and had been around forever. I mean, the area's called Jefferson Market, and that actually was the Jefferson Market.

The guy who bought it before us was only the second owner of that building. I don't know when they turned it into a rooming house, because it really was a somewhat intact New York brownstone, but in crumbling condition. Still, to this day, the common staircase has the same squeak in it. It was there when I was there, and we just never could figure out what to do with it. It's still there. And there still was a lot of period detail. The fireplaces were there, there was lots of very ornate molding, but sort of chopped up, so there was no way one could have restored it. It was habitable, but really a little bit crazy.

The interesting thing about 14th Street at the time was—if you got up early there was a parade. Not a literal parade, but there were lots of transvestites, guys in drag, walking up and down the street, because the Meatpacking District was where they all were. It also was a time in New York where there were a lot of homeless people. There would be homeless people camping out in the steps, because it was one of those brownstones where they have removed the stoop, so if you went down a few steps, there was an overhang, so it was sort of protective.

14th Street was never in beautiful shape when we were there. There was a funeral home, there was a church, but otherwise it was pretty residential. Then you went right into the Meatpacking District. It was slippery from the fat on the streets. It was mostly cobblestone down there, and on a hot day you didn't go there, because it smelled terribly. All the doors to these places had those plastic strips, but you could see inside the trucks when they were doing the loading.

The borderline between Chelsea and the Village goes through 14th Street, so we liked to say we live in the West Village, but we were on the edge of the West Village. I don't think anybody else considered it the Village but us.

This was not a luxury building. It's not like a Park Avenue story. It is the story of three tenants paying about $100 a month, and other people buying their apartments at that time for decent money. Over $100,000 for an apartment back then, which was decent money.

We lived on two floors, the parlor floor and the floor above. Later, when we left the city, we sold that apartment to a guy who did a gut job on the whole apartment. I thought we had done a decent job on the apartment, and he replaced everything pretty much one for one. He put in terrazzo floors and really big marble bathrooms, and a top-of-the-line kitchen, and then he went bankrupt in the middle of his project and he had to sell his apartment.

The two guys who bought the apartment from that guy, it was in the middle of a renovation, but they bought an apartment with really beautiful finishes, and when they sold their apartment, it was for something like $3.5 million or $4 million. So, you still have people downstairs paying $100 a month, and a $4 million apartment, at the same time.

WITH OUR TENANTS, I first sent them a note saying I wanted to introduce myself and meet them, and I got a lawyer's letter in response—from the one woman who's still there. But then, they somewhat came around. I would go there often to check construction, but while they were living through this, they didn't really complain. So, during that part, which was a little bit contentious, I really didn't see them much.

They once filed a complaint, I think when we turned off the water, when we were replacing the pipes and the water was coming back on. I gave them notice, but still they filed a complaint. But after that they were our neighbors, and we lived with them. Not that we were best friends, because I was the sponsor of the building so I was their landlord.

This one woman, she would have been a great super for the building, because she knows how to fix things. To this day, when she fixes something she writes me a letter explaining what she fixed, and they are the funniest letters in the world. She was the first person I met in New York who always rode a bike. That's how she got around New York, but even then there really weren't that many people who used it as their means of transportation. Still, to this day, that's how she gets around the city. She's a tough cookie, a very capable tough cookie.

She knew my kids when they were little, and she would say things to me about my kids (good things). She really watched my family grow up. Another tenant, Arthur, he was an artist, and he was also the super for a building on Gramercy Park for . . . I forget her name, but she was the woman who played the Good Witch in *The Wizard of Oz*. He was her super, and in her will, she left money to her daughter, to take care of Arthur in his old age.

These were rent-controlled tenants, and their rent was so little, and I wasn't allowed to raise it for a certain amount of years. The amount of paperwork to raise their rent was so involved that I just never did it.

After twenty-five years, for two months in a row, all of a sudden I didn't get a rent check from Arthur, and that had never happened before. I had an emergency number or something for him, and I ended up speaking to that woman, the Good Witch's daughter, I think it was. There was a dilemma because either Arthur wasn't doing so well or she didn't know what to do, because she was looking to move out to Colorado, and she was hoping that she could get Arthur to agree to move to Colorado. This was the time when my son Ben had graduated from college and he was about to go into graduate school in New York, and I thought, wow, if Arthur would leave, then Ben could have that studio apartment while he was a student. So, I said, "Listen, if Arthur wants to leave, I will gladly pay his moving costs."

A couple of times a year, Arthur would burn toast, and burnt toast, you can smell that all through the entire building. I'd go and knock on his door and I'd look in and I'd be like, "This is really a fire hazard." He never went through his stuff. I wouldn't call him a hoarder, because it sounds like he bought things and didn't get rid of them, but that studio apartment was . . . Well, he was a painter, and there was a bed, and then just racks and racks and racks of his paintings and stretched canvases and supplies, and these cupboards filled. There was an aisle to walk to the bed, and a little thing to go to the kitchen.

Arthur left and sent us postcards from Colorado. We really hardly saw him, because I didn't know when he went to work, I didn't know when he was home, and I only knew he was home when he burned toast. We had these movers come and move all his stuff. They couldn't believe we were asking them to move all this stuff, because it was all falling apart as it was getting on the truck. When it arrived in Colorado, this woman was like, "Why are you sending all this?" And I said, "There was no one to say send this or that."

Arthur had a storage space in the cellar, and we packed up that too, but that was just more of the same. It was just racks and racks of old sketchbooks that were falling apart. But he really was one of those New York characters. He wasn't an artist that showed his work or anything. He must have gone to drawing classes. Lots of nude sketches, that kind of thing, going to class with a model. Still lifes, you know, bowl of fruit, jug of wine kind of drawings. Just tons of them.

This was a guy who, when he moved, he was in his nineties, so I think he lived in a room in a rooming house in Greenwich Village and had a job as a super, and what he really probably wanted to be was an artist, and he practiced. Not measuring in terms of success or not success, but I don't think he ever showed it to anybody.

The other tenant, Frank, was in the apartment that was on the street. He was a guard at the Museum of Modern Art, and I even saw him there once. We saw Frank. "Hey, Frank," and he was like, "*Shhhh.*" We always thought it was interesting that he worked at the museum, and I think most literally starving artists need a job, but here's a guard who works at the Museum of Modern Art going home, able to afford to paint on his own.

Frank painted, so we knew when he was home, because you could smell the paint when you went past his door. Arthur's the burnt toast, and Frank's the linseed oil and oil paint. None of them ever really complained about anything. In all the years, nobody asked to have their apartment painted or anything like that, and one day when I was talking to a lawyer, they said, sure, but then something's going to happen, and they're going to say in front of the judge, "He never painted, he never fixed anything." Talking about me.

Frank had a heavy accent, and he really looked the part of a painter. He was very thin, so his pants were too big and really cinched with the belt. Big glasses. He did all different-sized paintings. Very abstract paintings. Unlike Arthur, who was a drawing-class kind of artist, that's how he practiced, Frank's were really abstract—color, big blotches of color. Smoked like a fiend. You would have thought his paintings would have been dark, but they weren't. They were vivid, big color-blocked kind of paintings. I don't know if he ever showed his work either. His work, it wasn't stored like Arthur's work. He didn't have a ton of work. I know that he was always painting.

I would say our tenants got lucky, because in the end they got these apartments that had kitchens and baths, and these rooms and windows. Frank lived in that place for probably twenty-five, thirty years.

One day my other rent-controlled tenant called me. We were living in Westchester . . . and said that Frank was in the hospital and was asking to see me. He was in Beth Israel, which is the same hospital my kids were born in, so I went to visit him. I didn't know, before they called me to say Frank wanted to speak to me, I didn't know that he was ill or in hospice, but he either rose to the occasion or, I don't know, but he was really chipper.

I was concerned to see him, because I thought he'd look terrible. He actually looked great. He was sitting up, and there was energy to his conversation. I didn't have to lean in with my ear to hear him.

He said to me, "I want to ask you something."

And I said, "Okay."

So he said, "How come you never raised my rent?"

I said, "Well, Frank, the paperwork was so complicated, and I could raise it two percent, and it just never seemed worth it."

He said he always wondered why I didn't do it. He wondered why I never tried to evict him.

I said, "But Frank, because you can't in New York. You're rent-controlled, you're at a certain age, and it's not legal."

He said that he never could have lived in New York without this gift from me, this rent, and he really wanted to thank me.

I said, "Frank, listen, it was really great to know you."

He said, "I don't know what's in there, but whatever's in the apartment, take whatever you want to take, and get rid of anything else."

I went home. He gave me the name of some friends of his who had a key. When I got into the apartment, his friends had, I guess, taken his art. There were a few unfinished things. Take anything you want, Frank said. He had a drafting table in there. So we took his glasses and the drafting table.

I got a call from a friend saying that right after I left, he died.

I mean, I knew he liked us all those years, but I think he just never wanted to rock the boat and say, "Hey, I'll give you more rent." I always did say, but I always said it as a joke, that this is my contribution to the arts, whenever people talked about it. I said it jokingly, not realizing that it was true. That we basically supported two living artists in New York, into their nineties.

In the end, even though people would always say to us, "You're crazy, you could have raised their rents," had I raised it, by the time I left there, or now, maybe it would be $200? I don't know what it would have been, but I'm happy not to have done that.

I was a reluctant landlord. I didn't mean to become a landlord. I just couldn't do anything about it. We bought that building as a place to live, the only way that we could afford to do it was to fix it up, sell off those apartments, get that tax abatement. I wasn't looking to make a profession out of being a landlord or renovating buildings or anything. There were people after I worked on that building who approached me and said, "I'd love to buy a building with you. You have the experience of doing all this." It was never my intention to do that.

The crazy thing, after all this, my kids were living in these studio apartments and outgrew their studio apartments, and I gave them each those apartments. We turned them over to them legally, so one of the things that they get now, is they rent out their apartments, these same studio apartments. We did fix them up a little bit, but they're tiny. Now I think they each get something like $2,500 a month rent.

There's talk of selling the building. Everybody in the co-op has agreed to sell the building, and we're talking about . . . So, from 1979 to now, we're selling the building to somebody who's basically going to demolish it to build something nice. I mean, the building's nice, but it's just not where everything else is going in the neighborhood. I think it's $12.5 million.

I think of it as a New York story. The city helped make it happen. There was incentive to keep these tenants, there was incentive to change the buildings, there were just things going on that don't go on nowadays. The one tenant that we still have, that we're going to work out some arrangement with, she's a rent-controlled tenant, she's over seventy-something years old. She's entitled to live in New York City, and if it was me, I wouldn't want somebody kicking me out.

It's a crazy little world in that one little building there.

I think nowadays we just think of artists showing their work, or posting their work, or whatever they do, and making a go of it, but we don't think about how many people are painters and artists in any which way, and they have a life and they go to work, but who they are, are artists, and they just do it because that's what they do. That's how those guys were.

My wife's a painter. She wears Frank's glasses when she paints.

LOUISE WEINBERG A curator at the Queens Museum

The Panorama of the City of New York is a repository of dreams. It's the heart of the Queens Museum. There's no flashing neon sign advertising it, but we'll get people from all over the world who will come in and quietly ask, "Panorama?" A guy knocked on the door once when we'd just closed. He was German. He'd trudged through the park. He said in his heavily accented voice, "Panorama?" If that was the only word he could say in English, hey, great. We let him in.

Seeing the Panorama for the first time is like when you came to New York for the first time, and you got out of the subway, and you didn't know where you were. That feeling, that exhilaration and terror. You have to orient yourself. The Bronx is up there, the Battery's downtown. But if you can't see a landmark, something that's obvious, you have to use all of your alien senses that you don't normally use. When you look at the Panorama, you can kind of get a sense of that, that euphoria.

There are few people left who remember the Panorama from the World's Fair era, so visitors that come to the museum today have the wow factor of the scale. But they have a completely different experience of it being open air, being able to stand right next to Manhattan and look right over it. Anybody from 1964 up to 1990, anybody in that era, had a completely different experience of it.

It's 10,000 square feet, approximately, so it's the world's largest architectural model. It is early 1960s design, materials, and engineering. It's old-school. I mean, it's gears and string basically. The planes that take off and land at LaGuardia: there's this huge gear underneath the floor. There's two gears, one at East and West Side, up at the ceiling. And it's squidding line, actually, like you'd use when you're going to go fishing. So, it's a fabric. It's not monofilament, not plastic. And those break periodically, or they get caught, and a plane will get trapped underneath, or stop dead in the middle somewhere. So, quick, we have to get the plane going again.

It was built originally on these two-by-four legs that shrink over time. If you look under there some of them have pulled themselves up and they're floating in their spaces. They've shored it up with a steel framework, so it's not going anywhere. When we clean, the curatorial department puts on blue booties and we'll go out and Swiffer all the areas with the water. You feel really big and you can't walk on anything. Over the years people have gone out with leaf blowers, which is not the best way to clean it because then your shrubs and your loose buildings blow all over.

I've actually painted all the water in the Panorama. I worked with one other person, and it took us a month. It was a lot of crawling around. The large gross bodies of water, I mean the Hudson and the East River, and then the Long Island Sound, are pretty obvious. But you don't realize that there's no blueprint of the actual waterway. So we were getting up and looking. See where there's a little inlet off of Flushing Bay, or the Flushing River? We did that every weekend for a month.

It was Robert Moses's intention that the Panorama be used as a tool for urban planning. It hasn't totally fulfilled that dream of his. But certain community groups have come and used it either as a bully pulpit to promote an idea, or to protest and point out, well, if you put this shopping mall right here instead of low-income housing, this is what's going to happen to the surrounding area. Now, of course, those voices get completely drowned out.

Generally during the school year there could be four groups of students here concurrently, with four different educators talking over each other. And what you find on the Panorama afterwards are pencils and crumpled-up pieces of paper and the little entry stickers. Once we found condoms, which was terrible because one of them left a wet oily spot on JFK.

When the Panorama was made it had about 830,000 buildings. Between the close of the World's Fair and 1990, about 10,000 buildings were added. In 1990, when the building started its first major renovation, the entire Panorama was taken out in sections and shipped up to Nyack, New York, where Lester & Associates was in business at that time. They updated it to about 895,000 buildings, and reinstalled it. But they had to cut off part of the Rockaways and part of New Jersey, because somehow it didn't quite fit as its original. On the Panorama itself, Jersey's just black.

MARVIN ABRAM A window cleaner

I was really hard up for a job. I was working in the Garment District, bringing home about $90 a week and it wasn't making it. My uncle, who was a second-generation window cleaner, I kept on asking him for a job. Finally I got one. He introduced me to a few people, I was sworn in at the union, and I went to cleaning windows. I've been cleaning windows since—twenty-eight years later.

I've been doing everything from ladder work, stick work, belt work—where you hang out the window on a belt—and scaffold. I'm a well-rounded person when it comes to window cleaning. Ground work and everything else. I wouldn't clean windows anyplace else in the world.

My first day was at the old Hanover National Building near Wall Street. They were showing me how to use a squeegee, how to clean the entrance doors, stuff of that nature. The belt was there for when I got there, I was a size 34 back then, and they took me up to the eighth floor and opened up the window, showing me how to put the belt on, how to reach out, and hook up, and how to proceed on climbing out of the window. I did that with no problem, because I wanted a job. I wasn't going to have any fear of heights. "Do what we tell you and don't fall." So that's the only advice I got. Short and sweet. They really took a special interest in making sure we did it the right way.

They taught me how to inspect the belt, even though it was brand new. You still have to inspect it, because the belt is primarily made out of fiberglass, and make sure the runners are intact, the springs are working on the clips, make sure it's not dry-rotted, make sure it wasn't kept in a dry place that has a lot of heat or a place that might have too much moisture.

Anything you do in window cleaning, the first thing you are taught is to inspect the equipment. That's first and foremost, before you go over the side of a building, or go out a window, before you climb a ladder, anything like that. Not just for your safety but for the safety of the public.

When you're doing belt work, it becomes your responsibility to protect your belt, protect your tool. Because that's something that now, physically, you take home with you or keep in your locker. Your life really does depend on it. Most of the time, scaffold men, they're rescued. There's very few fatalities on a scaffold. But when you're a belt worker, it's the complete opposite. Because if you haven't been taking care of your belt, doing the right things when it comes to being well kept, as far as your belt, you don't get any second chances at all. It's history. You're supposed to return a belt in every four years. They get broken down, get rebuilt, or they get destroyed and the company purchases a new belt.

That first day, I went out on the eighth floor. The ledges might've been about two inches wide. I wanted to get it over with. I just wanted to get out there and close the window, stand out there for a few seconds, and come back in and get it over with. But as time went on, it became second nature to just climb out a window and do what I have to do. It became second nature.

Five years ago I started cleaning the windows at 30 Rock. I got to learn about the rich history of Rockefeller Center and the reason it was the way it was built, you know, where Rockefeller could actually see his house, with his mountain in Pennsylvania, 'cause you could see all the way to Pennsylvania from the Top of the Rock.

I START WORK so early in the morning and usually we go straight up to the floors and it's just peace and tranquility. Serenity. You know, you're out there, you don't have any supervisors hovering over you, looking over your shoulders, that's a no-no. You're doing what you have to do that early in the morning, and you try to get your job done before people come into the offices.

We start hanging out the windows by six o'clock in the morning, so we can be done by nine.

I have some people take the squeegee from me saying, "I can do that," and it just comes out horrible. It's just practice. It's not like you're cleaning a glass table at home, or a mirror at home, or anything like that. There was one squeegee when I started, now they have a bunch of different brands of squeegee. I use Ettore, I'm an old-fashioned guy. I stick with the same squeegee. The Ettore squeegees have been around since the '30s. An Ettore handle, a brass handle, will last ten years. They have Sorbos, and the Ninjas, and all that and I think it's just to sell a product because, basically, you're doing the same job, the same function with the squeegee. One might be brass, the other one might be a plastic handle. It doesn't matter, I can clean a window with any squeegee you give me.

I was taught to never take a squeegee off the window, unless it's completely clean. I start from the left-hand corner, make my way to the right-hand corner. Don't remove the squeegee off the window until it's clean. With experience, I could take it off and know how to put it back on. And not leave a line, you know. When you're first starting out, you walk away from the window, you don't see the line. But when it dries and the sun hits it and you're like, *Wow*. There it is. And that's what the customer says too.

WINDOW CLEANERS SEE interesting stuff when we're out there. Sometimes you might be in a commercial building, where part of it is residential, and so you just stumble upon stuff. People don't expect to see you out there that early in the morning, you know? People might be walking around naked, or engaging in sexual intercourse or things of that nature. It startles the window cleaners. We are always listening for strange sounds on the scaffold. When we inspect it, we don't take the scaffold apart but we check the cables, you know. At least the cable that we can see, that's out. We might raise the scaffold up four or five feet to look under it, make sure there's no loose parts.

Then there's some stuff internally within a scaffold, that we can't get at, that we can't get to. But we know what we're supposed to hear and what we're not supposed to hear. We're listening for sounds that might be abnormal. Grinding, the cables being chewed up or something like that.

As a kid growing up in New York City, you're really not taken in by the big skylines or anything like that, the Statue of Liberty....I was never fascinated with the Empire State Building and the World Trade

Centers before they went down. They have always been there, so you expect them to be there.

Even when I started cleaning windows, I wasn't fascinated. I used to run and jump, play inside abandoned buildings and stuff like that. Jump from one window to the next, you know. I lived in Bushwick, we used to jump from this part of the roof, down to this part of the roof, you know, and roll over and get up and keep on running. So I never really had a fear of heights. People, they want to make that money, they want that good job, but you can't get over that fear of actually climbing out of windows. I didn't have that problem.

I've worked with people where you could actually see... They climb up the ladder, and you can feel the ladder shaking because their legs are shaking. You wonder like, *What's going on? What's wrong with you up there?* You see people, really hesitant, climbing out of the window. You have to talk people back in because they're scared. They're scared to actually lean back on a window.

When you go out of the window you have to lean back on the belt. You can't stand straight up on a window to clean a window, you know. You got to lean back. You've got people that are like, "Ah, no, I don't want to lean back, no!" It's funny, you laugh at it. It's not funny at the time. But you're like, "C'mon and do it, we have to do our jobs. Lean back."

STEVE ROSENTHAL The owner of a recording studio

I owned a studio called the Magic Shop. It was on Crosby Street between Spring and Broome. I built it in 1987, and I had to close it four months ago. I was altogether there for twenty-eight years.

In order to find a space, I had done a pretty wide search. I wanted to have a space with high ceilings and no columns. I wanted it to be in SoHo, I wanted the studio to be down there. So, I literally walked, not exaggerating, from Houston down to where the Towers were, across and back up to Lafayette, all the way back up to Houston. It took me about, I don't know, two and half, three months literally walking up and down every block. This was way before every block has a real estate broker and everyone's on their phone. It was a lot more analog.

I made these little notebooks that had "what space, how much it cost, who to call." And the space that I eventually found was one that I just literally walked in, knocked on the door. There was a sign that said, "Space for rent." Crosby Street was pretty funky back then. It was dangerous. But it was teeming with artists and painters, and sculptors, and musicians. And there was a really vibrant scene. I was happy to be on that block.

The studio was constructed properly, in the sense that they were rooms within rooms. It was literally like a structure inside another structure that's on a floating floor, and the walls are hanging from isolated hangers. It's expensive and time-consuming, but what you do is, you isolate your space from the rest of the building so that you can play loud and not have the sound travel into other parts of the building. Or have people's stuff coming into your space.

It took about six months to build the studio. It was constructed properly, but you never know whether it's gonna sound good or not. You can do everything right, and the room can sound like shit. You just don't know. It's sort of a combination of magic and science, really. When I opened, it was very hard to get people in there. Musicians, producers, record companies tend to be sort of superstitious. They want to go to a place that has a track record, if they're gonna spend money. Back in the day, you used to spend money to make a record.

It took almost two years of it basically being my sessions, before I started to have outside people come to the studio. At first, everybody that came would tell me all the things I did wrong. And what I should change.

"Everything should have carpets." "Everything should have Sheetrock." "Everything should be padded." "Everything should have wood." "You should put brick." I mean, everybody's a studio genius, right?

I also opened up a live room during a time period where it was mostly synth, squeaky girl dance music. The Madonna thing was really big at that point, and all of the imitators. And it was all machine based. Since I had the opportunity to build a studio, I wanted to build one like the classic ones that I got to go to when I was a kid. So I built a live room, which people thought was a little insane at the time.

I had gone on a Neve hunt, to England, and I found this very unique Neve console and had it shipped back here to America. That was 1987, the console was already sixteen, seventeen years old. The idea of vintage consoles and vintage gear, which now is a whole industry and everybody loves it—it was not looked at like that. In fact, most of the Neve consoles back then were being destroyed, and then you would take out a part of it to use with your digital stuff and your synths. But the actual console itself would usually be trashed. And so I found this really unique console that had been at the BBC in Maida Vale in 1971. It had a whole life at Maida Vale before I got it. It did broadcasts with Bowie and Pink Floyd and Badfinger.

Then it went to another studio in the East End of London, which is where I found it. People thought I was kind of daft to build a studio with a live room, and around this notion of an analog console. I would give my shtick and most people would just say, "Thank you very much and all," and leave. But there was this band called the Grace Pool on Warner Brothers, and they came in and I gave my spiel. I didn't even have to go more than three or four sentences after we walked around. They said, "Okay, great. We'll come for a month."

So that was the first gig. And then after that, I did a number of high-profile records. I'm a little vague on exactly what the order is. But Butch Vig came in and did *Dirty* by Sonic Youth, right? Then the Ramones came in with Ed Stasium and did *Mondo Bizarro*. Suzanne Vega came and I got to work with her. And then Lou Reed came, and he did *Magic and Loss* with Roger Moutenot. And then I did Charles Brown, the great blues artist, I did a Charles Brown record with Doctor John. And after those five records, I had a business and I had a place that people were like, "Oh, okay. We can come here now. It's okay." It had gotten a serious stamp of approval from a wide range of iconic artists.

Obviously that makes me happy, but at the time I was most happy that I could continue, 'cause I had put a bunch of money in. I had a wonderful partner, and he had put a bunch of money in. It was really hard to get going, but after those records I had a business. And then people would call and want to come.

A recording studio's unlike any other room. It's a really unique environment. But it's fascinating because it's a place where people get exposed in a true way. You see what they're actually like, which I always found really great. To some people it's very spiritual. To some people it's very mechanical. Does this work, does that work? Why the fuck doesn't this work?

The idea was, it was a live room. Acoustically, it was live, so that when people played, you could hear resonated frequencies sort of interacting. It wasn't a dead '70s environment. It was a live space where things would resonate. And so people could hear themselves and also hear the people that they were playing with.

It's a funny thing about making records, people want to see each other and play live, at least in the world that I created. But you need to have some isolation between the instruments and the sounds, so that when you sit in front of the mixing console, you can sort of put it together again. So I did have some isolated spaces. I had a big drum platform.

I had a big movable wall, which I built after Rick Rubin asked me to build it, and I thought it was a really good idea. And then I had two little iso-huts. But mostly, it was a space musicians interacted. And so most of the records that came out of the Magic Shop were what I would call played records.

Even David Bowie's last record, *Blackstar*, which was done at the Magic Shop, it's a played record. David was in the room singing and the band was playing. Yeah, he does the vocals, fixes this, but the energy created by the interaction of people playing together makes something very unique.

One of the fascinating parts about being in the studio is that when people are making something, they reveal themselves in all ways. Because most people who come to a studio want to make a great record, and want to make something that is a really... How should I say this? It's like an accurate document of what they care about at that particular moment.

And so even if it's, like, "Fuck you. I hate you." They want to make sure that it's clearly understood that it's "Fuck you. I hate you." And if it's "I love you dearly, and I want to spend my life with you," it's the same thing. It really needs to be an accurate representation of that.

So, no matter what the subject matter, or even the kind of music, it's a place where people reveal a lot about themselves. There's no cookie-cutter way, because everyone has a different process to get to that point where they can create. Some people need to be pricks and treat people like shit, whether they're engineers or artists or producers. Some people are incredibly loving. Some people are very quiet, don't say a word. Some people are nuts, they have to do drugs. They have to have sex in my bathroom downstairs.

You know what I mean? Everyone has their own sort of triggers to get them to the point where they can create. It's always different. Some people would come early in the morning. Phil Spector came and worked on the *Back to Mono* box, and he didn't show up until eleven o'clock at night. The place was pitch black, and completely freezing. So cold, it was incredible.

Kim Deal from the Breeders didn't start working until two o'clock a.m. When David Bowie came, he made his last two records at the studio, right? In total secret, and we kept that secret for both records for years. David would come every morning at 10:25 or 10:30 and Kabir, who's here now—he was one of the engineers on *Blackstar*, and was the head engineer at the Magic Shop for the last years—he would know when he was coming, and he would come. So he would show up. It's based on the process that the artist and the producer need to go through to get to that point where they can actually do the thing that they're supposed to do there.

I had this little room that was off back in the control room, which in the early days was my office. And then I moved downstairs into the dungeon. And that became a room where people would sit and write, and work on the lyrics. They could get out of the studio. I tried to keep it relaxed, because these people are under incredible amounts of pressure, especially when you're talking about the really super famous.

I did not bother anyone. I like to leave them alone. I respect their ability to either be pissed off or happy. You can do it all correctly, but that doesn't necessarily mean that people will be happy there.

With David Bowie, what happened was Tony Visconti called to come by the studio. He'd worked there a number of times and he wanted to see it again to see what was going on, and he was very vague about what was going on. This was during the time period when everyone thought Bowie was ill, but he wasn't. He was very healthy at that point. We were not told that it was him, at all. The way that we put it together was when we started getting calls from the guys that played in his band. We're like, "Oh, well, this is you-know-who's band." I don't know if we could even say his name, at that point. We were too freaked out.

I remember the first session for *The Next Day*, which was the first one Bowie did here. But we really didn't even know until he showed up. We all signed nondisclosures. And also, we pared the staff in half. Because some of the kids I just couldn't trust with the knowledge. Even if they had the best intentions, I just felt some of the really young ones couldn't deal with it.

There were many times I would go into the room and ask Tony, I would say like, "So, is it going to happen? Will it come out?" And he would be like, "I don't know, maybe." No one really knew whether it would be a record.

We kept the secret completely for over two years. I found out about *The Next Day* the same way everybody else did. My wife was on Facebook and she said, "There's something on the David Bowie page," and we both went, "Holy fuck." And that's how I found out and that's how I heard "Where Are We Now?" for the first time. I heard it through the walls, but that was the first time I heard it as a completed record.

Sadly, Bowie called the studio a couple of weeks before he passed away. Tony was in there working with someone else, and Kabir talked to him. He was saying that he wanted to come back again. And that, you know, he had more stuff.

WE WERE URBAN PIONEERS. Which basically is the notion that you go into a neighborhood that nobody wants to be in, and then you invest in that neighborhood both financially and artistically, with your blood, sweat, and everything. You build roots there. You create something, a place where people can flower in their art and music. And then you just get kicked out.

If you don't have enough money to purchase it at some point during the process, you're gonna get kicked out. And I get New York. I get it, it's like always reinventing itself, right? I walk down these streets and they're unrecognizable to me from five years ago. I understand how New York reinvents itself, 'cause there's always young people coming and they think what old people did sucked, and they want to redo it again. I get it. But the city has a bad problem now, it has this real estate disease. And so what's become most valuable in the world of New York City now, is real estate. Not what happens in the real estate, but the real estate itself.

And that's the defining sickness of our time. None of the mayors deals with it at all. It just happens. Large sections of the city get eaten by speculators. Shit gets torn down. They build these giant buildings, co-op and condo buildings that very rarely are going to be lived in. There are so many empty spaces in these buildings, because it's just speculative. It's all people from Dubai and Europe just speculating on New York's real estate, right? So both places became victims to this real estate disease.

It's really a bad disease, and it changes the focus of what life is about. I saw people walking around Crosby Street in SoHo in the later years, they're just wandering around. They don't know where to go. They're looking for a city that doesn't exist. If they want to go to CBGB's, well, there's this weird version of CB's that John Varvatos saved, even though it's a clothing store. But it's a weird version of it.

Most of the iconic places, they don't exist anymore. So, the tourists, whoever, are wandering around looking for history and it doesn't exist anymore. They can landmark buildings based on their structure, and they'll landmark streets based on whether they have cobblestone, but they don't landmark creative spaces. They don't say, "Okay, this place was valuable enough to the city of New York that it should be left alone."

At what point does something become valuable enough to New York that you think about it as something you want to preserve? For example, my friend owned the Bottom Line, which was this incredible music club for many, many, many years. A place that really deserved to continue in some form or another. And he was kicked out for the same reason. NYU wanted his building and he was done. What kind of city are we making? What kind of city is New York becoming? It's worrisome to me that the areas that we can create art, music, culture, are so thinned out by this real estate madness.

I get capitalism. I understand it. I ran a business, two businesses for a combined sixty years. I get capitalism. But I don't think this is capitalism. I think this real estate disease is something different. It's purely speculative. It doesn't offer any value to the city. There is nothing intrinsically that's valuable at the end of the real estate deal; the only value, incurred value, is that people make more money. Are they asked to do something with that money that helps the city in some way? No.

There should be parts of the city that are carved out, away from these speculators. Imagine if you had a three-year revolving program, and you took three or four blocks in an area. Of course, with all the real estate pigs, it would have to be some place way the fuck out; whatever, I don't care. But imagine if you had this protected art zone that couldn't be speculated, and the rents were really low, and that the purpose of it was to give people a chance to develop themselves as writers or artists or painters or musicians or whatever. You would set up a place where they couldn't be thrown out. Because Bushwick is not immune.

No location is immune to this real estate disease. At what point does either the government or the private sector or a combination of the government and the private sector say, "Okay, enough. We have to value something in the city of New York, culturally." You know what's weird? It doesn't affect the rich people. It doesn't affect the Museum of Modern Art, and all the super-well-funded stuff that rich people fund, but it's decimating the art scene that's created from the bottom up. The scene of kids who get out of college and can only pay 200 bucks a month. But, fuck, they can play guitar really great, and they think they have something, and they don't want to do it in Topeka.

The tourists come here all the time looking for a place that doesn't exist, so they just shop. You walk down Crosby Street, it's Millionaires Row. It's really safe, but there's nothing there. It's just a place to shop or go to the gym. How many fucking gyms can you have on one block?

There's that great story about Robert Moses, right? The guy that built all the highways around New York. He destroyed the Bronx, and then he was going to put a fucking highway through the West Village, and people just said, "No. No, you're not." Hopefully people will somehow get to the point where they'll say, "No. I don't want this to become the only version of New York that's left. I want to have one that's vibrant and gives meaning to people in areas besides money." Right?

I tried my best to save the studio. We tried everything we could, and we just lost to greed. Just out-and-out greed.

I'm completely pissed off. But I have to live, I have to continue. I have three kids. I got to make a living. So I have to figure out how to have some sort of sense of positive energy. I'm so deeply rooted in here, in New York City, that I'm going to continue to stay here, in some way or another. I have my guys who work with me who kick my ass all the time and say, "You can't be depressed. You got to try to keep going." Am I pissed off? Of course I'm fucking crazy pissed off.

But if I'm going to survive here, I have to figure out a way how to make peace with that part of my life. I'm not saying I have, because I sometimes wake up in the middle of the night and I'm fucking completely pissed off, or I'll be in a store and I'll hear a Magic Shop song or something, and I'll have a really nice memory and I'll think about it, and then I'll go, "Aw, fuck."

I get the sense of renewal. This is part of what makes New York a really incredible place, that everybody, each generation gets to make their stamp on it, culturally and artistically and financially. Each one gets to make their stamp on it. I think that that's wonderful. That doesn't freak me out. I'm down with that. The thing that freaks me out is that the opportunities that the next generation will have to do that are being limited by what's happening to spaces and to the value of spaces in New York City. So, that's my particular shtick about it. I come from the Bronx, so I know about neighborhoods going up, going down, coming back. I get that about the city. It's a good part of the city, that it reinvents itself.

It has been a really tough year, the city sort of kicking me in the ass. I got mugged six weeks after I closed. On 25th and Eighth Avenue. Somebody literally came up from behind me, clocked me, knocked me out. My head hit the subway stair. I got nine stitches on my eye. I have a torn rotator cuff. And all for my stupid telephone.

I think it scared my kids the most. It was a drag. Nobody helped me, so I had to walk all the way home and then show up bleeding in my house. The police were like, "Nobody gets mugged anymore." And I was like, "Well, I did."

The parts of it that I think are so special, and that I hope my kids can have experiences with? Manhattan is pretty much gone. You can go maybe up to Harlem or above Harlem or something, but Manhattan is pretty much gone.

It's certainly possible that this will all go to hell. That this whole real estate boom will just go bust and that eventually someone will ask, "Who are these people living in these buildings?" And they'll get a rent roll list and there won't be anybody on it. And they'll go, "Oh, that's probably not a good idea. Maybe we can do something else with these spaces, besides use them for speculation."

Think about it. You buy like a $7 million loft or a $10 million loft or something, and you come here hoping to find a version of New York that you read about and you see on the movies and stuff like that. Nothing gets romanticized more than New York. They come here and they spend all this money and then what do they do? They got to go to Bloomie's? And how many times can they go to Michael Kors's bag shop, or how many visits can they have at the Apple store?

SONDRA SHAYE A healer

I find it very hard to be in Manhattan. I don't like going into Manhattan at all, which is ironic because to me the whole point of living in this area is because you're close to Manhattan. I stay here in Brooklyn because I feel I can help the city a lot by being here. And then there are different areas of Manhattan that feel worse than others. Midtown is very hard to take. It's so intense. To me, and I assume everyone does this, because it seems very natural: imagine feeling the energy of every person. And buildings have energy and then you have all the cars coming through and the people in the cars. It's just too much. It doesn't feel good. It makes me feel uncomfortable, irritated, and then tired. I usually have to go home and lie down.

One of the things I do is space clearing, so I really feel all of the energies in a building. When you go into a building there is a lot of energy there from all the people who have been there. There's also energies coming in from outside. There's also—I know it sounds like a movie—but there are nonphysical beings who are there. Those are the ones who cause the most problems for people, I think. All of this effects everyone, they just don't know it. Which is why after a space clearing, when all of that energy is cleared and a tremendous amount of positive, sacred, blessed energy is brought in, everybody in the space feels so much better. If it's a workplace they get more done, they get along much better, they're much happier in a space. It completely changes the environment. You go from being a really negative low-vibration environment, not great, to being a high-vibration environment with no negative energy at all.

NEW YORK IS a small island, it's crazy. It's like Gilligan's Island being built up to the biggest city in the world. There's so many EMFs. There's so much technology, so much electro-smog, everything that's plugged in creates electro-smog, and cell-phone towers and computers and Wi-Fi. All of this makes you physically weaker. Which makes you more susceptible to getting sick. It's everywhere, but in Manhattan it's so intense. I only go into Manhattan now for work. I protect myself energetically. If I'm in a place that feels terrible to me, I just clear it. That's my way of dealing. If I get on a subway car and it feels awful, I clear it.

I get to see people's houses, gorgeous places in New York, which I love. There was an apartment on the Upper West Side, all the way on Riverside Drive, which these people called me in to clear. It would have been this really gorgeous old prewar apartment with twelve-foot ceilings, and all these rooms, and all of this detail, because I could see what it would look like when it was fixed up. There had been a terrible fire there, really bad, two people got killed. The guys who were in there fixing it up—they had to completely do everything over—they refused to work because they felt something there and it made them feel really bad and creepy. And they thought something's there, whether the souls of the people who died in the fire, I don't know. They wouldn't continue working until the owner or the realtor, whoever, brought someone in to clear it.

They called me and I cleared it. That was my favorite because I could see what that apartment would look like when it wasn't fire-damaged.

I do this for people who are trying to sell their place or just want their home to feel better. They sense that something's not right, or they're familiar with space clearing so they want it done because they know the benefits of it.

I do this a lot for realtors when they have a space they can't sell.

And then it usually sells very quickly. There was this one apartment a few years ago, it was beautiful, a duplex, with a terrace and a whole wall of windows on both floors. It was on and off the market for seven years and it wouldn't sell. A realtor brought me in and I cleared it. As I was doing the clearing the realtor got nauseous, which is because she needed healing, for one, but also because the vibration of the energy changed so much so quickly. She couldn't adjust fast enough.

That doesn't happen very often. But when all this positive energy came in so quickly it probably created something in her body, maybe her equilibrium, and she was nauseous. She went out into the hallway. She had scheduled someone to look at the apartment right when I left. They bought it. It sold fifteen minutes after the clearing.

Someone walks into a space, they have an immediate reaction. They feel like, *Oh, I like this.* Or, *I don't like this.* They haven't even looked at it. It's because they're reacting to the energy of the place. When I do this for realtors and you get rid of the negative energy and the low-vibration energy, they go into the place already liking it. This apartment makes me feel good.

It's basically a four- or five-step process. First I go in and out of every room. It looks like I'm just walking around mumbling to myself. I don't put on a big show, like they do on TV. I wear the same thing all the time: khaki pants and a white shirt. I used to wear a lot of necklaces with symbols on them, but I don't do that anymore. I just protect myself from the EMFs.

I go into every room and I'm talking to the higher energies. Any negative entities, any low-vibration energy. There could be beings who aren't in body anymore but are still hanging around. Or they could be worse, but I don't really like to talk about those. But they do exist. There are creepy things. I don't like to dwell on that because it's just kind of sensationalization. I don't want to feed into that. There are creepy things out there.

There were a couple times when there were super creepy things that if I didn't know what I was doing, I could have been in trouble.

These really negative energies feed on fear. You feel them. They feel horrible. I don't see, just feel it. I'm almost glad I don't see it. It feels so horrible. It's very easy to go into fear. It would scare anybody. Sometimes you feel it right when you go in and as you go through. Sometimes it feels so bad in a place, in an entrance way, I do a general clearing.

Those old buildings that used to be tenements? Terrible energy. More of them are getting cleared. Those places—when people came here, immigrants, there was a lot of hope for something new, but the primary feeling was fear, desperation, being uprooted from your home, a lot of them fleeing. It was just horrible. The conditions were so horrendous in those areas. Those tenement houses, if they haven't been cleared, they just feel terrible.

IT'S AMAZING HOW the universe works. I have a friend who works as a nanny. The family she works for has places all over the world. They're one of the wealthiest families in the world. She told the wife and mother about what I do, and she wanted to get it done, but it kept getting delayed. It wasn't that easy to schedule, and it kept getting delayed, and delayed, and delayed. Then I actually just felt, "Enough. We're doing your healing now. That's it. Talk to me."

It kept getting put on the schedule, and then getting taken off. I was getting a little annoyed. She says that she wants it. I know that it's going to be a good thing for her and her family. Somehow, my friend got her to commit to a day. And I went, and had no awareness of what day it was.

Of course, there was a little miscommunication getting me the address. I finally get the address, and I still had no idea. I just had the number and the street. Then I get out of the subway, and there's a lot of press vans. I still am thinking nothing, because this is New York City. This is in Manhattan. I'm like, *Oh, something must have happened.* Then there's cops. Then there's crowds of people. I'm just looking around, I'm looking up. I'm like, *As long as we're all safe here, this is okay.*

Then I get to the building. I still don't know what building it is that I'm going to. There's secret service guys all over the building, and there's people taking selfies, and videos. There are reporters talking into cameras, and guys in black suits, with black sunglasses, and a thing in their ear. "What is this?" Then I'm looking for the entrance to the building. And it's Trump Tower. Then I'm like, *Oh my God. It's election day.* I had no awareness that it was election day. It was the primary. It was the New York primary.

So I went in. It's funny in these buildings. The guys on the elevator, they're very chatty, and they like to talk.

"This is Trump Tower, right?"

"Oh, yeah."

"Is he . . . ?"

"He's home."

"He's here right now?"

"Oh, yeah. He's upstairs right now. That's why all the press is here."

When I got out of the elevator, the elevator guy was like, "He just lives two flights up," from where I was doing the clearing. When I got into the apartment I said to my friend, "Did you make this connection that I just made this second that I'm doing an energy clearing right below Trump's apartment on election day?"

"Yeah. Oh my God."

She's very spiritual too, and so she was like, "This is so meant to be. You so need to be here today."

I did the space clearing, a blessing for their apartment. I felt like it wasn't an accident that I was there. Nothing is really an accident, but that was *really* not an accident. So, maybe I'm intended to just facilitate some light coming into this building, and to him.

But I didn't want to give him enough light to risk any kind of success in the election. That was where I had my boundaries. God forbid. I did send some light up to him. Apparently his apartment was in the same line. It was literally two flights up from where I was standing.

I think I was there to bring healing to the building, to him. Maybe he could be a little less full of spewing hatred, maybe a little less divisive. Who knows? I was like, *Okay, I'll send light up there. But not enough light for him to win.* That was my deal with the universe. But the universe does what it wants.

JAIQUAN FAYSON A painter

I do have like a sort of philosophical thing about New York. And it's something that I don't notice anywhere else. And I'm pretty sure that for the most part is because of the buildings. Older buildings, especially when I'm in the city. 'Cause I really don't get this feeling in most other places in New York. But always when I'm in the city, and always when I'm in a building that's higher up. There's nothing but buildings, you know, just more buildings in the background. I always feel like I'm on stage, like there's a fucking big cardboard set, and if I push hard enough on one of those buildings, you know they'll all topple over, and it'll be a big thing. It'll be like a real sky back there. And it's usually at night too. It's almost always at night when I'm alone and I'm by myself. That I feel like if I push one of those buildings, this whole set will fall over and it'll be like a real nighttime sky. It's fucking weird.

A real, an actual world. You know like something about all those buildings just being a facade. They have those talk shows and they have the fake New York screen in the back. I always feel like that, I always feel like at some point . . . Particularly later on at night. There's less traffic, you know? It just doesn't feel as realistic, it feels like you can just . . . There's something back there, it's like the background is just a cardboard layer. And it'll just fall over.

DAVID FREEMAN An elevator repairman

People want what I have. Kids will ask you if you're an elevator man. They'll beg you for keys. They offer you money. All kind of kids. Old ladies. This old white lady on the Upper East Side said, "I know you guys have keys to put this on 'independent.'" She told me that she was going to give me $200 for the key. It's a $5 key. But I was like, "Nah, I can't do that. I could get in trouble if they found out I gave you a key."

This was an old patrician white lady. A war bonnet like Dan Quayle's wife. Got that war bonnet hairdo talking about giving me $200 for my key. She is the type of lady that has dogs and they're like little dog babies. So she wants them upstairs and in their dog box real fast.

People will buy those keys. Or if you leave your keys somewhere, and people see that ring, they will grab your elevator key ring and run off with it. Keep that shit on your ass. You put the key on "Access" and drop the car. If you leave it in the hall, there's people that see that key and they will steal it. It'll work all over the city.

In New York, I've seen an elevator that's a glorified horse pen: three walls of wood made out of pine and a floor made out of pine, hoisted by truck chains. You could be on an elevator that was built in 1904. Everybody that installed that is dead and it's still running. "Men of iron, rails, and wood." You do get a sense of mortality.

They're really smart guys who become the adjusters; the brilliant ones seem to have some kind of inborn obsession or love of what they're doing. One has a model elevator at home. He made the motherfucker and every part on it works. It's this big and he can show you every goddamned thing on the elevator. It's a scale model. People have told me they've been stumped and called this guy, at two in the morning, 'cause they had him as a teacher and he answers the phone and starts talking to them about elevators.

He can tell you exactly why a fuse blew, how it blew, how much power, by looking at it. He's insane. No, seriously.

You can have anything from a low-rise hydraulic elevator to a wheelchair lift, you can have a traction elevator and you have a gearless traction. In the Flatiron Building the hydraulic elevators were driven by water. With leather seals.

One time I hit the top of the car and it was covered in dead mice. It was in the projects and it was like the mice went there to die. Every mouse in this project went down on top of this motherfucking car and just went to hell. Right there, on the spot, like "I surrender to the will of God, I'm a dead mouse." And they're dried out, they're like mummies.

So I went up there with a broom and I tore the car apart. I looked down at the mice, and the guy I'm with is an ex-con—because the elevator industry is one of the few that hires an ex-con—and he's like, "I can't deal with this. This sucks."

I grab a broom, I start sweeping shit off 'cause I'm just a hillbilly, right? I'm a fucking Black hillbilly.

(I grew up in Indiana, but I'm half Black. My Black relatives were all from Tennessee and Kentucky. And Mississippi, originally. And all my English relatives, they're from Newcastle on Tyne. They're fucking Geordies. I am a fucking Afro Geordie. It's true.)

Sweep all the mice off. Okay. So now we are ready to start demolishing the car. So we hang it.

Gotta hang the counterweights up here 'cause you reuse them, get the car landed and then start cutting all the bolts on the dome. Then I got to get up there and cut off that crosshead and we started demolishing it.

We got down the pit.

What we hit was an inch of sludge, because the car had shoes, not rollers. Good shoes means that oil has been running up and down the rails for twenty years and dripping down there. But because people have pissed on it, it kind of turned into linoleum. So I had to take the scraper, like an ice scraper, and physically scrape this shit up. Big curls every time you did it. You get a blast of piss gas right up in your face.

The uric acid cured the oil into what looked like linoleum. And it was golden and it smelled like piss when you cut it. And I'm not lying to you, you could stand on it and it was like a sheet of ice. You're scraping the shit up to get down to the steel so you can clean up this area and build a new elevator.

What are you using to cut? One of them ice strippers. Just scraping it up in sheets and throwing it in bags.

New Yorkers

New York City can be divided into those people who piss in their elevators and those who don't.

Every housing project in New York, people pee in the elevator. Piss is like ocean salt water so it rots out the door locks because the door locks are run with copper wire or wires that have copper contacts.

It's rotting out the door bolt. That's made of steel. So even if you paint tar over that, eventually that piss finds a pinhole and starts rotting out the door bolt, unless it's made out of stainless.

So NYCHA uses a lot of stainless.

We're on top of these cars, cutting out these piss-soaked cars. I remember asking this dude, "Why do you piss in elevators over here in the projects?" He lives there and he's like, "I don't know. I guess the kids get tired. I think sometimes it's the kids, sometimes it's somebody's on drugs and they just pee in the elevator."

Dude, it destroys the elevator and every twenty years they have to build new elevators in NYCHA. I'm telling you the truth.

I DIDN'T HAVE a choice.

I had a baby coming, and I was laid off. But they made me realize I was more of a mechanical person than, honestly, I ever thought.

What's really weird is that it does involve intuition for some sets of people. But there's some people who have a mathematical mind, whereby their decisions are ruled by logic. My decisions are still mostly ruled by a kind of emotion, which detaches me from that higher level of knowledge.

There's the type of person I've worked with directly, who has an absolutely analytical understanding of an elevator, whereas mine is emotional and still based on hunches.

How you use a machine is a type of consumption. It is like drinking a beer. It is a consumption. You are having an experience. People kiss each other in elevators. They don't just pee in them. People meet their damn girlfriend. People hug each other coming home from a goddamn funeral.

I WORK WITH all kinds of people, everything from Soviet conscripts, which would have been my first mechanic, to bikers, racists, lesbians, you name it, all kind of weird people work with me. And I've got to get along with the sons of bitches.

Gay and straight. People that are libertarians slash labeled conservative politically. People that smoke reefer, people that don't. People are all different and they do have beliefs and you have to cope with them because you're part of a two-person team.

Oddly enough, most of the elevator guys I meet do something. I've seen a guy who makes some beautiful radio-controlled airplanes, I've seen guys that make hydraulics, and I've seen a man that guards the rosary and the host at his church, as a religious devotion.

Even the people that you don't necessarily agree with, you kind of come to an affirmation of love for them and friendship and forgiveness that takes you past differences. Why would a man sit around in front of a rosary and a host in a Catholic church at four in the morning? You look at the man and what he says and see how he treats people, and you realize he's got something going on.

You usually find out that most people on some level do have some kind of inner life, they have a place where they find joy. And even people whose beliefs you revile, they actually have saving graces that you don't understand completely at first but you see . . . It's like it's odd to say, but what it is is . . . a kind of forgiveness, where it really counts.

And it unfolds to you. It does end up being like a kind of forgiveness which you develop for people as you know them, which is probably what's wrong with the world because most people have the homogenous kind of experience. You don't meet people that do different than you, think different than you, and are different from you, so you don't see their humanity. But here, in a sense, you're in a situation where you have a lot of desperate people doing a dangerous goddamn job and, well, after a while you love them. Even if you don't agree with them.

I believe in managed risk. And ameliorating the worst parts of it.

It's like the kid telling me he was scared to get on the elevator because we're up in the air and I looked at him and said, "Man, if you wasn't scared you'd be fucking stupid. You got to know where your feet are and you got to know that the car is there. Those are the first two steps. Then you're going to put the stop switch in," and I started showing him. One hundred foot in the air. But he was almost in tears, he's a green helper, and I'm like, "Man, you got to understand something."

After he got up there he realized that what I was telling him was the truth, that it is possible to manage the risk.

If I had a lesson to add to anybody's life, it's about risk management. If you manage risk there's a possibility you can get out in one piece, but if you don't fail to reconcile that beforehand and have that presence of mind, that's when you get hurt.

YOU KNOW HOW MANY empty spaces there are in the city? You actually can go in these buildings. There's whole floors of buildings. You could actually house, very inexpensively, every homeless person in New York. There's enough building space. There's nice spaces. Everybody could have a $1,000 apartment. They're empty. They don't do shit with it.

There's one building that has the best room I've ever seen in my life and it's been empty for twenty-five years. It would be the most bomb studio you could ever have. I can't give you the address any more than I can give you Jerry Seinfeld's. (Which I've been to.) Curves in the wall, early twentieth century, high windows, spectacular light. Lower Manhattan, see the world, see the harbor. Look out the window. Nobody will rent this space. It has access by one elevator. Beautiful little space. It's wild, too, because nothing's been touched. All you have is outlets and sewing lights. You go in there and you can paint like a bastard for fucking fifty years. That's the most beautiful place I've ever come across. Did I feel hateful that I couldn't get in there? Yeah, I was angry. I looked at that empty ass space and I said, "Damn, That's how it oughta be."

There's whole floors like that throughout the city, wasted, empty space that no one uses and people restrict access to that. They're not going to rent it for less. So there's all this inert space all over Manhattan.

There doesn't have to be a homeless person in New York City.

MICHAEL RODRIGUEZ A seeker

It almost seems like things become more apparent here in New York than any freakin' where else. You know what I mean? I mean so much energy pulsating through the city. People's hearts and minds and sweat and blood and all that. You can imagine all the blood in the hospitals that's being spilled, on operating tables, and all this other stuff. Everything that's going on here. I swear this city just feeds you with energy. If you're a seeker, this is your city.

It's like a heart pulsating. Those pulsations activating everything, everybody's activated by this influence or this energy, you know what I mean? It's all a gift. Do you take and not give back?

Nobody got their ears open for it. I'm not saying everybody's dumb, deaf, and blind, but it takes a certain pizzazz you gotta have in order to see that. I see people walking around with their top hats and stuff like that back in those days and whatnot. They're here. They're trying to communicate with us, but we so dumb, deaf, and blind that we don't. Dogs have more fucking visions than we do. Because they look at us, *Dang, you guys so stupid, you all so clueless. You guys are so repetitious.*

People miss what the city used to be. They don't see New York as it was. The architecture and the clothing; the mannerisms, they miss that. They're still trying to seek that. You walk through the city tryin' to find out the history of the city. You're pretty much haunting *them*. Craig the ghost. The New York City haunter. You can almost see it, and know that it's real. There was a history. There was a past in this place. There were people here. Not enough people care about them.

I value this city so much. To me everything is priceless. I mean everything has a value. I don't see nothing as valueless. I see it all.

4

The Rich Are Different

YESIM AK A real estate agent

Initially, I was nervous to rent out a $6,000 or $7,000 apartment because I was paying $1,600 or $2,000. It's all relative. You're like, *Who's the person that can pay $6,000 a month?* They have to make forty times the rent to qualify. That's a lot of money! But I feel like I've been desensitized.

I mean, I'm no longer impressed when I hear these numbers—$20 million, $50 million, $100 million. . . . A lot of the buildings that we've sold are in the $3–15 million range. If you sell a condo, the seller pays 6 percent. If you sell a building, it's probably twenty times the amount of work, and the seller pays maybe 2 percent or 3 percent. From that, you give half to your office. Then you split the other half with however many people on your team that you're working with. So, in our biggest deal, I got paid $98,000. It always sounds like big numbers, but that's before taxes.

It's still a great way to make a living, don't get me wrong. But you're not a millionaire. The true millionaires are the people that have these properties taking all the tax deductions. That's really the only difference between a regular person earning $60,000 a year paying a 30 percent tax rate versus someone who's making $6 million who has a ton of tax shelters. He might pay zero or very low. That's how those people get ahead.

FOR ME, the hardest thing is that I'm always a deal away from freedom. For one deal, I was expecting a $300,000 paycheck. That could have been the life-changing thing. Maybe after that I would have taken some time off and worked on a creative project, just done the bare minimum to pay my bills.

Maybe I could stop drinking wine or having happy hour after a long day of work or not go out to restaurants as much. But when you're working twelve- or fourteen-hour days with high intensity, high stress, I'm not going to go to Whole Foods or wherever and make rice and beans for myself. I need a steak. I admit that's a choice I've made and

I'm going to have to suffer longer, but I'm always a deal away from it all being scrapped. Energy is the most important thing.

I'm always kind of dusty or slightly sweaty or something, because I'm constantly running up and down stairs or jumping from place to place. I used to call myself a pinball machine or a tour guide. I'd have hordes of people looking at apartments, going up and down the stairs, all day long. That's how I started. I was full-on. In my best month, I rented twelve apartments, which is a lot of work. Most people do two or three.

The drive came from having to pay back my student loans. I was waiting tables making $17,000 a year, and the monthly minimum on my student loan was $3,500 a month. I was afraid I'd have to leave the country. I was like, I want to work. I want to pay this back. How am I going to do this? I didn't know. I had it deferred but it kept gaining interest, interest added to the principal. How am I going to do any-thing? I can't be creative. I was like, I'll become successful overnight or something will happen. I'll get money.

When we first started, me and my partner made a deal. He said, "I want to just cold call and try to sell buildings." I said, "Okay, I'm going to do all the apartment rentals. All you have to do is sit at home all day and just cold call. We'll split everything fifty-fifty." He wasn't making any money. He was cold calling for at least six to eight months before we got lucky. I did every rental deal hustling, running around, and I gave him half of my paycheck at the time.

EVERYBODY WANTS TO BE here in New York. And as my broker always loves to say, "They're not making any more land." There's no land left to buy, actually. It topped out this last cycle. There's nearly zero plots of land to buy.

I once rented an apartment in a basement, and it would flood. This guy told me that once he had a friend staying over and he had a blow-up air mattress that his friend was sleeping on. He woke up after a thunderstorm and his friend was floating in the room.

I would have to tell people, "Look, this basement apartment has a tendency to flood. Although it's been renovated and you have tile floors, it's probably going to flood if it rains a lot, so we have this pump for you. You have to come home and turn the pump on."

I rented it. I had a line out the door. I think people paid like 15 percent broker's fee actually and a year's rent.

MAGGIE PARKER A nanny

Your relationship with the city asks you to confront so many gross things about yourself. Envy was a big thing for me. When I came here I didn't have a job. I was working part-time. Being around it, feeling envious, makes you feel gross. You're not in the safety of your own car, or far away from this. It's all next to you. Even if you don't open *Vogue*, you walk by all of the stuff.

I came from higher education, a lot of privilege. I got a car when I turned sixteen and for most of the world that's extreme privilege. We had a pool growing up. You know, wow! Then you come here and you're like, *This is a violent amount of wealth.* But it was also helpful because it redefined the term for me. People who are violently wealthy or aggressively wealthy, they don't seem very happy or that proportionately happy.

Everybody around you seems like they have so much purpose, and they're succeeding so much more. They're younger than you, they're better than you, they're cooler than you. Even if I was raised with all the money, that currency of cool I can't manufacture.

THE IDEA OF COMING to New York and making it with $30 in your pocket? That can't happen anymore. There's going to be a shift in what you see coming out of New York, and it's kind of sad. Because the people who are succeeding aren't succeeding because of coincidence or merit, it's because they're all connected. And they're in this weird insulated bubble.

All the babies that I've been close to will have all those opportunities, but because they were born into it. So you're not going to have this sort of Patti Smith, New York Dolls, Vivienne Westwood scene. It'll be a different scene. If you grew up reading *Please Kill Me*—that New York is gone.

The economy of cool is going to be a lot more important than money. And so how interesting your baby is like, "Is your baby taking ukulele lessons? Is your baby living in a yurt in the backyard?" You know, this sort of aggressive obscurity is becoming a weird trending thing. Like, "Is your kid named after an object?" The names: some of these names are ridiculous. *Noble. Whistler. Atlas. Midas*—he's going to be a great husband. What this says basically to the world is that this child will never work. Whistler's never going to work at Starbucks. Atlas will not be a waiter—for better or worse. There are experiences you can guarantee those children will not have.

These names are so aggressively cool and reflective of how you feel about yourself and your importance. It's not like you're named Krystal with a "K." What if she just wants to be a teacher? What if she just wants to get married? I would just protest if I ever had a child here. I would just name it "Thing 1."

They want to arm their child and I know they just want the best, but they're part of a society. You need your kid to stand out. And if you need your kid to be studying mindfulness or doing this stuff really early, I think it's well-intentioned but it's pressure to be a certain way. One toddler has to have kombucha and kimchi and foods that I haven't even heard of, and I actually had to tell them, "Have you considered a peanut butter sandwich?" And it never even occurred to them.

New York changes your perception of time, and your expectation of how much in reality that time is probably worth. I can feel it happening to myself. I know that if I were to raise a kid here, I would probably participate in a culture that I don't really like. You just do it. You get pressured into behaving that way. There's this industry of fear of your child not developing.

THE MORE YOU ARE in New York, the less comfortable you are sitting with your own thoughts because we don't get to do that ever. We are constantly distracted, so being comfortable being bored by your baby is *terrifying* without your phone.

What if your baby's boring? What if your baby wore Baby Gap? The threat of normalcy is so terrifying for them. I was talking to another nanny the other week, and we talked about what do you think a girl could be. And I was like, "What do you mean—do you think any of these kids are gonna be engineers or doctors or lawyers or teachers?" They don't have that choice. And ironically their parents think they're giving them more opportunity. They don't have that option. They don't have that freedom. They have to be aggressively cool for the rest of their lives. That's the option you give your child.

"I'm really into pesto." "I import vinaigrette." You know, they're gonna have some weird, niche, useless empty job.

They're a figurehead for something. They don't get any direction. They don't get to pick. They have to be cool. And it's a different currency than money. It's more threatening. Because the kids on the Upper East Side and the Upper West Side, their parents use money.

And that translates. That can go a lot of places. But cool is a really particular type of currency. And it's such an unfortunate ball and chain.

These kids are a reflection of the parents. I just have this visual of them looking into this pond like Narcissus and seeing their kids.

I want to give the kids a sense of agency. If you start in New York, where are you gonna go?

I'VE DEALT WITH nightmare children. You realized they were being bred for a certain type of lifestyle. Dark, evil money. You could sense it. I felt like if I turned on the tap, blood would run. I took that job because I thought I would humanize them.

With one family, when I first came over the kids were all wearing matching PJs, watching *Frozen* on their iPads. Pretty normal scene. But then it was the way they treated me: No eye contact, they didn't ask me anything about myself. I had to eat only after the children had finished their meals. I wasn't supposed to tell them "Say please" or "Thank you" or any of that stuff. It was not my job to raise them. I can appreciate that, but then I'm the wrong person to do that job. And you don't need a nanny with a master's degree.

It was so weird. "I'm sorry my husband couldn't be here, he's heli-skiing in the Alps." This sounds like a joke, but okay, alright, cool.

There was a lot of entitlement. If you are nine and cavalier about having your own private jet, nothing is ever going to be exciting to you. They had private chefs. Anything they wanted. Any amount, any time. Nutrition really didn't matter. To each their own, but just for your own sanity you want to try to throw a carrot or an almond down your kid.

They find pleasure from nothing inherently. Also, they play alone, they don't make friends. You have all this wonderful stuff, but you're alone. You have this horse ranch, pools and playgrounds, but it's just you. There's a lot of relational impoverishment going on. Those kids are never going to take the subway, ever. They don't say "thank you." They don't think that the people who work for them are people. That, I think, is really unhealthy, and I think it contributes to how people make political decisions.

I think adversity breeds strength. I don't think bullying is a good idea, but there is something called social facilitation that's really important. You have a kid who's sucking their thumb, they go to pre-school, they're going to get made fun of once, they'll never do it again. There's a level of checks and balances in a lot of child socialization that's healthy. You need that kind of thing. And they wanted to remove all adversity from these children's lives. I can respect the impulse, but it has the opposite effect. They can't handle stress.

If your brain doesn't know how to handle stress, and you get dumped? Remember the first time you really got your heart broken? You thought you were going to die. "How am I still breathing?" You get better at it, hopefully. You can touch down and then come back up. You use those systems of repair.

These rich kids that run around New York? Nothing. There's no repair and so those systems are really nominal. They're so lonely, they just want to find more drugs, fuck more people, buy more things. And they hurt other people. They haven't had to experiment with hurting other people's feelings when they were little. "Oh, I don't like it when my friend is mad at me . . ." There's none of that for these kids. And they're going to have so much power.

These children are not exposed to people of color at all, in any capacity other than working for them. And probably their parents talking poorly about them. I'm afraid of *the other*, we all sort of are—but you expose yourself naturally, gradually, and have positive experiences and you grow out from that and you become better. But you never do if you've never ridden the C train from Washington Heights.

Once we had to come up with an adjective for different animals. We were talking about polar bears, and I said, "Well, they're *endangered*." The boy was like, "No, they're not."

So I tried to explain, "The way we use the resources on our planet ends up changing the habitats that are available to different types of animals. Because there's a finite amount of Earth, right? We keep using it quicker and quicker, right? So polar bears' area to live is getting smaller and smaller. So it's harder for them to find food, have babies, all that stuff."

He was like, "Mom?"

And his mom said, "There's no such thing as climate change. That's made up. Polar bears are not endangered."

He ended up using an adjective for polar bears that I imagine they're very comfortable with: "*white*."

LIAM McCARTHY A private tutor

This kind of tutoring doesn't really exist in the wider world. You know, you're very solidly in the one percent world here. But I'm an educator. I approach each student's needs as important. Regardless of where you're coming from, I'm meeting you where you are.

If where you're coming from is Park Avenue and a big apartment and a family assistant and a driver and all those things, this is just the world that you were born into. You didn't choose your parents.

When you talk about the issues of these children, there's often a different reaction. "Poor little rich kid. The driver wasn't available to take you downtown. You had to learn how to hail a cab." The reality is that you have students who try to charge a ride in a pedicab on American Express. They try to swipe a credit card in the MetroCard slot to get on the subway. These are things that they're learning to do with no guidance. So I think it's important to respect every student's journey.

Among my students who are in boarding school or in private school in New York are those who do face special challenges. It's very competitive. It's very hard for these kids to let go and learn. It's very, very hard for them to embrace just learning, because there's such a focus on grades and scores. This hyper-competitive nature is fostered by the high schools at the same time as they deride it. In some performance notes, teachers will say, "So and so is too focused on his grades." I had a student who at an evaluation was told, "So and so is wonderful when she's engaged in the learning process, but when she seems to really focus on her grades it's frankly annoying"—which is a very hard thing for a student to read. A teacher saying, "I find your grade-grubbing annoying." And yet, that's this culture. You're not going to be admitted to the school you want to attend without the grades and the scores. Everyone knows it's a problem. Everyone knows that the emphasis on grades and scores is in many cases harming educational outcomes. What no one knows is how to fix it. Because the student who can focus on his or her passions and learn and not give a thought to grades and scores and yet get them? That student is exceptionally rare.

I look at my students, and I think if I could change one thing it would be more sleep. They're dealing with the competing pressures of all these demands. They look exhausted. They're so tired. Cognitively, when you watch them taking a test like the SAT, you watch them slowing down. You hear the malaprop. You watch the IQ drop from sleep deprivation. How do we solve that? You can buy a $5,000 bed but you can't buy more time to sleep.

These pressures. I was working for one family and I walked into the student's room for the first time. It looked like my office. There were custom-made curved desks with flat screens and a huge white board and a schedule and everything—multiple workstations. The room just happened to have a bed in one corner.

On the white board was the student's schedule. The student had six tutors in a row over a period of six hours with no break. One of my students talked about how he locks himself in the bathroom because it's the only place where there are no housekeepers, parents, tutors, drivers. He said sometimes I just go in there and lock myself in for ten minutes and sit on the floor. He's like, "I want to be alone."

That's a certain kind of Upper East Side experience. Apartments are never really empty. You don't get an appreciation as a teenager of how wonderful it is to be in an empty house sometimes. Doesn't that experience model adulthood a little bit? What will it be like when I'm an adult, when I'm out of school, and I have a job, my own apartment or home, and I come home? What will I do? What will I do when I have an unstructured block of time in my own environment? What choices will I make? Those experiences are important.

Many of my kids never have that. There's always someone at home. There's always staff there at least, if not family. There are many households on the Upper East Side where there's a family assistant who has some in-apartment office, and a live-in housekeeper who's there, plus another daytime housekeeper. So generally you're going to have three people wandering around. Maybe mom's around. Maybe dad's around. There are people bringing up the dry cleaning, people hanging a piece of art, people putting in the Christmas tree or taking out the Christmas tree. There is all sorts of activity always happening. I sometimes wish my kids had that moment of feeling alone, feeling solitude, feeling like king of the castle, even for an hour.

New York is unlike anywhere else. I have had parents who've taken the class list for their high school child and have put all the kids into a spreadsheet. Then they've put their parents into a spreadsheet and then googled them and done due diligence for every single one: where they went to college; where they went to graduate school; where they're giving; what their likely connections are. They'll figure out the kid's likely GPA and SAT scores. They'll try to make a map for where kids are likely to apply. "Looks like maybe Penn's going to be underrepresented in this class, so maybe I'll apply my kid to Penn." I have a parent like that every year.

There are moms who run these households in such tight, efficient fashions. If this were a company, they would be destroying their competition and gaining market share all over the place. In a way, that is enviable. In a way. But in another way, one is forced to reflect on what is it to be a parent. What is it to—in quotes—run a household? How much of that is strategic and logistic and how much of it is listening and empathy? I think in the best households there's more empathy, there's more reading, there's more listening, there's more debating, and there's less competition happening in terms of status and academic prestige. You meet a family where they are, and you try to nudge the value system into genuine, legitimate engagement, into scholarship and intellectual growth, civic engagement.

I deal with the one percent. But middle-class families will have to compete as well. These issues begin with one group of people, but they always find their way to others.

I remember opening my first bottle of wine for guests. I was in front of all my peers. I was one of the first tables in the restaurant. So everybody was still lined up against the wall. Full starch. White jackets. They could see me. I'm opening it and the cork gets saturated. It pops and then it starts to run over my hand. The pop sounded like bombs hitting the ground. And I watch one drop fly, like this, and land right on the cuff of this guy's white shirt.

So I continue to give him a quick taste and he's like, "Cool." I pour a round for the whole table and I come back to pour him and the lady next to him says, "Oh my God, isn't that your new shirt?" We had to pay for his dry cleaning and they made me come in early for two weeks to practice opening up a bottle of wine. I was like, *I know how to open up wine.* And I built from that.

I MOVED HERE in the beginning of 2003. I was working for a chef named Thomas Keller and I lived in Napa. Every year the restaurant, French Laundry, closes three weeks a year. Two weeks at the end of the year, because that's a slow season, then one week in the summer. This year was different, because they were closing for two months for renovations. They had taken this time to do renovations, and then they took a lot of the staff there and brought them here to New York to help train and open up Per Se.

We came. Part of my deal with them is that if I stayed to the end and helped them shut down the restaurant, they would give me two months rent free in New York. I had never been to New York.

It was the most anticipated restaurant opening in New York City in the last twenty years. I was like, *Fuck, I gotta go. I have to be a part of this.* I remember sitting down at a picnic table with the chef saying, *You know what, I need to be a part of this.*

I was a buyer at this really soon-to-be famous restaurant. You had a whole bunch of people taking you out and showing you around the city. You had this built in—a false sense of it, but you had all these people taking you around the city, doing these kinds of things. I got to see it from a different place. Not really struggling, in that sense.

I got here, like that was a big accomplishment, right? And then you just figure shit out. The next thing is how do you put a flag in this? How do you make it your own? How can you make it here? It was all these other things. Work would be done. It's 1:30 in the morning, 2:00 in the morning. I'm trying to make it down to Tribeca to go hang out and drink with some friends and I'll hop in a cab. It's bumper-to-bumper traffic in Times Square. It's that moment that, every single time, that blows my mind. I remember driving there, and calling my mom, calling my cousin, and I'm like, "Dude, I'm in New York City! It's 2:30 here, 1:30 your time, and it's bumper-to-bumper traffic. Can you believe this?" It was a sense of just reassuring you that it wasn't a dream.

I fucking *live* here. *That's where the Naked Cowboy dances right there*, you know what I mean? Then all this shit you find out. Oh, he doesn't get arrested because he has another pair of underwear underneath those pair of underwear. Right. If he was just in his underwear he'd get arrested, but he has to have another pair underneath. Now it's the outer garment, not undergarment.

I lucked out and I found this apartment on 69th and Central Park West. It was like nine short blocks to work, so I could walk down Central Park West to work. Walking to work what I quickly realized is that if I think that's John Lithgow, that's John Lithgow. If I think that's Axl Rose, you know what I mean? At some point you look, you're like, wow, that looks like a broke Axl Rose, right? Like if he had no money, and he was down and out. Oh, no. That is him.

On the walk you would pass by all these people. Where I was from, people would stop and approach them, but it's New York. No one here gives a fuck. Everybody just keeps moving, right? They might tap their hat, but I started to realize that pace in the city, and the thing is, you never have time. I remember being in line at this place, a pizza place, and it was busy, I was trying to make small talk. It's my turn and the guy says, "Hey, how can I help you?" I said, "What do you got?" He goes, "What do you mean? I got pizza. What's this guy mean, what I got?"

Oh, that's the Rock on the StairMaster. Oh, that's Marky Mark. Oh, isn't that the girl from the Vegas movie? You're like, oh, that's Elizabeth Berkley, from *Showgirls*, right? It's like, hey, that's Doogie Howser. As he was starting to make his comeback on Broadway. Then that's Keenen Ivory Wayans. Then in the gym, getting out of the shower, and I'm like, *That's Eddie George, right?*

It was just this constant unworldly kind of experiences, but you just took them as they come. That was your everyday life. You just ran into these people and you saw them. Mom used to say, "Act like you've been there before so when you get there you know how to be there."

I think being in New York is the whole driving force. I tell people that I don't think I'd be able to accomplish what I've accomplished, or continue to do what I do, if I didn't live here. It's like some battery that you plug into. It's charged. It's amped.

AT PER SE, we googled everybody before they came in. You're like, Wait a minute. Who's that? Oh, that's the guy who knocked up Elizabeth Hurley. He was the guy. It was like you knew who he was, because he came in with jeans. We don't allow that. He came in in these horrible tennis shoes, so we made him walk around in the back, and he had a trench coat on, and he sat down. He sat down with Mick Jagger and the editor of *Rolling Stone* and his boyfriend. You saw power couples.

That power that you saw, whether or not it was money, like the shipping tycoon. He would come and everybody loved him. He would always say, "Hey, did I take care of you?" Then you're like, "No, you haven't taken care of me, yet." Then he comes over to me and goes, "I take care of you?" "No, you didn't take care . . ." you know what I mean? No. I'm doing my job. Finally, at the end he just pulls out hundreds and he's dropping them. It's all falling on the floor and you're just like, oh. But they're all crumpled up and shit.

People lost themselves in a way. They consumed way too much. We used to have a wine cellar that was made out of this beautiful Jerusalem limestone, and it was cut and placed in ... It had limestone and then glass. There was the bathroom on the other side. People would walk out and run right into the glass. It was like a bird running into the glass. You'd see blood dripping down like someone just busted their nose.

Royalty from other countries. To me part of the fun was figuring out who these people were. Some of them weren't famous, but these are people who write the check. These people have fortunes. Hey, that's the richest guy in Canada. There's David Blaine sitting there. There's Tom Hanks over there. There's the head of CBS.

You got a sense how important the first bottle was. One guy, he ordered some bottle. Alright, cool. He sits talking. I say, "After this, I only have one left." So we went to that one. Then he's like, "We'll have another one." I said, no, I just said earlier that was the last of this bottle, and even when I came back to pour it to show it to you, I said this is the last bottle. He's like, "Ah! A restaurant of this caliber, you would think you would go out and go get one for me!"

I said, "Sir, we are that restaurant." You could tell when it was a big deal or not. What amazed me was how it wasn't a big deal to some people to constantly get up and get on the phone, which stalls the whole table. The big thing used to be smoking when we lived in California. California was everybody gets up to smoke.

People would come and they had to be somewhere in thirty minutes. Katie Couric would show up. You're running in here to get a snack? We don't do snacks. She's a busy person and I get that, but sometimes I was just amazed. You could tell that it was just another dinner for some people.

For other people it was an experience in a lifetime. Some wouldn't know if they were ever coming back. You can tell in their interaction. I waited on this kid, him and his girlfriend. I asked him about wine and he's like, "I'll let you choose." He wanted to give me back the wine list. He was shaking. He was that nervous.

And then you have someone with "Oh, I'm only going to be here for an hour." You had to wait sixty days to get the reservation. It was a lot of buildup. Expectations were high, but you could tell for some people that it wasn't. If someone like the Greek guy was coming in it was nothing for him to spend $8,000 on a bottle of wine.

We had these two brothers that used to come in, and it'd be nothing for them to spend $16,000 for wine that night. And they didn't like champagne. We talked about expensive wine, those are some big categories where you can rack up a big bill. I mean, shit. I dropped $49,000 worth of wine on them one night, on a party of ten.

PASSING THE WINE LIST around, they'll give it to the person who is supposed to know about wine. We figure out and gravitate to who that person is going to be. It's about managing egos of people, because that's a big deal. Then there's something standoffish about it too, because some people have that thought that sommeliers take advantage of you. It's like, dude, you can't walk in here and say that you wanted to spend $200 on a bottle and I'm going to bang you for $3,000 a bottle. It doesn't work that way.

The hard part was judging what was too much and not, because a lot of times they would say, "Oh, just bring us something." Then you say, "Something like this or something like this?"

Next thing you know, some people say, "Just bring us something. Don't bring us something that's like $900 a bottle." You're like, *alright, cool. $500.* But you kind of had to make that judgment call based on what you saw going on, or if you knew anything about the table.

Normally the people that you thought would spend a lot on wine, because you knew their net worth from the internet, weren't those people. Normally the person who spent a lot of money on wine wasn't a wine collector, because the simple fact is he probably already owned that wine. "So, why would I drink that when I have it in my cellar already, and pay four times the amount for it?"

When you say this dude's balling, like that dude's a baller, he's got to spend 16 grand. They weren't those guys. A lot of those guys were finance guys, those guys work with numbers. That's the whole end-game that I try to explain to everybody. Having money isn't about how much you can spend. It's how much you can keep. That's the game. That's why people evade taxes. These guys know that. These guys work with numbers.

Then you have the other people who try to beat the system and they would just bring their own wine in. There's service on that bottle. I think we had the highest corkage fee in the United States at one point. When I worked there it was $90. We had to try to explain to people. People balked at that price, but if this is a priceless bottle of wine, $90 is nothing. This bottle of wine went on auction for $60,000 two years ago. Ninety dollars for him and this guy to open it up doesn't mean anything. The fact is that we need to get paid for taking care of this. This is a priceless bottle of wine.

BUNNY WILLIAMS An interior designer

I grew up in Charlottesville, Virginia, and couldn't wait to get to New York City. I mean, that was the dream. How do you get there? How do you get your parents to let you come here, and what are you going to do? I had gone to a junior college; I knew I wanted to get into interior design. I mean, I knew it very early on. I didn't know that I'd have this career, but as a twenty-year-old, what job are you going to have? I wanted to be somehow in the art world, interior design, whatever.

I got to New York and I went to work for a very famous English antique shop called Stair & Company. It was on East 57th Street, and all the famous decorators came in to buy. Mrs. Paley came, and the Whitneys came, and every rich person that had beautiful furniture came to Stair & Company to buy it. Collectors came.

There were two salespeople there, including Mr. Morrison. I'll never forget: he treated everyone the same. He said, "You never know who's going to be a collector." It's a lesson I've learned. You can't assume about anything. There were young people who came in who would buy a piece of furniture and they'd pay for it over time, but they became collectors because they were interested. I was the receptionist; you are very nice to everybody, you never make any assumptions, and everybody's given the same service.

I worked there for two and a half years and got to know the designers, and I knew that the one design firm I really wanted to work for was Mrs. Parish. In those days, it was Mrs. Henry Parish II, but Albert Hadley was soon made a partner and it became Parish-Hadley. I decided to brave it and go up and knock on the door and see if there was a job.

They were on 59th Street. I walked up Madison Avenue to 59th Street and there was a lady there, Mrs. Elsie Emmett, who interviewed me. She introduced me to Mr. Hadley and Mrs. Parish and thought I would qualify; Mr. Hadley was looking for a secretary. Because I'd had the background in the antique shop, they thought, well, this is good. They remembered me from my job at Stair & Company.

That's what you need to do in life. You need to kind of find a path and make the steps to be in the right place and try to learn something from it. So I got a job as Mr. Hadley's secretary.

In those days, everyone dressed. There was a proper attire to go to work, and certainly working in a shop like Stair & Company where you saw the most elegant people in New York come in, you got dressed every day. It was hard when you're a struggling twenty-year-old. You learn to buy clothes at Filene's Basement. It teaches you to train your eye.

Ladies were always in dresses; they'd have short wool dresses—women didn't wear pants in those days—and beautiful shoes and elegant crocodile handbags, and very tailored. It was a Jackie O look: box suits and simple black dresses. I still have that, I'm just as comfortable now as I am in my blue jeans, but it's professional and to me, it's respect. When you lived through it and saw how beautiful people looked walking up and down Madison Avenue, men as well as women—it's a little shocking today.

I became Albert Hadley's secretary and assistant. I worked my way up in that company for twenty years, and I started my own business when I was forty-two.

I THINK I'D BEEN THERE maybe two weeks, and Mr. Hadley asked me to take some samples to an apartment on Fifth Avenue. I rang the bell and the butler opened the door, and there behind me was the Picasso painting of the boy standing next to the white pony. I'd studied art history and thought, "I do not think that is the poster version." It was the William Paley apartment. It was as grand and elegant as you could be in Manhattan, and yet it was a very comfortable room. It had big sofas, covered in brown satin with beautiful pillows on it. Even though it was formal, it was still informal at the same time. All the paintings are now at MoMA. I said, "I'm delivering the shopping bags for Mr. Hadley." I went into the living room that was painted taxicab yellow and had Gauguin paintings hanging on it between a pair of Coromandel screens.

In those days, Second and Third Avenue were antique shops all the way from 59th Street to 86th Street. You went looking, you went exploring. I spent every weekend going to museums, going to auction houses. I'd go to Sotheby's and Christie's every weekend when there was a sale. I'd get the catalog and study each piece.

I wouldn't have had that in Charlottesville, Virginia. I think everybody, I don't care what field you are in, you want to come to New York because you're going to be working with the top players and you're going to learn something. Then you may decide, "Okay, I'm going to go back and live at home, or I'm going to go back wherever." But you sure have had extraordinary training by being in New York.

Once Mrs. Astor's secretary called up and said the curtains need repair. They are silk and they are shattered, and Mr. Hadley said, "Well, go to the files and get out the file. It's all right there. You just order the same fabric and repeat the order," and so I found the file and I repeated the order, sent it to the workroom that had made it, they were still doing it. On the order, the person had reversed the colors of fabric, so the curtains were supposed to be pink with green lining and they ended up being green with pink lining. They reversed it and they got hung and there was a screech.

INTERIOR DESIGN SHOULD never be static. I have seen styles change and then reappear again. When I first started designing, most of my clients wanted what one refers to as traditional design—rooms filled with beautiful antique furniture, antique rugs, patterned fabrics, and realistic paintings. But as time goes on, we all evolve and what is exciting to me today is the mixture of new and old. Unfortunately, fewer people are buying antiques and the city has lost many of its great shops and dealers. The new large stores that produce simple furniture in China have made decorating a formula and easy to come by. But I feel that people with real taste and creativity will personalize their spaces. Mix up the old with the new. Make it their own.

An apartment's tired and so the new person buys it, and even I look at it and go, "Well, let's not have curtains now, let's have the light pour in and let's simplify the backgrounds and maybe have bigger-scale furniture." Life is different, we live more casually. A lot of people had more staff. Now they have a lady who comes and cleans one day a week or three days a week. They go out to dinner; there's certainly somebody in taking care of the apartment, but they're not entertaining every night. Important social people of the time had butlers and they had a chef, and dinner parties every night.

Over the past years, New York has seen the construction of new, very exciting, modern apartment buildings. Some of my clients are moving from traditional spaces to apartments high in the sky, with floor-to-ceiling windows with breathtaking views of the city. These high ceilings are a perfect place for large contemporary art. The older traditional spaces are getting updates to represent the new trends, but I only hope designers and architects will respect great interiors of the past and find ways of respecting the old while giving a room an update.

A classical space can look wonderful with a Rothko hanging on the wall and contemporary furniture. They all complement each other.

BEN GARDNER Personal staff

My old boss would go shopping on sprees on Amazon and international websites for clothes. She would buy clothes from Italy, seven of the same dress in different sizes. Have 'em all shipped to her and then just have someone return the other six, which of course is a fucking nightmare if you have to return stuff to Italy via US customs and duty issues and all that kind of stuff. I think when you relieve yourself of those sorts of responsibilities, you have no touchstone by which you can understand whether that's a rational decision. The wealthy in New York—what they're buying is time and so they don't care. The money isn't an issue.

With another former boss, his issue was always wanting people to make decisions and to execute decisions the way that he would if he had the time or the energy or the inclination to make those decisions.

So you would become versed in a way of decision-making that would be if this man is making a decision about what paper plate to buy, how would he do that? And the answer is he would look at every single paper plate available and he would try to figure out—probably dismissing cost in the first instance—what's the best paper plate and how do you determine what the best paper plate is? And the best paper plate is the one that you can put three food items on, let's say, at the same time without it drooping or dropping or cutting or any of those things. So that's automatically going to preclude fifty percent of the paper plates on the planet. Maybe seventy-five percent.

So you would then get samples of all the other paper plates and then you'd look at them and you'd say, "Okay, we have a paper plate that's made with plastic and a paper plate that's made with recycled bamboo and we have a paper plate that's made of a combination of Amazon tree pulp and something else. And we're going to figure out, based on who's going to use the paper plate, where the paper plate's going to be used, what kinds of foods might touch the paper plate . . . Is the paper plate going to be used with knives and forks? Or is the paper plate just going to be used with finger foods? Is the paper plate going to be a large paper plate or a small paper plate?

And then you would test the paper plates, one by one, based on that criteria. So you would have three paper plates. You'd put an apple . . . Do any of them bend with the apple? Okay, so they're all apple proof. What if you throw on a piece of pizza on top of the apple, now keeping in mind that this person isn't going to eat pizza because that's not in the nutritional guidelines. Nevertheless, if we're talking paper plates, there's a chance that someone might have something that is not one of the traditional acceptable foods on that plate. So, literally, this would go on for hours and you would look at which are the union-made paper plates and which are the paper plates made by companies with bad politics and which are the paper plates . . .

None of that would be part of the decision-making process in the end, but you'd want to be able to answer those questions when presenting the two finalists of the paper plate for the decision-making process or, worse, if you're not presenting two finalists and you just go out and pick the paper plate, you want to be able to justify the paper plate afterwards as to why this would be the paper plate that you would've chosen if you'd had the time or the energy. That's example one of what the whole bizarre place was about. It was, I want the optimized outcomes from every decision, knowing how I think, knowing how I would want to make a decision, what kind of information I would require on everything. Whether it be a piece of carpet, a paper plate, a hamster, you name it. And those are three actual examples.

THERE WERE FOUR PEOPLE devoted to travel for one person because again the travel is really an issue. You have an advance team who goes out and checks out the hotel room, not to see if it's a nice hotel room, 'cause there's no interest in nice . . . it's optimizing the room. Does the room have a nightlight so that you can get into the bathroom without tripping over? Does the room have a refrigerator located in the best possible place? If it doesn't, buy one, set it up, get it in there.

There's a perception that rich people want luxury. That's not what this guy aspired to or required. What this guy sought out was people who would extrapolate his way of thinking. Somebody who could ask the questions and get the information and be tenacious enough that he could be satisfied that the decisions would be made on his behalf in the best possible way. So instead of looking for the chef who has a three-star Michelin background, he looked for the chef who could follow instructions. The chef who could read a book and could know that if there were going to be no blueberries that were part of the daily requirement, could he substitute them with some other item that meets all of the blueberry requirements rather than taste good or is delicious, or looks like a blueberry or smells like a blueberry. There's no joy in this world of living.

In his bubble, everything is done for you. You pull out your wallet and there's always $500 cash in there, always. Every day. There's not less, there's not more. Every day there's $500 in your wallet. You don't know your PIN number because you never had to take out any cash. Not in the last fifteen, twenty years.

You've become inured to the stuff that you want to master, so suddenly you've become a product of this weird world that has no bearing on the outside planet. So you think you've mastered something, but in fact you've mastered nothing. You've mastered your universe, your domain, but God help if something slips and you have to actually function.

The super-rich don't go out to dinner because it's convenient. They go out to dinner because they have to. Convenient is having your chef whip you up something at home. It's a different world. They don't care. And it's funny, they don't care about restaurants. They don't care about bars. They don't care about fancy hotels. They don't care about the park. They don't care about gyms. They don't care about the status symbols of the salary man. The wealthy salary man is a different beast. The Anna Wintours who are at the top of the heap or the senior vice president for something at somewhere or the banker, you know, the vice president, she's been working in a bank for ten years and maybe gets paid $1 million a year. It's not that. They're beyond that.

New York for them is the status symbol, perhaps. New York for them is the restaurant reservation at Nobu for you or me or for the banker. But the rest of the stuff, not really. One wealthy person once said to me, when I said, "Why wouldn't you go and spend a week at the George V in Paris and luxuriate in that?" and he said, "Because it's not as luxurious as my home. The high level of customer service that we all get off on when we get it, which is rare in New York, but when you get it and you think, "Wow, I've been made to feel like a king." They feel like a fucking king all the time. They are the king. You know? It's a totally different planet.

NEW YORK IS a good place for these kinds of people. Here, everyone's allowed to indulge their neuroses. That's why people gravitate to New York, why there are young people who still come here and can be as fucked up as they were in their hometown, because people indulge it. People let it go. You can have a hissy fit in an office here. You can have a fucking meltdown in a way that would not be tolerated in any other place on the planet, but here's it's kind of, "Ooh, they're just having a bad day."

The thing about New York is you can buy anything. You can pay someone to do anything. I'll give you an example. One guy I worked for was looking to buy a kitchen countertop. And the kitchen countertop needed to be glass, because that's what he wanted and he designed it himself in some pique of 4:00-in-the-morning strangeness. But the problem with a glass countertop is that you put a hot pan on it and it cracks, right? So what can be used instead of glass or what kind of glass can be used that would potentially be able to expand and contract? And not immediately crack if you put a hot pan on there? Now, keep in mind that of course none of the cooking ever took place in this kitchen, so the chances of this ever occurring are a quarter of a percent. Nevertheless, this is an issue.

So, what do you do when you have unlimited funds? You say, "Okay, if glass is going to potentially be a problem, what kind of material can I use?" Well, how do you figure these sorts of things out? Well, the first thing you do is you start calling people and in New York you can call lots and lots and lots of people to answer these questions. You can call furniture places, you can call kitchen installers. You can call glass blowers, artists, people in museums who work with glass.

First you have to have the conversation with the person you're calling, you have to explain that you're just trying to get this information. "Have you ever worked with the material?" "Well, I've worked with this material, and this person is the person who sold it to me and got it to me. Call them."

You call them and they don't return your call. And then you have to call them again and you have to say, "Look, I'm working for a very well-resourced human being. He really wants the answer to this question. How much can I pay you to get on the phone and call me back and answer the question?" And then they call you back. And they say things like, "Look, I don't have the time to deal with this for some rich person. What is it you want to know?" "Well, I want to use the material." "This is going to take an hour to talk to you about all the different kinds of materials and the different vagaries and the chemical compounds." And you'd say, "Fine, how much is it going to cost for an hour of your time?" "Well, I'll just throw a number out. Why don't we say, $5,000 for an hour?" "Fine." And this conversation plays out ten times a day where you're retrieving information and you're finding that everybody has a price and you just have to find out what the price is.

So finally, we get down to the material that we're talking about and it looks like it's a material that has been used by NASA on Space Shuttle tiles, because they expand and contract when they go up into the fucking atmosphere. So now you're in this surreal moment where you know that the material exists, you know that NASA knows what it is. How do you call NASA and find out about this material for a kitchen table for some dude in New York? And yet you do. You call NASA and you get the receptionist and you spend hours and hours on the phone going from person to person to person to person and finally you get the guy in the tile department who deals with the tiles. And this has taken weeks at this point. And you get to the person who's on the tiles and he says, "Listen, I can't have this conversation with you. This is really ridiculous. It doesn't make any sense."

And you say, "Can I pay for your kid's school fees for a year to have this conversation?" And they can't deal with it and they freak out and they go home and they talk to their wife and they come back and they say, "If you're really willing to pay for my kid's school fees for a year, I can talk to you about this."

There's no question in New York that hasn't been asked before. There are only questions that haven't been answered yet. And when you have unlimited resources, those questions will be answered.

The hard thing is taking the leap from admiring the desire for the best possible solution to whatever it is you're working on, to being utterly appalled that you're enabling this person's neuroses and psychoses and inuring him to the reality of not knowing anything about anything anymore.

WHEN THE CORONAVIRUS HIT, and everything in New York shut down around the middle of March 2020, I remember seeing town cars and SUVs all over the place, picking up people and people throwing their luggage in the back and taking off. I think a lot of those people had the opportunity to go to a family or a second home out of town. But what is increasingly apparent is a lot of those people have come back and the people who are still gone are the rich. I look outside my window onto an apartment building which had apartments selling a couple of years ago for $1.5 million for a studio and then moving up to $27, $28 million. And for months, I've not seen a light on. These immensely wealthy people have just taken off to somewhere else.

I don't know where they've gone. But I do wonder what they're going to find when they come back. Will life resume where it left off with the only noticeable impact on their lives being some social distancing at their favorite restaurant? Sometimes I wonder whether the rest of us—the nonrich, who didn't leave—are going to be more wary and resentful of those people.

Perhaps we are part of a New York that those rich people can't possibly understand anymore. One that has been irrevocably changed psychologically, if not materially. The rich have always lived in a different city from 90 percent of the rest of us. I don't know whether those of us who've kept the place running for them while they've been gone are going to be as happy as we might've been before to let it go back to what it was. I mean, none of us can live without those rich people going out and spending $175 on a theater ticket or overspending at restaurants. That's the part that scares me. We're sort of subjugated to those people. I wonder whether there will be a mass reckoning.

TWO ANONYMOUS BANKERS
On what it takes to live in New York

A banker and an ex-banker eat Thai food on the Lower East Side.

Banker: "At the risk of sounding like a banker, when I think about how much would I need to make per year in New York to support a wife, two kids, and save for my future . . . $400,000? I'm not sure it's all that disconnected."

Ex-banker: "It absolutely is!"

B: "People are doing it with less, but are they saving for their future? I'm sorry, I just don't think that's true."

Ex: "I know people who own brownstones in Brooklyn, have families with two kids, and earn $200k, $250k tops."

B: "Which by the way is a ton."

Ex: "Which *is* a ton, which is a ton. It's not anywhere near $400,000. . . . But let's not paint New Yorkers as vulnerable people who have no choice of where they choose to live their lives. You could choose to up and move to Austin, where your cost of living is one-third of what it is here."

B: "This person you're talking about in the brownstone? I'm not saying they're not good at their job, I'm not saying they're not good at providing for their family. I just don't believe that they are saving for their future. Put it this way: when they retire, they can't stay here."

Ex: "If they own their home, they can. As long as the cost of food isn't that expensive."

B: "I'm sorry, do that math. Two hundred fifty thousand, okay? So, what are you netting? You're netting one hundred fifty, maybe. How much is that brownstone?"

Ex: "Purchased ten years ago for 600k."

B: "Yeah, but count that mortgage. I'm sorry, the math doesn't work, just doesn't work."

Ex: "People also have very different retirement calculations than you do."

B: "Maybe people don't plan on staying, which maybe is part of it."

Ex: "Maybe people are stupid a little bit as well, and don't actually realize how expensive retirement is. The problem is, ultimately people make choices, right? People with whatever their salaries are in the city want to have everything. They want to have the one-bedroom apartment in the West Village that takes up sixty percent of their income, and they are choosing to do that, and that's a dumb choice. They don't make enough money to do that. So, fucking move to Jackson Heights because that's where it's possible. Everyone comes to the city thinking, *I can earn my freelancer salary, I can live with a roommate in a great part of town, and I won't care about saving for the future.* I don't want to paint New Yorkers as being victims because we've chosen to live here."

B: "If you're painting a picture of somewhere you live in the moment, what you're effectively saying is it's a transient culture, which it probably is. I mean, that's what scares me. As much as I've saved, if I left today, I wouldn't feel comfortable. . . . Let's say I spent six months unemployed. I'm not going to spend six months unemployed paying X on New York rent. That bleed is so quick and so fast. It's like, *Man, I'm doing pretty damn good, and I got a nice little egg, and I'm not willing to take that hit.*"

Ex: "You're also smarter than the average, and more conservative than the average."

B: "I don't think the average person in New York has more than $10,000 in their bank account."

Ex: "That's fair, but the average person in America is not actually saving, period. This isn't a New York phenomenon."

B: "It's worse."

Ex: "The average person in the United States who earns more than $100,000 is actually living paycheck to paycheck."

B: "But, no, it's worse in New York. Anything you do in New York, you make more than you would make in Topeka, but the only industry that outpays the cost of living is finance. In other industries, you may make fifty percent more, but you're doing worse, is my point. . . . That's what I found most upsetting about a lot of Occupy Wall Street and the pushback into finance. Don't feel bad for me; I'm fine. But ninety percent of the people at my firm, they're no different than the guy who's working at some consumer company. They may be working in finance, but they're making the same if they'd work anywhere else."

Ex: "These are people that are helping deliver the fundamental products of finance, and then not sharing in the profits because there's not an equal pay structure. So the executive assistant that's scheduling all of the meetings that allows for the managing director to meet with the client gets a nice bonus at Christmastime, but for the most part doesn't get a fair share."

B: "Does it really surprise you that the people who understand money as a job have the most money, and the people who understand fashion as a job are the best dressed? There are a lot of people who do finance because of the same reasons that I do it, which is I add up my numbers, and it doesn't add up. I think we are so much deeper, and more screwed than people ever imagined. No one likes to be told like, 'I know better than you.' That's one of the problems with Wall Street. There's a lot of things where it's like, 'You're actually wrong.' But in order for me to tell you you're wrong, it's almost a condescending social class kind of thing. I'm just telling you. I mean, I look at a lot of my really smart friends. People are hopelessly naive about retirement. I know it's twenty, thirty, forty years away, but people are living thirty years in retirement, and the attitude of, like, *I'll deal with it when I get there* just doesn't work. I never want to be that person."

Ex: "I think you take it to extremes."

B: "When I'm in retirement, I'm not going to be taking round-the-world vacations. I may be the extreme, but I'm not like living large. I look at it as I'm going to be able to maintain my status of living, and everyone else is going to be fucked. I look at every dollar I've saved to date as untouchable, absolutely untouchable. It doesn't fund a lifestyle. Every dollar I have is locked away until I'm sixty. Again, I think that supports the fact that it's not about working on Wall Street to buy your yacht. It's about security."

Ex: "We have no social welfare system. Social security is broke, and ninety-nine percent of America doesn't make what you make. Even if they were saving, even if they were more frugal and as thoughtful about their future as you are, ninety percent of America wouldn't have anything compared to what you're going to have for your retirement."

B: "I agree."

Ex: "That's a structural inequity that in some ways finance is perpetuating."

B: "It's not because I don't love New York and think it's a great place. For me and how I view the life and quality I want to live, it's not sustainable. I wouldn't raise a family here. I have a boss who told me that he thinks that he spends $25,000 a month. He has two kids and a wife, lives in Westchester, so there you go. I mean, look, I'm not even judging. I have to believe he's living bigger than he should, but he's not living huge. All I know is I never want to get to a place in my life where I'm living $25,000 a month."

[The food arrives.]

B: "Here is something that crushed me this week. I am at this point where I hate wearing ties to the office, because I ruin them. Last weekend I bought five ties. They cost me a thousand bucks."

Ex: "It's Ferragamo."

B: "There it is. You can believe me when I say this or not, but I would have no problem wearing no tie, or a $20 tie. I truly and honestly take no special pride out of my $200 tie; I don't. It's a pay for play. There are portions of my expenses which are directly related to doing this job."

Ex: "I think you give Wall Street way too much credit, because ninety percent of the dudes that are buying Ferragamo ties are doing it because they actually think four-inch ties with dolphins on them are attractive. It's like, *No, dude. You have no taste whatsoever. Sort it out. That's a fucking waste of your money.*"

B: "Dude, who justifies a $200 tie?"

Ex: "It's a status symbol. Everyone knows when someone's wearing a Ferragamo tie."

B: "When I eat dinner after the office, I either take my tie off or I tuck it. It's taken every ounce of me to be like a real person, and not tuck my tie in a restaurant."

Ex: "But you don't care about the Ferragamo. Right. Ferragamo gets spaghetti on it, you'd be like, *Whatever, I'll just buy another.*"

B: "The last time I cried—true story—was about a tie. It wasn't a Ferragamo; it was more like a $100 tie. I cut myself shaving my chin, and then I went to tie my tie, and I did the flip. Not bad, but a little blood came straight down, and you can't save ties. And I cried."

Ex: "Not because you were devastated about having lost a tie."

B: "It was wasted money."

DAN BAUSO A personal injury lawyer

Instead of taking the subway everywhere, I occasionally caught a ride to different neighborhoods with a personal injury lawyer from Queens who drove a Nissan Quest with a dented sliding door. It was his office on wheels. There were pizza boxes in the back from Phillies in Middle Village, an old nativity set, a half-bottle of Prestone antifreeze, a beach chair, his Con Law textbook, and an old, rusty wheel clamp. As we drove around Sunnyside and Jackson Heights, Dan provided a commentary that only paused when the Quest did. One cold afternoon in January we ended up on Roosevelt Avenue under the elevated train. The Quest stalled. A red light flared on the dashboard. Dan wrenched the van into park. Someone behind us honked. "Okay, okay," Dan said. He started up the minivan. Beside us, on the pavement, a man in a foam Statue of Liberty crown handed out flyers. We rolled toward La Abundancia bakery, but the Quest stalled again in front of Spicy Tibet. Someone honked behind us, a different car. "Okay, okay, okay," Dan called out. We drove on until we eventually reached Long Island City.

So here's the thing. The five boroughs joined in 1898. Manhattan was busting and thriving, but so was Brooklyn; Brooklyn was just a step behind. When you go to Brooklyn Heights you see it's the remnants of a big city, just never continued to develop. The Bronx was so-so, Queens was basically built up over here, but the rest of it was farmland. And Staten Island was like a penal colony. I don't even know what was going on with Staten Island.

So the big tug was between Brooklyn and Manhattan. Manhattan had to convince Brooklyn. Basically, the other three were the three little sisters. They were gonna follow what Brooklyn did and Brooklyn regrets to this day that they did it. You talk to real salty Brooklynites, they're like, *We should have never done it. We would have rocked the universe.*

Queens, on the other hand, has an inferiority complex.

[The red dashboard light flashes. Dan pulls over and puts the Quest in park.]

The Queensboro Bridge is at the end of this strip, the end of 21st; there are several entrances. If you live in Manhattan, the Queensboro Bridge enters under 59th Street. They don't call it the Queensboro Bridge. They call it the 59th Street Bridge. Simon and Garfunkel wrote their famous song "The 59th Street Bridge Song" and they're *from* Queens. You'd think they would know better! Now they've just named it the Ed Koch Queensboro Bridge. You wouldn't name the Brooklyn Bridge after somebody, why you naming this one? But nobody cares.

Another crazy thing: Queens streets. I love my borough, but you'll go from 45th Road to 23rd Street. There's no rhyme or reason.

For months I rode in the Quest with Dan. We visited Forest Hills, Astoria, Howard Beach, the Rockaways. The van mostly didn't stall. The trips were always memorable. For instance: It's Christmas. Dan stops the minivan outside my apartment on the Lower East Side after driving to Dyker Heights and then helping me buy a last-minute turkey from a local butcher shop. My mother, visiting for the holidays, sits in the back seat. The conversation turns to his work. One of his cases involves representing a young woman who lost part of her finger in an escalator at Macy's. He suggests, as a joke, that if things get bad enough in New York, if the city is too much for me, I should start looking for my own lawsuit. There is a company, he says, that keeps track of all the cracks in the sidewalks of New York.

When there are cracks in sidewalks, they send the information to the city. So now the city has notice, so now you can sue them. Let's just pick the right crack.

Hold on. They know every crack?

They go through the city.

Who does that?

The Big Apple Pothole Company.

Do you know them?

They're a friend of the plaintiff's bar. I'll order the map. For instance, we see a crack in front of a city housing project. I'll order that map.

[My mother chimes in:] And then you have to fall.

Don't fall yet. Let's make sure the crack is acknowledged. *Then* fall on the crack. Listen. You're a good-looking kid, Craig, but your modeling days are over. So, face first. Let's maximize the amount of damage we can get here.

[My mother again:] I wish I'd had you as my lawyer.

Then we'll bring Mom in. A grandchild? No way. The damages, ladies and gentlemen, are manifold. I'm not even going to put a number on it. I'm going to ask you to do that which is right. Could you do the right thing for Craig Taylor? Craig Taylor was a guest in our city. I don't know. When I have guests in my home, I invite them in. I let them sit down and make them comfortable. Is this what we want people thinking of our city? That poor, wayward Canadians can come here and be maimed, *grotesquely* deformed. Look at him. Look at his face. It's incalculable. If there was a machine . . .

[My mother:] Couldn't it just be his arm or his leg?

We'll go with the face. We're on a roll here. If there was a machine, ladies and gentlemen, that I could put Craig in and press buttons like in a science fiction movie, and smoke would come out, and he would come out as his old self, don't you know I would do that?

[Dan smacks the dashboard.]

Don't you know I would do that? But I can't do that. Neither can you. What can you do? You can award a large cash compensation and you should do that. You know what? The city will know. Not only will you be putting Craig back in a position where he was and making him whole again, but this city will know, this great city, they will know. It's time to make this city a better place, a place where we can all live and walk without fear of a sudden, traumatic and violent throwing of the body to the pavement. How many Canadians, ladies and gentlemen, have to come to these shores and suffer like this?

What would the judge say to that?

It's summation. It's bad form to argue during summation. It's bad form to object or interrupt. You've really got to be bad. There's a lot of latitude. That's what lawyers live for, the summation, as long as you argue the evidence that's in. You can't argue for stuff that's not in. That's the stuff that drives judges crazy. If this didn't come into evidence, then don't argue it. That era—they say that era is over. For criminal defense attorneys in the 1950s, '60s, '70s, it was like a Shakespearean play. One guy, he would get down on his knees and start to cry, it was amazing. Another guy, he was so theatrical, he used to wear capes and he had a walking stick and a handlebar mustache. Then there's the magician, Tommy Moore, the medical malpractice guy. He was from Ireland, in his sixties now, an avid marathon runner, he's the king of the med/mal, he has over one hundred million-dollar verdicts, he gets all the cases, they all come to him. When he does summation, the Irish brogue comes out.

[Dan dips into a brogue.]

"Never again will she feel the blush of a kiss. She will not feel the blush of a kiss on her wedding day due to this." He'll bring them in on a gurney. He's ruthless. I'm gonna go that route with you. "Craig Taylor was an author. Now you give a book reading looking like this? Can you imagine?" That's if you go face-first. It writes itself. "When Craig Taylor exited the Nissan Quest and tripped over that crack and smashed his face beyond recognition, the policemen came and did everything they could for him. They called the paramedics, and they did everything they could for him. They took him to the hospital where the emergency doctors and emergency room attendants and the nurses—they did everything they could for him. They discharged him to months of therapy and plastic surgery, and those therapists and plastic surgeons did everything they could for him. Then he came to my office. And he retained me. And I have brought this case. And I have done everything I can for him. Ladies and gentlemen of the jury, only you are left. And I know when you get into the jury room, you are going to do everything you can for him."

TOM MOORE A lawyer

New York juries. When I say New York juries, I really mean New Yorkers, right? That's what we get, and there is something about New Yorkers that can be endearing and frustrating and annoying and uplifting and all of these things and myriads more that I could mention. I think most of all that New Yorkers see the essence of things more quickly than others do, and see through things. They'll see through you. It's rather frightening, you know? I really believe that.

They have a healthy skepticism about anything that people say to them. They're going to examine it, and they're going to analyze it. I see it in their manner. I see it in the body language, and I see it in their eye. I hear it in their questioning. We have the ability to do what's called a voir dire to talk to the jurors ahead of time before we select them. That process can go on for a couple of days, maybe three days sometimes. It's quite a bit of back and forth before you finally end up with the people that are going to sit on the jury.

You're getting to know them, and they're getting to know you, and they're rather probative in their questioning. They want to know what they're getting into. They want to tell you that they're going to reserve judgment. I mean, I've had jurors say to me after they've been excused from the case, "You know, you were kind of entertaining in there, but I was very open minded, and I would have been fair on the case." They made a point of saying that even though they'd been excused.

I feel less constrained in a New York courtroom than I did in a Kentucky courtroom and than I would in a Michigan or California or a Florida courtroom. The best example I can give you is that the federal court in New York and the state court in New York are separate. The state court is my court. I see the difference. The federal court is like the United States court. Federal court, United States district court of the southern district here, the eastern district across the river in Brooklyn, and all the other districts throughout the United States. They're rather similar whether you go from New York to Kentucky to Jersey or whatever. The New York state court, and the New York state courtrooms, and the New York state judges, and the New York state juries, they're different. They allow for someone to be themselves and to present their case in a fashion that they see appropriate—within certain constraints, of course. I'll give you one brief example of this.

Back in the 1970s, when even I was young and starting to try cases, I tried several cases in the federal court. A couple in the eastern district, which is, as I say, just across the river in Brooklyn. Then, in Foley Square, in the southern district, I tried a few more. Something happened in my last case that I tried at federal court, which was in 1978.

The judge said to me as I was cross-examining a witness, "Mr. Moore, you have to stand at the podium when you're examining the witness." Well, you have no idea how devastating that was to me, and I mean this literally. I can't think unless I'm moving.

In the hurly-burly of a courtroom, in the back and forth, I feed off movement, and I think, and I respond, and my thoughts are so much aided by my movement that they go together. If you tie me to a podium, I'm not a shadow of what I would be otherwise. I don't know if he was the first judge to do it, but it was around the time that it became de rigueur throughout federal courts in New York state and throughout the United States. There would be these restrictions to be placed on lawyers in terms of movement when they're cross-examining witnesses. Just appalling to me.

To this day, that's not the rule in New York state courts. We can move around.

I'm moving, sometimes deliberately, sometimes quickly. I'm looking at the witness. I'm looking at the jury. I'm turning, I'm pacing, and I'm trying to keep it interesting. There were some great actors that have stood and done monologues without much movement. We all know the courtroom is theater. It's real-life theater.

It's monumentally important theater, but it's theater. It's real. It's reality. Jurors have their own lives and their own issues and personal things.

There's a job issue or a family issue on their minds. You want to keep them with you during those hours that they're in the courtroom and through those days they're going to be with you, and during those weeks that they're going to be with you. I think it helps if you can do more than just allow the case by itself to persuade them, but to allow them a little of the theater.

When I first came, I was always a proud Irishman. When I arrived, and I still am, but I was a little self-conscious I must admit as a seventeen-year-old, and an eighteen-year-old, and a nineteen-year-old and for some years later about my brogue. I probably made an effort to control it and to change it. I wish I had it back now, as strong as it was the day I got off the plane, but little did I know that I would think that way. There's no doubt that in the courtroom my brogue even still, even though many people would say I don't notice when I speak to them on the street or in a room or whatever, say, "I don't notice that you have an Irish accent."

Then I'll say, "You didn't notice I had an Irish accent," and they'll say, "Oh, now I notice it." Once they make me conscious of it, it comes out.

There's something primordial about the courtroom.

So the people that say his brogue comes out are correct. When they say he does it deliberately, they're not correct, okay? I do change my voice in terms of volume constantly. That is deliberate, particularly when I'm summing up on a case. I think some people have accused me of shouting. I don't consciously shout, but I do raise my voice. I raise my voice when there's a particular point to be made or where the witness is particularly vulnerable and I know that I have that vulnerable spot and I'm going for the jugular, so to speak. Then there are other times that my voice is already soft, and hearken back to when I said movement is part of keeping juries' attention. The raising and the softening of the voice is an attention-getter I really believe rather than speaking in the same monotone the whole time.

THERE ARE SOME great courtrooms in New York. Almost all the rooms in 60 Centre Street, the *Law & Order* facade courtroom, even though the courtrooms in *Law & Order* were not in the building, the pillars and the steps going up. They're great. Then, just adjacent is the federal court that's not nearly as impressive, and the pillars are not as impressive. Practically every courtroom in that building is a wonderful place to try a case. Queens County out at Sutphin Boulevard is a relatively old court. It's a wonderful courthouse with some great, great courtrooms. What I like in a courtroom is big. I like a large courtroom because I feel confined if it's not, and my manner of trying a case is inhibited a great deal by a confined space and a small courtroom and low. . . . I like it large so that when I raise my voice, the jurors are saying, "Well, he has to raise his voice. Otherwise he couldn't be heard."

I love a symposium courtroom. I mean not all are large as a symposium, right, but a courtroom that *looks* like a courtroom, that was meant to be a courtroom, that gives the sense of a cathedral of justice, a holy place, a hallowed place. It's evident once you walk in and then it becomes more evident once a trial begins and the whole process continues and everything becomes evident and more evident as time goes on. People say this had to happen in this place. This is the place it had to happen, you know?

The juries overwhelmingly, not invariably, but overwhelmingly do the right thing, because they want to do the right thing. Let's face it, why am I so proud to be a New Yorker? I'm so proud to be a New Yorker because we're difficult sometimes and we don't have time for small talk sometimes, and we're abrupt sometimes, but when the chips are down, when really serious matters are afoot, we're there, and we can be counted on. I say we. I mean New Yorkers can be counted on. I say that about New York jurors. They take their job as jurors very seriously. They may not be jumping for joy that they were selected to take three weeks or four weeks off from work to sit on a case, but once they're committed, they stay committed.

I think my admiration for that knows no bounds really.

MR. M A car thief

You got to be a good driver.

What's the secret? Every corner, turn. Going uptown, every corner you turn. As long as you're going up, towards the division of Manhattan and the Bronx, every corner you turn. Every corner. Don't go on the right path because they going to lock you in.

They're going to put the chains in the front and blow your tires. So every corner—they don't know what's on your mind—so every corner you turn. They can say, "He's on 138. Oh, he's going over, yeah, he's going to 139 now." Throw them off. I done that for years. Every time they chased me, I never go straight.

If I got a fast car, I'm booking. And I get away.

MARILYN ALICEA Whose son has been incarcerated on Rikers Island

At first, when he wasn't going out to the yard, I said to him, "You have to go outside and you have to get a mental break. You need to breathe in that air. You know, you have to get out." So he's been going outside, but it's been really hard, facing fifteen years for what he did.

I feel hopeless because I've always fought for him. I've always advocated for him and now I can't. I can't save him now, and that's my problem. That's what I'm going through. Sometimes I feel like I failed him. I'm a single mom, his dad wasn't really in the picture, it was always me taking care of him. And one day he said that he chose the streets because he was tired of not having money. I mean, I used to give him money, but how much money can you give a kid when you're doing everything on your own and you're not on public assistance or anything? So he went to the streets because he wanted to have things. I mean, he had nice things, but he wanted more. I really didn't want to lose him to the streets, but what can you do?

It's been a mess. I cut my hair. I used to have long hair. I almost lost my mind because of this. It rattled me. It shut me down. I've been numb for a year. I've isolated myself. I've been angry.

Sometimes I go visit him and I break down like a baby. I try to go with a straight face, I tell myself, *I'm not gonna cry today.* But once I see him in that situation I can't help it. I tell him, if you see me like this you have to understand, I haven't seen you in a week. Or, I haven't seen you the two weeks you've been on lockdown. Of course I'm gonna feel like this. We have great visits. But there's gonna be days where I can't control myself.

I get up at 4:30 a.m. on the days I visit him. It's dark. Where I live, there's a lotta crackheads. You never know what's happening when you come out of a building. When I get on that bus I'm excited, I have anxiety, and I get nervous. My mind is racing. It's funny 'cause when I go in there I feel nervous, like *I've* done something.

So the 101 bus to Rikers pulls up, and they have the corrections officers outside of the doors, waiting to check the visitors. The doors open, they come on the bus. They give a speech about if anybody has any drugs, any contraband. Anything, you know, this is your last chance. They make it seem like you have something in your pocket. They give this speech and then you get off. You have to show your ID. They explain what they are going to do. They tell the employees to get off the bus first. Then you get off the bus and you form a line into the building, and you wait to be called into that building and you have to stand side by side. You can't touch anybody, hands on your side.

If you have a hat, take it off. If you have a bag, you have to take it off your shoulder. You have to bring it down to your side, and then they come to the door, and they tell you, "If you have anything" again, and they check you. The dog sniffs you out, and then you go about your business.

A world of guilt. That's what it is.

You get off the bus. There's the line. They check your ID. You go on this line. You get in. You have to take off your shoes, everything outta your pockets. You can't wear hoodies. You can't wear this, you can't wear that. Women cannot wear bras that have wires, because you have to go through a pat down. Then you go, you register. You go through whatever window.

And then you wait for the bus that takes you to the building to where my son is at. When you get there, that's another search.

When you first get to Rikers there's a locker. In that locker you leave your phone. Everything stays there. Your wallet, your money, not a problem, but everything else stays outside. Then when you get to the building, you leave whatever else in that last locker to go in.

From the moment you walk in the building, it smells like cleaning stuff. I'll never forget that smell. Everything is cold. It's cold and uncomfortable, dreary, and there's like a dimness in the building. Echo-y. Despair, right?

Now you wait 'till you're called. They call you. You go upstairs for one hour. They sit him in the front. One because he's a adolescent, and two because they're watching him. I already know that. Because it's always in the front, in the front, in the front, in the front. Why are you watching him? Don't know, don't care. You know? You got one hour, one hour.

He comes out in the jumpsuits. If you wear orange, that's something special, that means you've done something. Otherwise, it's gray. You get your hour and then you go home. You go back down, you wait for the bus again, and then you go. I leave . . . Sometimes I'm happy. I'm not gonna say *happy* . . . I'm kind of like relieved that I saw him, that's he's okay, and frustrated that I can't help him, that I can't bring him home.

I go three times a week.

AND THEN THEY put him in the box. He told me that they told him it was gonna only be twenty days in the box. They gave him thirty. It was thirty days.

What they do is that they put 'em in a cage. Those are the better visits, believe it or not, the cage visits. Because there's more contact. It's weird, but it's true. We're both in a cage—you know, like a dog cage, that's what it is. With a partition, right? And then a chair and a chair, that's it. It's a cage. When you want to see your kid you don't care. It hurts me to see him that way, but what can I do?

He's gonna be alright. I don't know why I'm saying that, but I feel that. Yeah, he's gonna be alright. I'm just scared. Fifteen years is a long time. And I'm gonna be honest with you, I don't know how I'm gonna live without him fifteen years. I don't know how I'm gonna do that. How do you do that? It's been a year, imagine fifteen. Sometimes I go see him and I'm like, "Why did you leave me alone?"

It's crazy how much I love him. How much you can love somebody.

I DON'T THINK that Rikers Island can be fixed. They need to shut that place down. They need to rebuild. They need to train these people how to deal with situations like this on a different level. They need to retrain their correction officers. They need to be supervised and retrained. You're dealing with these kids; challenge them in a positive way. I don't know how. Challenge them instead of beating them up or degrading them.

These people are dehumanized. Sometimes you need to pull in somebody. I'm challenging you to pull that kid in. Don't curse him or berate him. Pull him in. Talk to him. Wisdom, say something. You never know. Maybe that way, you can get through.

There's a lot going on there. They have to keep their milks in the toilet bowls. Imagine that. You know the cartons of milk? They put it in the toilet bowl to keep their milk cold.

The doors are the big thing. You know when they shut? That's the biggest thing. I would go home and I could still hear the doors being shut. The slamming of the cells, that stayed with me. You're in the visiting room, you don't really hear anything else but that. And that stays with you. Every time they open that door, you know somebody's coming out.

When we went to the cage, there was a window. And my son just got up to look. Mind you, we're in a cage. Where is he going? He got up to look out the window; they wouldn't let him look out the window. Something so simple, to look out a window . . . just to glance. He wasn't even allowed to look. The guard said no.

YOU KNOW HOW I live? Do you know when you act like that person doesn't exist? That's how I'm living every day. The moment I think about it too much, it hits me. So I can't think about him. That's the only way I can live.

So I don't go in his room much. I just cleaned it up. His dirty laundry was still dirty a year later. Imagine. Just avoiding. "Okay, I'll be ready one day," and I'm just never ready to go in the room and clean it. It's almost like when someone says I'm in mourning.

And now the bed is not there because he broke the frame, so I threw that out. I just threw out the box spring the day before yesterday. Little by little. I take baby steps to clean the room. That's how I deal with things now. I make believe they don't exist.

That's gonna be my art room. It's gotta be something positive. It's gotta be something, because if I leave it like that I'm always gonna feel that way.

I thought about moving out of New York. I stayed. I stayed and I prayed.

[In October 2019, the New York City Council voted to close the jail complex on Rikers Island by 2026, and replace it with four smaller jails in Brooklyn, Queens, Manhattan, and the Bronx.]

JAIQUAN FAYSON

A painter who used to be incarcerated on Rikers Island

My first time being locked up, I got locked up for a robbery. Just random, stupid, you know, running around, point a gun at somebody and tell them to give you their wallet and they'll do it. And people won't call the cops—oh shit, this guy actually called the cops. And, you know, I got arrested. I was sixteen years old.

That was my first time on Rikers Island, and that was a horrible experience. The smell was fucking horrible. It is something that is almost unrecognizable out here, but when you're in there it's like, you know where you are. It's kind of a mix of like Pine-Sol and some other weird, violent whatever. It's there.

Once you're in Rikers, it's just like a switch is on. Like werewolf mode, like holy shit I know I smell it. I can feel it. It's stale, stagnant, like desolation. This is your last stop. You know? Even though you know it's not, that's kind of what it feels like.

Going to Rikers really saved my art. I always drew. I was always an artist. I was always known for drawing. I drew a lot of comic books. I was able to make money by selling drawings. People would ask me, "I'm up here for five years, can you draw a picture for my daughter so I can send it home to her?" Or "Can you draw a card so I can send it home to my wife?"

Mostly, it was cards. But handkerchiefs were also popular. People would always want you to draw on a handkerchief for whatever tacky reason. And they would pay me in cigarettes, stamps, cookies, snacks, food, whatever. So that was how I survived in jail, and I did really well.

Prison helped my art because I realized the therapeutic values to it, which was major. I had ants in my cell. I was feeding the ants, I thought they were my pets. Once a bat flew into my cell. It literally died on the wall and it sat there for maybe a day or two. I'm wondering, "Why the fuck is this bat . . . ?" I told them I had a bat in my cell. They didn't want to come clean it up. Prison, as long as they can make you suffer. These guys take pride in making you suffer. It's hell.

So I drew a shitload of pictures. Particularly I drew hands. They allowed you to have a certain number of things, like five magazines and three books. I would ask for any magazines I could get. The thing that I could always draw was the position these people's hands were in. I could always draw their hands and I drew hands, I drew feet, I drew faces. Those were important things to me. I remember coming out and having a book full of fucking hands and feet.

Drawing is like drugs. It can take me away from all these circumstances because I'm only focused on getting this drawing done and the details of this drawing. The whole world is absent. It's like reading a book and you're reading and everything that is going on suddenly becomes mute. The TV is on and then all of a sudden you don't even hear the TV anymore. You don't feel anything besides what you're thinking about this book.

There were times when I just wanted to punch whatever I could. There were times I *did* punch stuff. Eventually you punch the walls too much, hurt your hands pretty bad. That happened a lot. You exercise too much, your body gets tired. It was like I'm exhausting myself in these ways and I'm going to keep fucking my hand up. I won't be able to draw. I might as well just keep drawing.

Even now it's something I automatically gravitate to. If I have a bad day I'm looking forward to going home and painting. I'm looking forward to it. It makes me feel like I'm putting my energy into that pen and I'm also getting something out of it because I'm keeping myself calm in a constructive way. I'm actually getting something done.

Now I worry about my line quality, my line control, these kinds of things. I draw people on the subway. The best way I can describe it is

I feel like I have something in common with everybody, but I feel like because of that I'm not like anybody. I feel like I can empathize with pretty much everybody because of the situations I've been in.

Everybody is really an individual. Even when you find people that look very similar. When you get into it they have nuances. To me, that's really important, to actually show that these are *people*. They're not just mannequins with a nose and eyes and a face on them. These people— not only are their faces different but their body types are different. Their mannerisms are different. I can't capture their movements but I can try to capture some of what their mannerisms are.

Lately I've been painting a series of homeless people in the city. I take a bunch of photos. I choose maybe five or six photos from the same angle. The most important things to me are the emotion in their face and their hands because those are the things that I feel like are going to speak. So all of my attention is focused into that and if I take five or six pictures I'm going to find out of those five or six pictures two moments that I like the face and the hands.

Immediately when I walk in, I see people's hands. They're so emotive and they have so much personality. You're not communicating with your elbows, but you are with your hands and your face. They're like everything in New York. New York is less of a melting pot and more of a mosaic. It's really like different colored tiles, and different people being who they are.

It's hard because hands are moving more than anything. They're moving so much more than your face. Even when somebody's hand is just on a pole.

[He shows off the painting on his phone.]

I wanted to show the heaviness, and the weight, and you can see how swollen it is at the top of his palm, at the top of his hand. The back side of it. The guy's an alcoholic. He's drinking, he's probably used some drugs and I know a fair amount of people who use drugs. They tend to get these sort of swollen, really swollen, heavy, slow hands. To me that was a big part of his character.

The curve of the fingers and the face . . . I went into it feeling like these characters should be given some respect. They're not characters, they're people. They should be given some respect.

I want you to look at my painting when it's finished and say, *Damn, this kid knows how to paint.* And I want you to go, *This makes me feel some kind of way.* Whether you like it, whether you don't like it. Whether it pissed you off, whether it made you think of something. You gotta feel something.

I need you to feel something and I want you to realize that I'm upholding a legacy. I'm doing the same thing that Goya did. You remember *Third of May*? You ever seen *Third of May*? It's a guy with his hands up. There are officers getting ready to execute him.

I happen to love Goya.

SOMETIMES I MEET people from LA or Chicago and I ask them, "You know this song? You know that song?" And they're like, "No." Then when you look the song up, you see all the comments on You-Tube are like, "Yo, this was a New York anthem." And you look the person up and it's like, this person was born and raised in New York.

Back then we didn't have the internet, and we didn't have satellite radio. We had local radio stations that broadcast local popular singers.

There's one I was listening to recently, the song was called "Getting Over Like a Fat Rat." There it goes right there. I listen to that song pretty often.

[A woman beside us in the café is nodding her head.]

You remember that one? Is it only a New York song?

[Woman in café:] I don't know, but I been listening to what you were saying. I had cousins that lived up in New Jersey, like Atlantic City area, and it seemed like there was songs and dances that we would get in New York and when we would go to Jersey and visit them in the summertime we'd be like, "Do you know this song?" And they'd be like, "We never heard that song before." "Do you know this dance?" But they hadn't seen that

dance before. It was like New York kind of had music first, and we had it for a period of time and then maybe if it was popular ...

Enough.

Enough, then maybe it would get to them. But it didn't happen until like months later that they would finally get it.

Yeah.

And then New York would already be on to something else. It was almost like a delayed kind of thing for the rest of the world. New York always got it first. I think that does give us a lot of that kind of music, especially around hip-hop and that kind of R&B, like De La Soul. Leaders of the New School, and it was kind of like based out of New York.

I'm thirty-eight, so I remember a lot of just music and dances and different things. And then I would go visit my cousins in Baltimore or somewhere like that and they just had no clue. It almost seemed like it was such a different world.

I think that the internet and YouTube and all those things have something to do with it. But I also think music is able to expand in a way, so that everyone is able to watch at the same time; whereas before it was just focused on a specific geographical location. You only had two stations. You had WBLS and you had KISS-FM. In the beginning, just those two. Then they added like—

Hot 97.

There was a time when 98.7 played hip-hop, and they played R&B at night. You had a countdown, you had your slow jams. And then, you know, WBLS had like The Quiet Storm at night.

There was also one point where there wasn't really much separation between R&B and hip-hop.

They ran together. Back in the day, artists wasn't traveling abroad to ... I mean if they did it was because they finally had enough money and maybe they went on a tour. But that was just like so far and in between. It was like you only rhymed about what you really knew about, and what you knew about was your hood. Like, this is our world, this is our commu-

nity, and this is what we take care of. So they can't rhyme about any of that other stuff.

Stuff that ain't going on.

Because they didn't really know about that other stuff. They could only rap about Queens Boulevard because that's where they were from.

And I think people, even in New York anyway, regardless of whether somebody said they were from Queens or whether they were from the Bronx, there were things that were universal.

So New York.

INTERLUDE

A Sunday on the Street

AFTER NEARLY A YEAR of conducting interviews in New York, I learned about a free lunch served on Sundays in the basement of St. Francis Xavier, a neobaroque church built in 1878, on 16th Street and Sixth Avenue. Over the course of a typical Sunday afternoon, the kitchen staff of the Welcome Table served around 1,300 hot meals, often meatloaf, sometimes turkey loaf.

Those who came to eat or work at the meal would gather outside on the sidewalk beyond the church's gabled portico. The wealthier residents of the Flatiron District mostly crossed the street to stay away from the crowds, but some rushed past with fruit juices in hand and yoga mats underarm. One Sunday I volunteered, and the next weekend I drifted back. I'm not religious but I began to look forward to my Sunday mornings.

Two lines fed into the basement, one for men and the other for women, children, and anyone with special needs. One ticket entitled the recipient to a meal, and after eating at one of the long tables a guest could get his spine cracked by an osteopath, or play one of the two pianos set against the wall. Student lawyers offered help with tenancy agreements, and more tickets were available for those who circled back again for another meal, and maybe another meal, and even a fourth.

My job, at the end of the lunch, was to stand by a Japanese pagoda tree that towered over the iron exit gate and bid people goodbye. Various men stood near me on the sidewalk and offered cigarettes for sale. They said, "Loosies," and I said, "Thanks for coming" and "See you next time." When I was feeling down or discouraged or homesick, I knew I could at the very least hold the iron gate open on 16th Street.

One day, the doorkeeper, Ralph, asked if he could introduce me to someone. He gestured toward a man I'd noticed before, mostly because he walked around bent over at the waist, staring down at the pavement. Joe was a white guy with military-short hair, the skin on his hands a mottled combination of blue and pink and red—raw and even blackened around the nails—and the back of his neck tanned chestnut, even in winter. He was so bent, I worried he might headbutt a person or an iron gate—he'd mistakenly headbutted a bus shelter before. Joe watched the behavior of the feet of different guests as he stood, bent over, with his hands on his thighs. He watched the pavement, the shins, the footwear, the cracks, the foot movements. When he sat down on a step near my exit gate and finally tilted back, his face emerged, and he surveyed the last of the lunchtime crowd with calm gray eyes. At these moments late in the afternoon, he liked to say he was "getting it," as in "*Oh, I'm getting it now.*" He often got it from Ralph the doorkeeper, who took pleasure in making fun of him for coming from Pennsylvania.

"I'm getting it big time," Joe muttered, with obvious enjoyment.

Joe had a mouth that flapped because he no longer had teeth; his nose was curved and much broken. He'd served as a marine in Vietnam, and many years later he'd taken a blow to the head, which had brought on glaucoma and taken away his ability to read. Even while sitting, he emanated both pain and fortitude, and he hated being called Popeye as much as I hated being called The Canadian.

"Would you like to meet The Canadian?" Ralph asked Joe after a bout of giving it.

"Would I like to meet a Pennsylvanian?" Joe responded loudly in a show of willful inaccuracy. "Sure I would."

"Hi," I said to Joe.

"I'd rather meet a Pennsylvanian," he replied. Regardless, he offered up his hand.

Since moving to New York I had met hundreds of people. Some I knew for the length of a five-minute conversation. Others sat down with me for hours. Others kept popping up in my life, month after month. Because I'd known no one when I got to New York, these became the people I knew.

Starting that Sunday, I would stand around talking with Joe for an hour, sometimes two. He would linger at the gate, smoking a cigarette or just sitting on a concrete block, stretching out time. Week after week we talked and looked down at the pavement with lots of long pauses in between. His interest was less New York and more the wilderness I'd known growing up, so I told my own story and con-jured a few leafy and rocky descriptions of British Columbia, and he responded with tableaus of Pittsburgh, where he'd grown up, and the Allegheny River, and the forests where he'd once hunted.

"I guess we're both visitors to *New York*," he said once, pronouncing the name of the city with distaste.

ONE SUNDAY IN MAY, after several weeks of hanging out at St. Francis Xavier, Joe and I walked around the corner to a coffee shop on Sixth Avenue. Joe squeezed his walker into the small space to the right of the door and stacked a couple stuffed plastic bags atop its seat.

"Do you know what?" he asked after he'd doused his coffee with sugar and collected a stack of napkins. "This is the longest I've ever had my hair."

It was military-short only when he could afford it.

"Why can't you afford it, Joe?"

He told me he was often robbed. He'd sleep on any crosstown bus, completely dead to the world, and his pockets would get rifled.

"It looks good on you," I said.

He gave me a look and then spread out a couple napkins on the table.

"I'm getting it now," he said.

As it often did, our talk soon turned to Joe's time in Vietnam. Joe was a marine. He *is* a marine, he said, because being a marine is never placed in the past tense.

"There's a piece of metal in my left leg," he said. It lodged in when he was blown up by a mortar in 1969 and Joe can still feel the edge. "And do you know what I do?" he asked me. "I pick at it. Can you believe that? I *pick* at it. Why would any normal person do that?"

I asked him if he would go to the hospital. He didn't like the so-called care he'd received, the attitude. He had a problem with doctors, and nurses. And he had a problem with those who worked at reception, as well as with traffic wardens and police officers and security guards, which was why he was well known in his neighborhood.

In the evening, when the traffic on Park Avenue started to abate, Joe would set up camp in the alcove in front of a tanning and waxing salon at Park and 23rd Street. A man who worked at a nearby hotel passed him whatever was left behind by guests. If Joe wasn't careful, the police would question the provenance of these objects. He often gave the NYPD a list of made-up names when they would check up on him in cold weather thanks to the Code Blue initiative, which allowed the police to forcibly remove people when the temperature dropped below a certain point. Joe didn't like being touched, and the cops often pushed on his shoulder and prodded his blanket at night. So he offered them phony names and told them he'd stay no matter the weather.

He didn't react well to cops, doctors, nurses. When we were in the coffee shop he asked me, "Do you know what the first question is on the PTSD questionnaire?"

I said I didn't.

"It's, *Do you have a problem with authority?*"

When we finished our coffees, we often stood around outside. Bent over, Joe took a drag on his cigarette and the smoke drifted up and wreathed his head.

The skin of Joe's left forearm was a plasticized swirl where the mortar had hit and peeled the skin away. Sometimes we would talk about the shrapnel still in his body, more than twenty pieces, which would lead back to the subject of Vietnam. Most subjects were, in some way, related to his time in the marines. Some of these threads were strong, some slender, but they all pulled him into the past. Vietnam was not just inside him, but nearby, alongside. It revealed itself. I knew New York was big but this was the first time I saw that it actually contained other places. For Joe, the smell of gasoline brought forth Vietnam, as did the sound of a traffic helicopter. Once a nearby car backfired and Joe threw himself down onto the pavement. He broke his nose. He'd been ashamed—that was the dominant feeling, he said, and he looked around to find out if anyone had witnessed the act.

Sometimes, too, we would talk about my family, and then Vietnam, and his hometown of Pittsburgh, and then Vietnam, and then more Pittsburgh, especially that feeling of confidence at a Steelers game when they were up by fourteen points at the half. "You could leave," Joe said, "knowing they'd win." He said that the great athletes walked the streets of Pittsburgh, like gods touching down on earth.

Once, standing at our usual spot on the corner of Sixth Avenue at 16th Street on a warm evening after a parade down the avenue, we leaned on an NYPD police barricade. The barricade had been painted such a recent blue that I kept checking my palms to see if the color had transferred. It was nearly seven o'clock. The staff at the Welcome Table were long gone, the volunteers were gone, the gate was closed, and the parade had passed.

"I wish you'd known me," he said.

"I do know you."

"You know remnants."

There's a moment that arrives when you know you've spent too much time on a sidewalk, watching buses pull up and pull past. It was time to go. I didn't want to leave. I was lonely, and I told Joe maybe we should do something else. I'd love it if he came with me around the corner to a bar. He didn't drink, he said. Then maybe a restaurant? Joe couldn't. He said he was waiting on a check. When I told him I didn't care, he told me not to do this to him, so I relented.

"I feel embarrassed for you," he said.

"You don't get to do that."

Joe had started offering me things during our conversations. That day he gave me a metal utility clip for my belt that he'd picked up somewhere. I spent the entire conversation rolling it around my palm, sliding my fingers through it so that they resembled silver brass knuckles.

"Why do you get to give me things?" I asked him. "Why can't I give back?"

"Don't do that to me." A bus went past on Sixth Avenue with an ad for a TV show on the side. Joe read out the text: "*We get the world we deserve.* We sure do," he said. "I'm losing weight. Do you know that Stephen King book?"

"*Thinner?*"

"Thinner," he replied.

"Do you have some sort of curse?"

"A Vietnamese curse."

Just before he got on the next bus, I gave him a hug and followed the lead of Ralph, the doorkeeper, who often said tender things to the people who waited in his line.

"Love you."

Joe turned around and said, "Love you too, buddy." He pushed a new piece of luggage, a bright pink suitcase, toward the curb. I watched him wrestle it on board. He pushed toward the back of the bus, head down, dragging the case. It was nearly dark. I descended into the subway, where the Seamless ads reminded me of my hunger.

IN THE WINTER I walked with Joe as he pushed his walker through the slush to the corner of Sixth Avenue before taking refuge in the coffee shop. In the summer, we stood in the shade of that Japanese pagoda tree outside the gate, trying to remain still in the heat. My own sense of the city changed. I pushed out into its borders, went on endless subway rides, recognized its gargantuan size, which was hard to conceive of even while looking out at the Panorama at the Queens Museum. One day I got talking to a train conductor who told me the subway map was "all possibility, all the time." Everything tempted me to speak to more people: the scraps of diner conversation; the person with the interesting face still on the train at Van Cortlandt Park; the stories in the Metro section of the *Times*; every train sliding by, packed with anxiety and humor and ambition.

At moments I caught a glimpse of the city's intensity, its might. I kept feeling variations on the city's forcefulness from different angles—from the brutal wind out on Governors Island, to the way it transformed and amplified or diminished its residents. I kept feeling thankful: most days I had a new person to meet, an address to head to, a phone number to call, an introduction, a reason, an apartment to buzz. I was changing, getting older, but this power was working on me too. Mostly, I was enriched by it, even by my many misfires, all the interviews that didn't end up in the book, all the days that didn't have a tangible outcome. On the subway I felt I had a secret knowledge—I probably wasn't the only one—a secret reason to travel, knowing that this exercise was ultimately for me, all these encounters brought with them lessons on how to live. And also how to shut up. In these years of increasing volume I had so many great reasons to stay quiet and bear witness. The days featured assertion and negation. I pushed myself to reach Canarsie and Sheepshead Bay—often late for my appointment, often flustered—and when I got there I learned to listen, or tried to. And then on Sundays I'd go back to 16th Street and often recount these travels to Joe.

After a while I saw he had no real wardrobe. It was like he was gradually wearing all of New York. I rarely saw the same shirt twice. He moved through clothing—a T-shirt from an amateur basketball league, a dress shirt with the name of a financial company on the breast pocket, boat shoes, boots. His clothes flowed, first clean, then gone. He was lucid some days; on others, he drooped. His nose hovered above his meal. His coffee cup tilted. The conversation paused and I watched, from the coffee shop, the passing faces on Sixth Avenue.

After saying goodbye and wondering where he went off to, I'd descend onto the platform on 14th Street, with its pools of dank water around me, and I'd begin my journey home. I started to imagine where Joe spent his evenings.

"Come and see me," he said one Sunday, after a few moments of consideration. "You don't have to," he clarified.

"I want to."

"But I'm only there later at night. 23rd and Park."

A few nights later, I stayed out late and walked down Park to see Joe, but when I reached the alcove of the European Tanning and Waxing Center I nearly overshot the mark and missed him. Joe was there, wrapped under a duvet, the edges tucked in. I walked up the ramp and crouched down. I didn't want to shake him. I didn't want to scare him, so I just kept repeating "Joe, Joe" softly. I was aware of the people walking south on Park. I looked up at a few faces as they passed.

I reached out and placed a hand on the duvet. "Joe," I said louder. He lay on top of a flattened cardboard box with a bottle of water near his head. His pink suitcase stood nearby, but tonight it was wrapped in a black garbage bag. What was the best possible outcome here? I could shake him awake and he'd emerge, worried.

Rain started to fall on Park Avenue. I circled the block and returned. I had nothing better to do that night. But how helpful was it to be there crouched on the ramp to the European Tanning and Waxing Center, with my fingertips resting on this duvet?

WHEN WE TALKED about our lives, I was often unable to refrain from reaching out and offering optimism. I should have been more careful with it. On some Sundays, instead of asking about who I'd spoken to, Joe would ask me about the West Coast, about British Columbia, and I said to him—in a voice infected with that same West Coast naivete I despised—"You can visit." Sometimes when he talked about Pittsburgh I said to him I'd be happy to rent a car and drive us there. He was bent over, but he looked up to see if I was telling the truth.

"You believe that?" I asked him.

"That's my line," he said.

We made plans and promises. We talked about that rental car.

I came back to Park Avenue another night before Joe was asleep and sat down with him. The traffic was quiet.

"Welcome to my porch," he said.

He'd set up his bedding as well as the cardboard wall he used to block out the noise of the street.

"You know what?" he asked me. "Those people inside the tanning salon, they all call me different names. Sometimes it's Mike. Sometimes it's Dave."

He went on: "People are always, always coming up to me. I'll be sitting on my porch, getting set up, and people will always stop and say, 'How are you, Joey?' Or they'll ask me, 'Are you Joey?' Craig—I don't *know* these people. I've never seen them before. But they know me somehow."

He told me he used to swim in the East River behind the VA hospital, which he knew well. He'd go down there with his pants over his trunks. "I didn't think of them as adventures. I'd just go swimming to feel the water on my skin."

"Good feeling?"

"Good feeling."

I told Joe about phosphorescence where I grew up and what it was like to swim in the stuff, what it was like to draw your hands through water and watch the paths of shimmering algae.

"I would love to see that," he said. "Sometimes you talk about a place, and I get sad that I won't see it."

"Anytime you want," I said. "You believe that?"

He nodded.

"You've got places," I told him.

"Don't say New York," he replied.

He knew Park Avenue in a way few people did. He knew so much about New York. But instead he thought back to Pittsburgh, spoke about the water of the Allegheny and what it looked like when the mills were running.

"When I was a kid," he told me, "the water was so filthy, a greenish green, a marine green. Back then, objects floated in the water—silver from the pounded ingots. I had never heard of metal floating," he said. "This floated. You could see the silver in the undulation of the water."

"We took it for granted," he said of the Allegheny. "It was part of us."

Sometimes the past slipped into the present, and he was not amid the green of the Vietnam jungle but instead the green of the industrial Allegheny. This Pittsburgh: his old house, the house of his aunt, the parks, his work, the bricklaying and pressure-washing businesses, the quiet streets, the moments when he would drive home to his family.

When I asked him why he came to New York, his answers were always different. There were some subjects he wouldn't discuss. I asked him one day about getting a NYC ID. He shook his head. He said he didn't want anything that would tie him to this hole.

"New York," he said, "isn't a real place."

Part
Two

PART

TWO

6

Clashing in the Streets

DAREE LEWIS A philanthropic foundation officer

Some interviewees I went back to again and again. Daree Lewis was one of them, and our meetings took place all over the city. A Black woman who had grown up in Queens, she would always thoughtfully describe her New York. When I first met her, she talked about the New York subway and the mysterious water that drips from the ceiling. Later we spoke about her school days in Howard Beach, where a hate crime that transfixed New York had taken place in the 1980s. One hot July evening, a few days after the 2016 police shooting of Philando Castile in Minnesota had sparked national outrage, I walked to a bar on First Avenue in Manhattan to meet up with her. That evening, Daree looked as dejected as I'd ever seen her. She looked me over and laughed, then sighed, then we ordered drinks. "So, yes," she said, "I have a white man to work this out with. . . ." She'd come straight from work, and we drank a couple cocktails.

These conversations have to happen one on one. They *have* to happen one on one, because what you never have to think about you never have to experience, and what I always have to think about I always have to experience.

The only way that anything can actually change is if the people who don't have to experience this help carry the burden for the people who do. Right? Because there is an actual burden that comes along with being in this skin, and that is separate from having to educate other people what the burden is. And so the only way that you get to help me carry my burden is by learning about my experiences. What it feels like, what it is like, what I do about it, what other people do about it. And then, because of your skin privilege, go and tell other people about it because you have an access that I don't have, right?

You are immediately validated when you walk in the door. No one thinks you're mediocre. No one questions whether you belong in a room. Depending on the room, that question will be asked about me.

And I never get to rid myself of that. Ever. Ever. Right? And that is very, very heavy to carry.

Not even here in New York City. I can be anonymous in this city, I'm another person on the subway, I'm another person walking down the street. But even that, in its neutrality . . . It affects the things that I carry around, because I think about the things that people have said to me along my way and wonder if when people look at me, those are the things that they think. Like, "You're not that kind of Black person. You're like the Huxtables." White people have said that to me. Black people have said things like, "Oh, it's very clear you grew up middle class," or "You grew up in a house, didn't you?" There are so many assumptions about what I am and who I am when I walk through their door that are very particular to my gender and my race. And my class, even my upbringing.

So, even in the neutrality of walking down the street or riding the subway like anyone else, there is still the concern about the perception. It's going to affect any interaction. In addition to the burden I carry, then, I have to make other people feel comfortable with me. I have to make you feel comfortable with me so that we can even have an interaction that's going to be beneficial to me.

This is the burden: there is a constant noise in the background for me that other people don't have. People who don't have to think about their race because they're in the majority. And that is all kinds of questions. Does it matter who I'm with right now? Does it matter how many of us are together right now? Does it matter who I love? And the people whom I don't choose to love, like my family members, there's always a constant worry about them. There's a worry about: "Will a police officer think that my brother is intimidating?" Six foot four and 240 pounds, and that could be intimidating, right? He drives a big SUV—that is threatening to some people too. And then the children in our family and the cousins and the other brothers. I don't choose those people for my family, but if I love them, I worry. As a person of color in this country, you're not without that worry.

There are situations where people dismiss what I have to say because it's just invalid because I'm the one saying it. When you have a lot of those moments, you have to either develop a thick skin or have enough resilience to say, *This is not about me, this is them.* But it is about me because of who I am and what that makes the other person feel.

This is the noise that never goes away. This is the noise that never shuts down. I can't walk into a room and think automatically.... I can think I'm their equal, I can think I'm their intellectual superior, even. But I know that I have to prove it every single time. I have to prove that I belong in that room. Even if the person doesn't have bias, I have to prove it for all the people who come after me. That's a lot to carry.

People have asked me a lot of times, *Why aren't you more angry? Why don't you show anger?* I'm like, *I don't get to be angry.* If I get angry, I'll probably just lose it because of all the things that I have to carry around. I can't show too much aggressive emotion because I'm a woman and that makes me a bitch, but as a Black woman it makes me an angry Black woman. And if I'm threatening, then you shut down. You, the listener who has all these beliefs and has heard all these same things that people tell me about *me* all the time. I don't get to connect with you. I have to make it my business to connect with you so that you don't completely just dismiss me as one of these things that the world has told you I am.

Anger, to me, is an emotion of privilege because no one tells white men they can't be angry. Actually, it's probably encouraged. White women get to be angry some of the time. They still get called catty and bitchy and all of these things, but they're much more forgiven for it. When I express that I am fearful for my brother's life because of his stature, or that I feel vulnerable when I see a group of police officers . . .

Somehow even expressing that makes other people feel that I'm expressing anger. What I'm actually expressing is disbelief and dis-illusionment and sadness and fear and a lament for the things that are not there. A mourning for an innocence lost, a mourning for the people who lose people, who were just driving home with their kid in the back.

Anger is a privileged emotion. It is only allowed to be displayed by the people who have enough skin privilege. Only the people who get enough forgiveness. And we don't get it. We don't. Our parents teach us not to show that anger to the world because they're trying to keep us safe.

Negating or nullifying anger is really, I think, what our parents and our grandparents and our ancestors hoped for us. Don't be too angry. Don't be too angry, because then you get accepted and you get to be in that room. Don't be too angry, because we have hope for you. We're doing all this for you to be in that room, for you to go to college, for you to go change something.

PETE MEEHAN A cop

I became a cop when the murder rate was at its highest and I left on its huge decline. Things kind of reached critical mass. The police department is not going to solve the city's problems. It was a collaborative effort of people who just had enough, cops who just had enough, businesses that just had enough. How much worse could you have done? The only thing you really could have done was pulled the plug and let it sink into the Atlantic Ocean. That's where you were at. It could only have gotten better, 'cause it would've been nothing.

I'd always say, "Today's not a good day to die." I'd say it every day. *Today is not a good day to die.* When I was single, I'd hug my dog. I'd go, "Don't worry, Daddy's going to be okay. Today's not a good day to die." I'd hug her and I'd go, "Hugs are better than drugs," and I'd go to work. The commute was an adventure. You've got to remember, you're carrying a gun wherever you go. You're armed. Being a cop, you start to see a lot of things that no one else would see.

Just like a heart surgeon could probably look at somebody and tell they have a heart condition. A beautician could look at a woman and say she has a really bad hair issue or really bad skin issue or whatever it might be, even though she's got makeup on. As a cop, you start to see things that no one else will see. You see it and you feel it. Smell. Touch. And your sixth sense of being in a situation. *This doesn't feel right.*

What you see on the camera is not the reality of a lot of things. When did the camera start? When didn't it start? What angle did it get? It is very philosophical. But can you see the wind? No. You can see particles flying in the wind. You can see the wind affecting trees. But you can't see the wind. How do you know it's windy? Right? Can you see the sound of a gunshot? You can hear it. What does it sound like on a CCTV camera? You don't know. But that explosion, that auditory exclusion, that visceral physical experience you go through when these things happen. That's you living in the moment.

You smell the aftereffect of a gunshot. You smell the gunpowder. You smell the burnt chemicals. The nitrates. It's a real thing. A dead body. A gunshot. They're unforgettable smells. You see a CCTV or a video someone took on a cell phone, when the cop is confronting an individual, and that tape can't show you the smell of alcohol on that guy's breath. Or the reek of marijuana from that person's body. You know? Or you might not be able to see the spit coming from a guy's mouth as he's talking so viscerally. Arrogant or aggravating, or angrily. You just don't see that stuff. You don't see a guy's chest puffing out on these grainy, shitty videos.

Hands. Everything's hands.

I could tell a lot with someone's hands. There's no scientific reasoning behind this. There's no way to prove this, not one hundred percent, but hands are what get you in trouble. You never really hear about a cop getting kicked to death. You hear about a cop getting his gun taken away from him, choked, someone going in their pocket.

I studied people's hands, and for some reason—I don't know the scientific research behind it—but in my brain I can tell an alcoholic, a heroin addict, a pill taker. You can tell a smoker, someone who smokes crack. There's dirty hands and there's *dirty hands*. A guy that smokes crack, he can't get those burn marks off of his fingers. There's a bloating that happens when you're so heavily into heroin. I don't know how to explain it, and I don't know the medical terms behind it, but I'm sure there's some truth to it. Someone who is a really big drinker and they're doing some type of narcotics, they can get a discoloration in their hands. Their hands are bloated, the nails are very unhealthy.

Nobody puts makeup on their hands, so your hands are like a window to your inner health. The way people's hands shake when they're nervous. It's the actions, and the physical health. The physical presence of the hand was an insight into that person's soul. Fidgeting hands, hardworking hands, delicate hands. It's amazing the shit you see. Articulating actions. They wouldn't get their hands out of their pocket, they kept going for their pocket.

If someone's doing something bad, they're doing it with their hands. The hands tell it.

FORGET ABOUT THE JOB stress—just the stress of living in New York really takes a toll on you. New Yorkers live a little bit longer, I just think we're preserved a little bit longer. We might have more years on earth, but that's not living. To live longer—yeah, you might be alive longer in New York. The mortality age in New York might be higher, but that doesn't mean you live. Living and being alive are two separate things. To live . . . I like to live, and that was the whole thing. Even in New York, I embraced the suck. I embraced the suck. If it sucked, I embraced it. If it was good, I embraced it. And so I live. And I have pretty much a terminal debilitating aggressive horrendous illness, and I live. You can't do it any other way.

Being a New York City cop taught me how to be safe. It taught me how to be cautious. It taught me that even shit can be repurposed and used as fertilizer to grow beautiful things. Not everything is garbage. Not everything is shit. The way I would view things, I would look in a neighborhood and be like, "Oh, look at this shit"—if I wasn't a cop. But I would look at a neighborhood and be like, "Oh my God, this is a beautiful neighborhood. I see the potential. I see the beautiful people here. I see the wonderful people here."

You know, I wasn't a cop that lived in my police car. I was a cop that got out and spoke to people and talked to everybody.

There's a distinction between when you're talking about a *cop* and when you're talking about a *police officer*. If you have to ask, you're a police officer. That's the way it is. It's the same thing in a police department, in business, in the military, in anything. You have managers and you have leaders. Sometimes they don't mix too well. Sometimes a good manager doesn't do well as a leader and sometimes a good leader doesn't do well as a manager. There's a delicate balance.

You have the hairbag mentality in the police department. You always will. I call it the "fuck that" mentality. You can go into precinct roll call and be like, "Guys, listen, no strings attached, I'm gonna give you a 15 percent pay raise this year and next year. I'm gonna give you a $1,000 holiday bonus on top of what you got. I'm gonna shorten your tours by ten minutes, and I'm gonna give you two more vacation days." And you'd get a resounding "Fuck that!" Always. From the few guys who got that fuck-that mentality. It's embedded in that hairbag police officer mentality. That's a police officer. That's not a cop.

A hairbag is a widely used term. You could say it's a guy that's very disheveled—shitty uniform—but then there's also the guy that has a very disheveled attitude. Just a hairbag. They don't give a fuck. They don't care. They don't give a shit about the greater good. They don't give a shit about anybody else. A guy you don't wanna work with, people you don't want in your squad. You don't want them working with you. Everybody's got them in every walk of life.

The one thing I would say to the cops at the time. They were going through a transition. I said, you guys don't believe in change. I said, think about it, we have new police cars, right? They're pretty decent. I go, they're better cars, it's a change. We got new uniforms. We got rid of these baby-powder-blue uniforms. That's a change. I go, guys, we got rid of our 38s and you can get a 9 mm if you'd like to. You get guys, "Fuck that!" Alright, you don't want a 9 mm? That's fine. You can still carry a 9 mm and your 38, but you just want one gun and you want to carry a 38, I get that. There's an affinity. You came out of the academy with it and maybe in fifteen years on the job that gun's gone through some gun battles, I understand that. I want the best fighting chance I can. I carry two guns in my work. Always. I always carry two guns. I carry my 38 and I carry my 9 mm. Tactically, it's just a wiser decision.

The police department is full of those guys. It's everywhere in the world. Now, I would tell these guys, we do have change. We used to have Mace, old CN-CS gas, and then we went to pepper spray. I said, "There is change, guys." You know, you can look at things different ways. Yeah, the city's always gonna suck. That's a given. It's always gonna suck, meaning the administration and the city itself. It's always gonna suck. But there's only one thing that can change in this whole equation and that's your attitude.

The majority of cops become cops because they want to help people. And if your intention is to not help people, you either already are or you turn into the "fuck that" guy. Because you always want to help and if you're not there to help, you're in the wrong job.

NEW YORK IS A FAST-PACED city, and everything is happening at that fast pace. I don't know about so much aggression. A lot of anger, but that's all over the world, just anger. In New York, it's condensed because there's so many people. It's magnified in New York because everything is so close and so tight.

What makes New York different is the concentration of people from so many different backgrounds. I don't think it's really a challenge. I think it's a benefit. It's a deal that, to deal with so many different aspects, different languages, different customs. I remember going into a Japanese lady's house and taking my shoes off before taking her to court for a stolen vehicle. Why wouldn't you?

If someone I worked with had a problem with that, that means they're police officers, they're not a cop. A cop would take his shoes off. It's not like it's an emergency. I remember one time, my partner was like, "I ain't taking my fucking shoes off." I said, "Well, you should mend the holes in your socks and sit in the car you fucking baby." And he took his shoes off because he was the "fuck that" guy. It is what it is.

I remember going into an Orthodox Jewish household. I could not greet the wife and my female partner could not have any contact with the man. And the kosher kitchen and the Sabbath and things of that nature and dealing with it, so many different cultures and so many different cultural aspects—it's awesome. It wasn't a challenge, it was a benefit.

If you work with it, there's nothing that can't be accomplished. And because we deal with everything, I think we can accomplish it. New York City is so huge, other than downhill skiing and maybe desert kite sailing, I don't think there really is an activity that we don't have in the city.

The weather's rough. The summers are brutal, the winters are brutal, the fall can be brutal, and the spring is usually nice but can be brutal. The commutes are horrible and there's always something going on, whether it's a protest or a riot or whatever. There's always something. Forget about the job stress; just the stress of living in New York really takes a toll on you. You're running from call to call. You're chasing people. You're running over fields. Wherever people may work. If it's in the sand, you're taking 'em in the sand, and if it's in the hills, you're taking 'em in the hills. You're taking it over people's front yards. You're going up on curbs. You're weaving in and out, hitting shit roads. You're banging into everything. You're hitting telephone poles. You're hitting light poles. You're hitting mailboxes. Whatever. You're pushing people out of the way to get to guys screaming for help. It's life and death.

In no way, at no time ever, can you allow people to become unlawful, ever. Ever. That's a disservice to the people that you're serving. You can never allow people to become unlawful. Whether it's the West

Indian parade, the St. Patrick's Day parade, the Puerto Rican Day parade, the Sikh parade—if you allow people at that parade to become unlawful, then you're doing a disservice to the citizens of the city and you just can't allow that to happen.

SONIA RODRIGUEZ A protester

The NYPD have free rein. They can violate your ass and you can't do anything about it. Imagine the feeling, if you ever had it, of when you were a kid and someone who is not your mom or your dad, some adult, yells at you and tells you what to do. The kind of disorientation that you feel, but then the immediate recognition that you have no power, right? This is an adult who, at a basic level, can overpower you physically and you know it. Ideally, you don't have dealings with the police where they're barking an order at you and being aggressive. If you haven't, all I can say is congratulations. I'm happy for you that you haven't had to deal with that.

My eyes go to the gun, right? It's like, I know that this person has the capacity to shoot me, kill me. They can come to my body and grab me, and handcuff me, abuse me, beat me down, throw me in a car. I'll be in jail and who knows what can happen from there. These people have the immediate capacity to inflict this kind of harm on my body, on my life, on my future. Immediately I'm frozen in that moment and, oh God, filled with dread. Just hope that I can do what I can to keep them from taking my life, ruining my life, from abusing me.

Your body heats up. It feels like you're in a nightmare. That moment that you realize you're in a nightmare and you try to wake yourself up—it is exactly that feeling. Like, please, don't let this be real. You can feel the world spinning, because you don't actually have the capacity to resist in that moment. While technically, legally, you have rights and I know I have rights and this is something I'm going to need to work on going forward, because I have been through ACLU trainings, I do know that I have rights; except, I also know very acutely that the police regularly violate people's rights and there's no justice. That they actually do what they want to do. That the rights that we feel like we have are on paper, but there's very rarely any justice for when the police violate those rights.

Oh my God, if the police do hurt me, kill me, I think about how heartbroken my mother will be when she reads the news article that intentionally misgenders me, right? That will probably write my dead name, that will refer to me as he and him, that will say that I either dressed or lived as a woman, right? That language is intentionally made to negate who I know I am and to signal to other people that it's perfectly fine to do that too.

I'm stunned that the logic of broken windows and stop-and-frisk, that logic can be so widely accepted as true, and valid, and a model to take up, that believes that something like a broken window, or a small, petty crime—that these things give way to social ills that need to be heavily policed. That you can have a kind of crude, misguided material conception about where social problems come from, but yet refuse to engage with the fact that it is poverty itself that yields these problems and a refusal to alleviate that poverty. Well, then, I know that you're not really serious about solving the problem. That policing, and the kind of policing that we're seeing, is substitution for it.

"Since I refuse to actually do something about the poverty that is endemic to my system, I will impose a heavy and brutal police presence." You're substituting one for the other. That's why the NYPD is what it is. If everyone had what they needed, right? If there were no homeless people in New York City, if everyone had a home, if everyone had enough to eat, if everyone had access to education and basic dignity, the police department would be a tenth of its size and budget. That's what the police is there for. The police is there because they know that you don't have what you need and they don't have any intention to do something about it for you.

So the police is what you get.

I THINK NEW YORKERS ARE very accustomed to a progressive or liberal rhetoric and facade, except the material reality is very much in line with a neoliberal agenda. Very much in line with conservatism. That's why we have potholes overrunning our streets. This is Bushwick. They're all over.

That's not just like a, "Oh, isn't that so terrible." Well, yeah it is. And behind that is a very concretely well-thought-out conservative government planning of austerity that says that it is not worth it. If we have a finite budget, we're going to spend it on tax breaks for developers, not on fixing the roads. That's a classic, conservative approach to social problems. And then it goes out from there.

Our schools. There's a school across the street that's severely underfunded. It might be shut down. And the list goes on and on. And that's saying nothing about gentrification. So I think that New Yorkers are used to extremely right-wing policies that affect their lives in the material world, while having a sort of feeling, a mood, a facade, of being a liberal haven.

Both of those things can be true. With all that contradiction, as I say.

SO I BECAME POLITICIZED. First at the place where I work now, a trans and gender nonconforming people of color organization. And then Occupy Wall Street Right? Zuccotti Park. That changed my life.

Occupy really changed my mind around a lot of this stuff. I'd never heard the term "income inequality" before. Right? I sort of thought about poor and rich as these natural categories. I didn't think about the system itself.

But then once I started to conceive of it, not even be able to see it, but even conceive of it as a factor that leads to the intense poverty that I endured my whole life, suddenly all that stuff that I internalized, suddenly I had laser focus on an entity that was actually causing it for me and for billions of other people on this planet. So I'm like, *Okay, that seems like a worthwhile project*, and I'm still in the process of making that project come to be.

So, no shame, I'm going to say what it is: I have one of those Republican-nightmare fixations of a welfare mother. That was my mom. We lived in bad neighborhoods and shitty apartments and I went to a severely underfunded school. On and on and on.

I internalized that. I just thought that some people are rich, some people are poor, and if I work hard enough, maybe I can be rich. I fully understood that it was shitty and I was not happy to be in it, and as soon as I became an adult I made some pretty drastic steps to try to get out of poverty. But even that individualized model of trying to get out of the hood, and trying to shake off a legacy of poverty and abuse and all of that, even if I was able to successfully shake that off, and I'm not sure that I totally have, that's not a sustainable model. That's the rugged individualism that now I have a conception of, and I blatantly, severely rejected.

For a lot of queer and trans kids that are from New Jersey, there is a sort of fantasy about New York City. I had wanted to be here for a long time, I even tried to maneuver a way to move in with relatives that live here so that I could go to Harvey Milk High School, which is a high school for queer and trans kids. It didn't work out. I was in the youth enrichment services program at the center on 13th Street, and very quickly found community there, and really clung to it and tried to find a way to be here instead of there. I cut a lot of class to come to the city, and as soon as I graduated, I couch-surfed, stayed with friends, did everything that I could to be here. And then once being here, living here, I became really disenchanted, like a lot of other people, because New York City doesn't care about you. The feeling is not mutual. It's not magically tolerant and affirming, that was hard to accept. And then of course it's so expensive that when I actually got the chance to travel and saw how much cheaper it was to go to other places, I was like, *Okay, I think I'm okay with not being in New York City.*

WHEN I'M GOING OVER the bridge and I see the skyline, my class antagonism really rages and I have fantasies about expropriating all of that wealth, to be honest.

Oh God. I think about walking in with a box full of checks of $40,000 to hand to people who are multimillionaires. They're looking at the $40,000 check like, *What is this for?* And I say, *Oh, that's your salary. That's what you'll be living on. We're taking all your other shit. Thank you.* I don't know how that could possibly happen but I dream about it, to be honest.

I think about how there's a very good chance that it'll all be under water, right? The apocalyptic movies that we've seen where the city is abandoned and drowning. I think, *Oh God, if we don't get smart, this is what's going to happen.* That crosses my mind. Sometimes I think about the old IWW, Upton Sinclair, Big Bill Haywood. People who used to take the ideas of infiltration very seriously, and would find children of the oligarchs, and seduce them, get them to be class traitors.

The Communist Party in the sixties who would throw parties to fabulous people in the city who would never organize with a party, who didn't want to be political activists but, hey, you throw a party in a penthouse, and you have champagne pouring, and everyone knows it's all going to the Communist Party. It's a fabulous thing, right? You're sitting around in your cocktail dresses and you get to think, hey, solidarity. Yeah, what does it look like to start to build that again?

Building resources for our organizations and hopefully our future parties, but also to make those alliances and to have the capacity and a winning strategy to actually be able to change popular consciousness to make people think critically again about the role of the state in our lives.

IN MY DAYS I've met a lot of rich people through sex work. Wall Street guys love to get their ass beat. That's a thing. That trope is real.

Yeah. The ideas around excess, that these people have so much wealth. That I've been to penthouse apartments on Fifth Avenue or

Park Avenue and seen how the other side lives. Then to know that I'm only there to service their primal needs, right, for a fee. That before becoming politicized I, of course, just had an uneasy feeling about it but couldn't name it. Now, I think, I'm so resentful that in order to be able to pay my rent and eat enough food, I had to engage in work that I didn't feel good about. I know that there's a lot of discourse around sex work positivity and I support that. If there are any sex workers who are listening, or reading, or whatever, I'm like, yeah. One hundred percent. Self-determination, if that makes you feel good. If it doesn't make you feel like shit, I hope you do it. I always felt like shit doing it.

Now that I'm looking back, part of what makes me feel like shit is the fact that if I had enough to live, and survive, and thrive by right of being alive, being a human being, right—which foundationally is an idea of socialism; its failures in its attempts throughout history don't obfuscate that foundation for me—it means that because I was born, I have a right to my basic needs. That is not something that was available to me. That I had to engage with people who very directly were the reason that I didn't have what I needed? It makes me very bitter.

Those apartments? Sprawling. Ornate. Some of them upscale minimal, industrial. Beautiful. In New York, even middle-class people live in 500-square-feet apartments that are still $1 million. The pipe is leaking in the bathroom, right? It hasn't been remodeled since the seventies. But it's like another world. The juxtaposition of what's on the street versus what's in their apartment is really stark. It is a metaphor for the kind of refusal to invest, right? The hoarding of money. Trillions of dollars are tied up in banks who refuse to invest.

All the money goes to executives and paying out dividends to people who are shareholders. The failure of trickle down . . . Not the failure, the lie, right? The intentional lie of trickle down is really personified. You can see it when you go into these places. This is what happens when you enact those policies—not just enact those policies but when you make them a point of ruling ideology. People think that if the other half, if they're doing well, they will create jobs—and do all of these things and then everyone will get what they need. When you walk into one of these apartments it's very obvious that that's a big fucking lie. It's a joke and the joke is on us. They're laughing.

The road from Park Ave to the South Bronx? Yeah, well, that's where rebellion comes from. That's why we see lulls, right? Nothing, everything's fine, and then it explodes.

Me and other people who are on the organized left. Come on. How many panel discussions do we go to? How many rallies and organizing meetings? We see the same people over and over again. We all know each other. A lot of us don't like each other, but we all know each other. Then, when you see these explosions, you see people you've never seen before and you see people that are screaming revolution, right? People who are talking about social justice, and income inequality, and redistribution; by another name sometimes, but that's what it is.

NEW YORK IS BECOMING a playground for the rich. Or maybe it's not even the question of being able to afford, but also the degradation of people's standards of living are falling so much that even if I might be able to eke out a living, if the quality is so bad, why? Why would I? The refusal to see that as a social ill, a reflection of a failing society, of a crumbling empire.

No pun: empire state, you know. The refusal to engage in that shows me that there is a tacit agenda at play.

Oftentimes there's this thing that happens in this neighborhood, right, because Williamsburg is right here. And moving over into Bushwick. People here that have a righteous fear about what's going to come. Sometimes I notice that there's a kind of thinking of gentrification of this wall, right, that has no consciousness and it's just coming, rather than key decision makers in the city who are signing contracts, right? Sending them to their lawyers, having their assistants read them over, actually signing off, shaking hands, sitting in meetings with people who are going to get tax breaks to do the development that will actually create the gentrification that we talk about in the abstract.

It's actually not abstract. There are people with faces, and names, and mothers, right, who are actually creating the policies that give way to it. It's not a natural phenomenon.

BOB SAUTER A former bus driver

Listen, don't get me wrong, people call the country racist now. From where I sit, it was more racist when I was growing up. This isn't to denigrate the Greatest Generation, but it was very segregated. We were brought up that way. I'm not going to say that I wasn't brought up being afraid of Black people coming into the neighborhood.

They say change is hard. And it is hard, especially for older people. Even now, okay, we're becoming a diversified country. But it was always a problem with the country becoming diversified and who didn't want to live near the Italians, and who didn't want to live . . . You know?

I saw it in my own family. They were wary of the neighborhood changing. *We've got to get out of here . . .*

There's Brooklyn and then the rest of the universe. That's how unique I think Brooklyn is. The family home I'm going to show you, they sold it when I'm eighteen. I still consider that house my home.

I'm very religious, so rightfully or wrongfully, I believe what I believe, you know? I can say, for the most part, I'm kind of firm. I hate to sound that rigid, but I am. I am. It's not that I'm the most brilliant guy in the world, but my debate strategy is to make people defend stupid things they say.

It's ideological now. It's two different views of what America should be. And they're never going to reconcile. I'm not going to say it never used to be that way, because you look at the Civil War. But I think it's as contentious now as it was in the lead-up to the Civil War. I don't believe you'll see a Civil War like we had then.

I'm a militia member. I'm an Oath Keeper, and I'm in APIII, I'm an NRA member. I hope I don't offend you. I'm only an associate member.

The Oath Keepers are . . . To be a full-fledged member you either have to be active or retired military or law enforcement.

Actually, if you remember in Ferguson when they were burning the city down. They had on the news, there was guys walking around in camouflage with guns, they were Oath Keepers. If they're asked in, they'll protect your property. So, there. I'll protect their property.

I would like the red states to secede from the blue states, but when the left talks about civil war, I have no problem with that. If they start shootin' . . . I don't think it will come to that, I don't think it will get that far where it's all-out. What I think is, I think once my side punches them in the nose and says *enough*, then things will get back to the talking stage. But right now they have no reason to talk, they get everything.

You seek out people with your point of view. That's what you do, and you know why? I think it's because it's come down to two ideologies. But in the old days you could talk. When I was a kid they had the Democratic club up the block from where I lived and there was a Republican club a few blocks away, but they were all in church together on Sunday. That's no more. There's a lot of people out in Staten Island like me. In Brooklyn they used to be like me.

I WOULD HAVE EMPATHY for anyone who is genuinely afraid, but that's a narrative that comes from the left. It's identity politics. I'm a friggin' old white guy, I'm the devil incarnate. Am I wrong? People tell me, "Die soon. I hope you die." Who'd I ever bother? I worked, I raised my family. Why am I the devil all of a sudden?

So why am I evil? I've never jumped a Black guy, but I've been jumped five times if not more. I never pulled a gun on a Black guy, I had one pull a gun on me. I had a Black shoot a friend that was standing pretty close to me.

I have a few gun people that are like, "Oh, too bad you live in New York, move by me." Listen, this is the greatest freaking city in the world. Like I said, to some people it's still Disneyland. If they disparage it by saying it's a cesspool, yeah. If they say, "You live with all them freaking liberals," I say, "Hey, listen, I grew up here, okay?" They're not all bad. But, listen ... how can I explain it? Liberals ... with anybody, you deal one on one, you see how they really are.

I'm very snobby, I honestly believe that there's Brooklyn, and the rest of the universe comes in second, is tied for second. Listen, wherever you grow up, you had the best childhood. Okay? But it's kind of like if you haven't tasted honey, you don't know how good it is. Your childhood was good, but if you knew what we had in Brooklyn, you'd be like, "Damn." Okay? That's the way I feel about it, alright?

My father worked in a brewery, he used to put melted candles into the bottle caps to give them weight to play skully. I always had brand-new bottle caps from Piels Brothers' brewery. Like I say to my kids, "For you, you had the greatest childhood because you didn't taste the honey." And so did you. You didn't taste the honey.

So, listen, I hope when you're done we still remain friends.

LAURA HENDERSON An activist and political organizer

I always wanted to be in New York. So, when I finally got to New York after I graduated, I was like, *Thank God, I'm here. This is where I'm supposed to be.*

My uncle. I love him so much but he has such strange politics. He lives in Indiana and he was talking and he's like, "Oh, how's it going in New York?" I said, "Oh, fine, New York's the greatest city in the world!" And he's like, "But what about ISIS?"

"What?"

"How's security taking the train?"

"What?"

And he's like, "ISIS?"

"I know you're saying that but ... I can't really put any meaning to the words that are coming out of your mouth, so please help. What are you getting at?" For some reason he was concerned about ISIS. I'm not gonna sit here and be like, "ISIS is just an organization." No, I'm not gonna sit here and defend ISIS, of course.

But ISIS is not my top priority. My top priority is like, *Will the G train come in the next thirty minutes?* Edge of my seat! ISIS, no.

He was just like, "You just need to be careful. You're driving through the Holland Tunnel."

Look, I freak out when I drive through the Holland Tunnel but less because of terrorism and more because I think infrastructure is pretty bad around here. That tunnel's gotta be real old. Sometimes, when I'm driving, water will drip on my car and I'm like, "What is that? And where is it coming from? And why haven't they fixed it?" That makes me so nervous, I hate the Holland Tunnel. Oh my God. I think sometimes people think I'm crazy 'cause I . . . I'm always like, "People are so worried about terrorism!"

OCCUPY HAPPENED the second year I was here. I heard about it before. I was friends of some of the folks. There was the Adbusters call, and there was the first flyer that went out for it. There was a group of people before Occupy who were doing this weird sleeping on the street shit. Bloombergville, did you hear about that?

They were really trying to make Bloombergville happen. And it just didn't. And through the summer right before Occupy, people were doing these general assembly things that, again, weren't really sticking. It just seemed like a lot of weird people doing weird stuff. Maybe it was the Adbusters call, people kind of hearing more about it. All of the sudden there was the whole thing of go down to Zuccotti Park.

But even the first couple of days it still wasn't very big, I don't think. The first day my friends were like, *we're going to Zuccotti Park, are you going?* No, I have other things to do. I'm obviously not going to that. Y'all call me when you're done. I'll be at home. I'll be at work.

I didn't actually go until, I remember, it was the Troy Davis execution. That's what it was. It was at night, I was talking to my brother, we were just watching the news, being like, is it gonna happen? And they were like, yeah, Troy Davis is about to be executed. I remember being so upset. My brother cried. I was talking to my mom, everyone. It was just a bad, bad moment. I remember being upset, working for a union, having done student activism, they did everything right. They had the marches, they had the rallies, people were calling their legislators, people were writing to whoever they had to write to. No one did anything completely outrageous. They did everything by the book, they did it right. And it didn't matter. They're like, *We're gonna kill this guy.* They had made up their mind to kill this guy, because this is how it works.

I remember feeling so hurt and defeated. Like this is it. This is what our lives are gonna be like. I went to work the next day and I felt like shit. I was working in New Jersey at the time, I'm always working in New Jersey. And my friend called me. "There's this Troy Davis march happening. We're gonna start in Union Square to march, can you get here?"

"I'm at work, I'm gonna be late." And she was like, "Just call me, I'll keep you posted where we're going." So I'm driving back from Jersey, racing to get to Union Square. And they were texting me, "We're going to Zuccotti Park."

"What the hell is in Zuccotti Park?"

Oh, right, for the Occupy thing. So I drove over there, parked my car, met up with some of my friends, 'cause the march kind of ended there. And I was just looking around, it looked kind of weird. It was just random people around who looked kinda gross. I think there was a general assembly and I think they were talking about sleeping bags or something. And I just sat down on the ground. I'm in business casual wearing a fancy pencil skirt and some heels, and I just sit on the ground. On the dirt. 'Cause I'm just so dejected. Just looking around, feeling sad. Feeling torn apart and upset about all this.

I'm looking at this really weird-ass scene, and maybe we do just need to do something kind of weird. It didn't make sense to me then, but I'm like, if we did all this other stuff, maybe we should try something different. Maybe we should shake shit up a little bit. I don't know if this is it, but we should probably give it a shot. So I remember going back the next day, calling a friend who worked there, and I was like, *Come with me to this Occupy thing. Let's figure this out.* So we went back one day in early October.

A bunch of people came that day. And it was huge. I think I remember Radiohead was supposed to be there, but Radiohead did not show up. But all these people were there and this spontaneous march, whatever, happened. And I think it just hooked people, and people just kept coming back. Because people were in the streets. It was like a weird hippie utopia, but it felt really white too.

So my friend just out of nowhere convened as many people of color as she could find, which was like ten of us. And we were on a street corner like, alright, let's talk about race and class. Let's figure out what we should write. So that was our first people of color working-group meeting. And then we announced it, put it out on the internet, sent emails to our friends, whatever. And just literally yelled about it in the park, 'cause that's what you did. And people showed up. The next day it was twenty people, then thirty people. Then at one point it covered an entire block. People just being like, *let's talk about this.*

I was probably going there every day.

After work I would be there. I would be there on the weekends. If I wasn't working I would be there all day. I'd be there late into the night. The belly of the beast, oh hell yeah. Wall Street was not that far. That's why Occupy Wall Street was so funny. All of that inequality and anti-capitalism conversations popping up and—oh shit, it's right over there. I'd see them walking by and think, *Your suits are ill-fitting. Your fashion is horrible. You have money, fix it.* That was my first thought. I used to wear fancier clothes. I think I was caught in a live-stream Occupy Wall Street and then screamed at a cop to not touch me 'cause I was wearing designer clothes. *Don't touch me, this is Dior!* Then I was like, "Oh, no, people just heard me, I'm losing my leftist credibility."

What was interesting was seeing the younger Wall Street folks running around. They looked so weird, walking really fast, kind of running to the train. I was like, "Your lives must really suck. They must be really, really bad."

Empathy is not the word, but there was some type of this . . . I don't know. I had a friend who I was a lot closer with. He worked in that finance world, grew up in Jersey. He would sleep in his office a lot and I remember him talking about how he got a couple of hours over the holidays that he could leave and drive home, spend two or three hours with his family, and make it back to his office and finish up work. I was just like, "Mm."

And I remember going to his apartment and seeing all this really fancy new shit that he bought online. But it was also boxed up and all still wrapped up. "Wow, you make a fuck ton of money for playing with fake money on computers"—whatever they do. "But your life is bleak."

I SPENT A LOT of time in that park, but I spent a lot of time in those bars. I spent so much time in those bars.

The Raccoon Lodge smelled bad, it was small. It had all these weird union pins and stickers all over. Because I think it was a bunch of union New York dudes.

Part of me was like, Occupy was great. But also, it's like, I was twenty-three. And I was acting like I was twenty-three. There was gonna be a working-group meeting. This working group makes me so angry, so let's go up to the Raccoon Lodge, get a shot and a beer really quick. Then we're going to the meeting.

That was part of Occupy for me. We would have a crew, like this is our squad. We're going in, grabbing a shot and a beer, then we're going into this meeting, we're gonna yell at these old people about politics. That's what's gonna happen. So I spent a lot of time at that bar. Raccoon Lodge, White Horse Tavern, which we still go to sometimes for nostalgia. The Patriot. Because there's the like really ritzy Wall Street. Then there's these old-school Irish tavern bars down there.

Which was also weird 'cause it's like these old-school New York Irish bars, and you're bringing in a bunch of kids from Occupy. So it's like me, I'm Black, then all my queer friends, rolling into the old-school downtown Irish bar. The bartenders are like, *Who the fuck are you?* And we would become regulars at some of these places, whether they liked it or not.

Sometimes they would be like, "So, what are you guys doing here?" "We're just having a meeting, Occupy Wall Street." People would bring up any issue they had. People would talk about gentrification, Wall Street banks, or all this other stuff. Anything that they had an issue with, they felt that somehow what we were doing there related.

A lot of old-school movements or organizations were like, it doesn't have any demands. What are your demands? I think it's really fitting for a lot of us young folks to be part of this, 'cause we're that generation of: we essentially demand nothing because we want it all. We want it all. We want everything. I'm not gonna give you a list of ten things, 'cause I want it all.

Give us what you owe us.

People had this idea that Occupy should make demands or turn into a political party or turn into an organization. No, no. I'm glad it died when it did. Because any longer it would have gotten real weird. It already started to get weird. It was just like a surge, kind of like a movement injection. And I think there is something to be said about how that works. Where you have organizations that are kind of plugging along and doing the work long term.

Then you have these movement surge injections that in a really short period of time break open space for these organizations to take up a little bit more. And that's what it did.

I LOVE THE Black Lives Matter movement. I love that it is so focused. It will not stray. It's like, nope, this one is for Black people. It feels great and amazing and wonderful, the whole phrase or term of unapologetically Black, that is so awesome. So excited for that to be a thing. I love it. I really do. You get tired of hearing things that are like this is for people of color or POC. They don't mean Black. They don't. That's why they said POC. That's why they said people of color, because they don't want it to mean Black. That's why. This is it. We will not waiver. This is for Black Lives Matter. That's what it's for. It's wonderful. It makes me so giddy.

I think movements just come in waves sometimes. There are peaks and valleys, and we're at a Black-ass peak right now. That's what it is.

Sometimes I think Black Lives Matter has done better than Occupy Wall Street. One, it's not afraid of leadership, because Black people aren't. We love it. We want it. It needs to happen. There's this network of families that have been affected by police violence, and a lot of them know each other now, when they didn't know each other before. They go to events together. We had this really, really big march as Black Lives Matter was really starting to rise up in New York.

You could hear it everywhere. I was on tactical team, so I was running around in the front with the banner. And I was talking to my friend. We had these little, weird secret-service walkie-talkie things. It was so silly. And I was trying to figure out where the back of the march was, and they were telling me it was like ten blocks away or something insane. It was just like y'all are in another neighborhood. It was huge.

The funny thing is, most of these marches are big for marches, but as far as the numbers of people involved, and the number of people in New York City, it's a small fraction. But it gives you a sense of how powerful all these people are. If we really want something to be done, we can get that done.

I was just doing things strategically to make sure this goes as planned. So I had to get ahead of the march. So I'm in the march, jump on the train, go a couple stops to get ahead of it just to scope out and be like, where are the police? 'Cause we're about to turn this corner. I'm just standing there, waiting for them. And I'm on some weird secret-service walkie-talkie looking thing. And they're like, *Alright, we're cool, we're all set, this is gonna be great.*

And you can just hear it as they start to turn the corner. That sound is just like this crescendo. It's beautiful. You hear it first coming through the blocks. You know they're out there. Then they turn the corner, and it's just like, oh my God. That sound. I live for that sound.

The recent BLM marches felt really, really different. Even the way people have been talking about policing and the energy around defunding the police. That is not something that has ever been main-streamed, right? Movements break open this space that creates the ability to do more.

I was pretty nervous at first, mostly because of coronavirus. It was also nice to see my old crew. A lot of us who were very active during Occupy were right back out in the streets together again. Maybe it's nostalgic but it was really cool to be there. And to be there as just activists in the march, you know, not planning or leading things, and seeing so many people we didn't know.

There were thousands of people at Barclays, thousands of people closer into Crown Heights, thousands of people would be downtown. All the neighborhoods are right next to each other. So all these differ-ent marches would join. There'd be feeder marches, and all of a sud-den more and more marches would combine. We're hearing people are taking the Brooklyn Bridge, but we're on the Manhattan Bridge. Then apparently there might be people on the Williamsburg Bridge. It was nuts. There were so many people, so many people.

The police presence felt different too. One night I was coming back from a march. We had taken the Manhattan Bridge. Oh God, we're in Manhattan now, I gotta get back to Brooklyn. So we're walking down Atlantic. I was about to go pick up my car. We're passing Barclays. I look over. It was late, like eleven o'clock at night, and there were still maybe a couple hundred protesters out. In front of Barclays, that area before you get into the train is just covered in cops in formation in their riot gear. It looked like an occupying army.

Taking the bridges, it's the disruptive element, right? Everyone going over the bridge and now you have to wait. I know some people are like, "That's terrible!" No, that's the point: it's not business as usual. It's not like everything is fine, you can go about your day. The world isn't okay. Things are not okay. This is New York protesting. You gotta take a bridge. *Take a bridge.* If you can't take a bridge, then why are we even out here?

JIM EIGO A gay-rights activist

By 1986 my neighborhood and my kind were being decimated by AIDS. So I, and a lot of people like me, were just searching for ways to help . . . What do we do? The first things we did were the GMHCs of the world. Take care of real day-to-day needs. We never even used the term "living with HIV." You had AIDS. So we called them PWAs, because they were People With AIDS.

Every person who got AIDs could go to GMHC and have a one-on-one financial adviser, and you can imagine if you're in your mid-twenties and have a salary one week, and the next week you're in the hospital, and you're told, "You're never having a job again, kid. And not only that, you don't have insurance anymore." Health care in America was even worse then. Now you can get Medicaid, but it's a byzantine nightmare to go through to get it. So you need what we now would call a navigator.

A whole bunch of us realized this was not just a health-care crisis—it was a political crisis. And certain populations were being left to die because they're marginalized. Until we made a political stink of it and—by any means we could—gained a voice for ourselves, we would go nowhere.

We had the neighborhood, we had the art networks, we had the literary networks, we had the network of venues. Downtown New York was really networked pre-internet, a real physical interaction. We had our gay networks and we were starting to have our HIV networks with things like GMHC. When ACT UP came along, it was incendiary. It could combust immediately; almost from the beginning we had two hundred bodies a week, and after the first year we had five hundred bodies a week in that small room.

It was really almost a natural, given the theater space of downtown New York. Is there a greater theater space than the canyons of Manhattan? Just think of those acoustics. Just think of those backdrops. Just think of the havoc you wreak when you just block two streets. Imagine how it is when you can block six! Imagine how far the traffic is backed up into New Jersey when you can fan across Wall Street and Rector Street.... It all came together so quickly because of New York. Because of the networks we had, because of the setting, because of the theater that nowhere else in the world would have given us.

IN DECEMBER 1987, it was illegal to have a demonstration on the City Hall steps, but my city councilwoman for this district, a woman named Miriam Friedlander, smuggled about a hundred of us onto the steps at sundown. I still remember how stunningly beautiful it was. You have the Woolworth Building on one side and on the other the Brooklyn Bridge and the Metropolitan Building, which is one of the most gorgeous but strange architectural monstrosities in New York, because it's this strange double-building, half of which doesn't at all relate to the other. But that's what makes it so charming. And City Hall Park, in the middle of that, and City Hall on other side. And all the voices! Hundreds of people chanting the same things amid the acoustics of downtown Manhattan.

A month and a half later, the president's AIDS commission came to New York. We went up to the MetLife building, because that's where they were meeting. It would have been the same winter, early '88 rather than late '87. At sundown, we marched outside, because ACT UP had a full demonstration. At dusk, there's this reduced visibility, so it makes the audio portions so much more. So just that ringing of the canyons of Manhattan, when you had voices. And some chants just beg for double voices, call and response. It's just magical, acoustically. You can't do that everywhere, physically, in the states.

ACT UP: we were so tied to New York spaces, our opening demonstration was Wall Street, our first birthday was Wall Street, our second birthday was City Hall, and later we took over Grand Central Station. Our very first Gay Pride Day, June 1987, ACT UP won a prize. Because what did it do? It took a quarantine prison and we marched it down Fifth Avenue. All the newspaper and TV coverage we got because we had people in jail cells being wheeled down Fifth Avenue. We won a prize from Heritage of Pride as the best float. But for me, even more importantly, because I'm a downtown New Yorker, in 1988 we won an honorary Bessie for it.

You needed New York. You needed theater people, or at least people who thought theatrically. Wall Street. Where's a better site for carrying bodies away?

7

Song of the Rockaways

Dan Bauso pulls over the Nissan Quest.

DAN BAUSO: Somebody used to say Rockaway is a poor man's Hamptons. It's more like the rich man's Coney Island. The neighborhoods on the peninsula are Far Rockaway, Rockaway Beach, Rockaway Park. Now, Rockaway Park, it starts to get nice. Rockaway Park, Bell Harbor, very nice; Neponsit is very nice. And then Roxbury and then Breezy Point.

Rockaway guys are known to stick together. They're very tribal. They love their neighborhood. The houses are gorgeous. The ocean is right there. It's beautiful, and you're still a city resident. So it's got really the best of everything.

They're sorta working-class nuts-and-bolts union Irish from a bygone era that ran city politics. They're really a dying breed. They're still big into the cops and firemen. They have three or four kids, and their kids are all like, you know, "Shaun." They name their kids "Shaun" and "John," you know it means the same fucking thing. They don't get it. The girls are all "Kira" or "Kaitlyn," and they all play sports.

They're phenomenal swimmers, they are. And they're ocean swimmers, all of them. Every one of them. They're surfers. They all been swimming since they were very little. The DFDers, like me—"down for the day'ers," that's what they call us—we would go to the beach in dungaree shorts and Rolling Stones concert shirts and they're wearing Hobie Cat rash guards and Oakley shades. They got like a California vibe. They're very surfer-chic, with surfer ponchos and shell necklaces. And Woodside would show up with the 30-pack of Coors Light, getting off the bus with the Def Leppard 3/4 T-shirt and jeans. We had no panache.

JERRY REA: When I first moved to Rockaway, I was kind of bummed because I grew up in Brooklyn and Manhattan was the big city. Then

I moved to Rockaway and Brooklyn was the big city. The only thing I really liked about Rockaway was that the lights turned green fast. You didn't have to wait too long for the light to turn green.

Now I love it. It's a one-horse town. You get to know everybody. You know the mother, the father, the brother. Even though there are a few bad people, you know who they are so you stay away from them.

I started out when I was fifty years old. I got on the DSNY. I was lucky enough to become an officer a couple of years later. I didn't pick up that much garbage. They work very hard, these guys. It's a great job. You make good money. You have camaraderie. It's open 24/7 so if you work the graveyard shift or 4–12, you can still do other things during the day. Such as, *Need a car, call JR. He's not far. He's on his way to the bar.*

My mother always said when I was little that I was so good at cleaning ovens. I worked for the newspaper, so I put an ad in there. "Does your oven smell? JR makes it well." People would give me like $20. I clean their oven. The next week, month, two, six months later, $40. When it got to like $50 or $60 I remember being in Howard Beach. There was this old Italian lady that was dying, she was like, "Oh, you clean my oven one more time before I die." I was like, *man, I gotta get outta this. This is like enough. I'm cleaning people's ovens before they die.* I was always good. I always sprayed it. Let it dry, then I got steel wool and cleaned it. There's something about a spotless oven. It's virginal.

This is the third-poorest neighborhood in the city of New York. There's 59 community boards in the city of New York, right? We were number 57. We might have went up a couple of notches, maybe there's five or six, but these people are so poor, they can't even pay attention. But there's very little crime. When we leave, there's no lock on my fence.

I sold a car to a guy not too long ago, he's like, "I can't fucking believe you don't have a lock on your fence." I lied. I go, "Oh, there's cameras up there." There's no cameras. The only time I've been robbed in thirty years was by people that worked for me.

Under sanitation, I got benefits, I make good money, but it's just an inconvenience. But this, my friends, on nice days we put music on, we have a couple of beers. I'll get ammonia and steel wool and like, see those alloy wheels? If they're dirty, I'll just spray it, put the music on, clean it. To me, that's my art.

You have to know people, and you have to know psychology.

You know, I had a lady here yesterday. She was walking around and she was looking at this blue Hyundai and I said, "That car, you don't want that car. That car's got problems." She's like, "Man, I like you. You true." I said, "If I screw you, I'll never get your money again. If I treat you good, you ain't dying, God forbid. You're still gonna buy twenty more cars before you do." That's how you make money.

Aristotle, or one of the fucking philosophers, said it's better to be good than bad. I mean, I really don't know what that means, but it sounded good.

One of the reasons why Americans are so spoiled is because we haven't had to suffer. I had a girl buy a car the other day and she was like, "Oh my God. I'll be without a car for a day." And I think that you need a certain amount of pain. I think you need disappointment. Remember Hegelian logic. Georg Hegel, the German philosopher? You need pain. You need a rainy, shitty day, or you're never gonna appreciate a sunny day. If every day is sunny, it's ridiculous. You need a certain amount of conflict in order to grow.

I'm affable, and I like what I do. Sometimes I'll get someone, we'll be driving around, I'll know her whole life story. She'll know my whole life story. You know, it's more than just selling a car. And don't forget, Rockaway's a one-horse town, so I see these stickers, these Jerry Rea stickers, on the back of cars sometimes. You know what? It makes me feel important.

Business is slow, though. It's tough. There's not enough money in Rockaway. We're the third-poorest neighborhood, but the second-safest. The only precinct with less crime is Central Park.

I love Rockaway, bro.

DAN BAUSO: During Hurricane Sandy, we stayed. My ex had her hip surgery, she couldn't get around, and my kid didn't want to leave. So it was me and my daughter Nora, who was fourteen. I made a big pot of sauce.

We eat dinner and we settled down. And we lost light, but I have the radio. At the window I can smell the gas. My car is in the driveway, but the driveway is on a bit of an incline, and the car is already flooded. I keep looking out the window, monitoring it, when a guy across the street above the—it used to be a drugstore, it's not anymore—he's flashing me with a flashlight. I look down the block and everything's ablaze. Just a wall of flames.

I run to the back of my house and look in my backyard. The water's up to maybe my second step. I'm petrified. I smell the gas, everybody's siphoning the gas out of the cars, the smell of gas was everywhere. And these houses are all on fire. We gotta get out of here.

So I grab a sweatshirt and I tie one sleeve to her wrist and one to mine. I said, "We gotta go." She was okay. I said, "We're gonna be okay. We just gotta get out." I said, "We gotta leave the cat." When she got more nervous, I said, "The cat will be fine." I didn't know at the time the gas I was smelling was from the walk-in basement over there.

I go up to get the old, stubborn, Irish landlady and she says, "I'm not goin' anywhere." She's like, "I'll die in this house, I'm not goin' out, I'll die in this house, I've been here about fifty years." I'm glad she didn't go, 'cause she would've died. She wouldn't have made it. I said, "I love you," I gave her a kiss, and we went out the side door.

The first thing I hit was a table. Furniture from everybody's houses had been lifted up and taken out. There was shit everywhere. It was like a raft, coming up the block from the ocean. The fortunate thing is you could see on this block, everything's connected. We were able to stay on the houses. We were tethered, right, with the sweatshirt, to her wrist and my wrist. I just kept saying, "We're gonna be fine. We're gonna be fine." And we knew it was gonna be okay. And she kept saying, "I know. I know." She didn't cry.

We get up to the corner. My house was on the corner. Rockaway is a long, narrow peninsula jutting out from southeastern Queens. Its northern boundary is Jamaica Bay, contained by a six-foot concrete wall with metal piping on top. Its southern boundary is the Atlantic Ocean. The numbers go from Beach 1st Street all the way east in Far Rockaway to the 260s all the way west in Breezy Point.

Now, my house was on the corner of B. 129th Street and Newport Avenue, as I said the midpoint of the whole damn thing. I start talking it out for Nora. We are going to leave the house, on the corner of 129th and Newport, and turn left, away from Newport, and the ocean beyond it and the burning buildings, and head north on 129th Street towards the bay wall, with the metal piping. You could see the flooding was coming from the ocean towards the bay, so we would just follow the water, and take 129th north to Cronston, cross Cronston, continue north to Beach Channel Drive, cross Beach Channel Drive, and hug the bay wall at 129th and turn left again and head west towards 137th Street and Amy's house. My ex-wife, Amy, lived on the second floor of a private home, safe from the water's reach, and there were no fires in the vicinity. We would be safe.

Well, nothing goes according to plan. The problem was, when we got to cross the next avenue up, the water was up to mid-chest on me. It was up to Nora's chin. Right below her chin. You take a step off the curb, and that water's up to here on me and it'd be over her fucking head. I'd have had to carry her. I woulda had to grab her and she woulda weighed me down. Wasn't gonna happen.

When I got to that corner, I turned around. I couldn't go back. I looked down the block, it was all ablaze. It was biblical: fire and water. There's fire behind me, there's rising water in front of me. I gotta do something. And then I saw this house, across the street. A huge brick house. We were gonna go in. Here's a little history of Rockaway. This used to be small houses, bungalow community. You still see some. But over the years, those bungalows have been bought. A lot of resentment from the old Irish here. Someone buys the bungalow, they tear down the bungalow, they put up a monstrosity. This was one of those houses, right there, and all the lights were out. So I said to Nora, "We're goin' in that house. We gotta break the window, we're goin' in that house."

She went with it. She was great. Not that I pat myself on the back . . . but I had this approach to parenthood . . . I have had this mantra with my daughter since she was four years old. Whether she couldn't figure out the words on her vocabulary test, or she couldn't figure out a dance move, or how to ride a bike, or roller-skate, I would always calm her down. I would say, "What do we do? We solve problems." I've been telling her that. I've always used that for mundane things, such as learning to roller-skate and learning how to spell "facetious," stuff that's not life and death. I didn't say that in this moment, but I like to think it was ingrained in her. To think, we got a job to do, let's get the job done.

She's never manifested any anxiety over it or anything. In fact, I think quite the contrary. Family and friends were all, "Oh my God, the poor thing," and she almost kind of gets a kick out of it. She didn't panic and I didn't panic. That's all I can say, you know? Now she goes to pieces over every other little thing these days, drives me . . . I try to remind her. *Remember when we went out in the fucking flood? So your girlfriend didn't call you for the party, why you goin' crazy? This'll pass . . .*

Anyway, we step into the water. As we walk, a guy hits me with a flashlight beam. "Come here, come here, come here." And he brought us into another home. "Don't go there, come here, come here, come here." He took us in. There was a restaurant with three stories, and it was on fire. And then one house set another after another on fire.

The guy that took us in was really, really smart. We were gonna wait until the house two doors down caught on fire. When that house goes on fire, we're goin' out. And to compound matters? I went out at 9:22. The weird things you remember, the time was 9:22. Full moon. Full moon for 9:30. So, not only is the hurricane pushing the water in, but the full moon's lifting it up. It's a double bust. His thought was, let the moon let the tide go out. We stayed there for three hours, two and a half hours . . . Took us a half hour to get there. We were there 10 to

12. Then the house two houses away caught on fire, so we had to abandon again.

He had a bay window. It was like you were in a snow globe with embers. Embers instead of snow, it was just big, fat embers. 'Cause the wind was blowing the embers, and the embers were hitting the roof. People's roofs were goin' down. It took a while because everything was wet too. When we went out the second time, the water was up to our shoulders. This guy, he got us to another house too. We stayed there until five in the morning. Then there was no water, then we went out and we finally got to my ex's.

It looked like . . . well, it looked like I would imagine it would look like if it got bombed. There was furniture everywhere, people's photos, wires hanging. Some blocks were impassable with bookcases, grandfather clocks. Everybody's got a basement, and they were getting washed away. The water was coming in and sucking it out.

The oil. That's one thing I remember. And taste. Afterwards, a perfect, Irish American family, the O'Connells, they sit us down . . . I'm in this guy's house, I'm just in from this tragedy, this terrible calamity, and within twenty minutes I'm having a cup of tea and cookies. His wife comes with a pot of tea and cookies. I never tasted such a good cup of tea.

JERRY REA: When there's a tragedy, it doesn't matter if you're black, if you're green, if you're yellow, we're on the same level. And I saw the hipsters were coming over the bridge from Williamsburg, like fifty of them on bicycles. I was like, look at this. To come to Rockaway, to feed people. What else? The Mormons. Who are the other people that don't put on lights and shit? From Pennsylvania.

The Amish came, bro. The Amish, this skinny guy and his son. I'm like, "What are these guys doing?" Eight hours later, they were still working. I was like, "Oh my." They don't drink and, you know, they don't, they just, they just . . .

The good came out of it, after a tragedy, I guess.

And the Sikhs came too.

What happened was, I worked sanitation that night, and nine guys went emergency. I was the only officer that stayed the whole night. Next morning I came home. *[He points at a car.]* It was the only car that was saved. Everything else went under water. The water, come here, I'll show you where the water came up.

But then, what happened was I got back to Rockaway, and I was like, "My cars are gone. What the fuck?" Everything. I didn't get a dollar, except for when we jumped them. And then, somebody tells me that my friend's wife ran in the basement to save the Christmas lights or something. And the water was so strong that it broke the window and it cut her femur vein. There's this one vein in your body, that's the main vein?

And she just fucking bled to death in front of her kids.

So then I'm like, *I'm worried about these cars?* My fucking friend lost his wife. His wife's dead, she's dead! The army had to come in two days later, to get in the house, to get her out of the basement. Okay? So I'm like, just the same, it's the old story. I was upset because I had no shoes, but then I saw a man who had no feet. Right? So then the next day I worked until the next morning. I was supposed to come in that night. I guess I called and said, "I'm going sick," because I have unlimited sick, sanitation.

So this guy goes, "Well, what are you going sick for, Jerry?" And I was like, I didn't know what to say. I went, "Depression." Hung up. When I tried to get my friends to call me, they're going, "We're making money like crazy. We're making like ten hours of overtime a day. Come back." I couldn't. They go, "You gotta go to your doctor." I go, "My doctor? There's no doctors," there was nothing. It was anarchy, bro.

It was anarchy. There was no lights. You could fucking do anything you wanted. There was a little looting. I don't think there was a *lot* of looting.

And we helped people and then I saw how other people . . . I remember my friend calling me. It was hard to get through with a cell phone, but I was on 116th Street and my friend Billy goes, "What are you doing?" I said, "I'm on a soup line." It was the first and last time in my life I was on a soup line. I was on a little thing, and they gave us free soup. Hipsters. Fucking hipsters.

There was no lights. It was pretty much, we got up in the daylight. There was no heat. I got blood clots from it. The next year I got diagnosed with blood clots. Because I was sleeping in cars, I was sleeping on my couch. I believe it was from Sandy.

A lot of people split. A lot of people from Breezy split. I had the car lot. I had an apartment. I live on the second floor, on 117th, so the apartment didn't get wet, but there was no electricity, it was cold.

And you know what it taught me? Out of all the things I want, hot water is the most important thing. That first hot shower, I was like, "Whoa, Dada." It was fucking great. I don't care if my food's cold.

The first couple of days I went out and bought cars and sold them, like that. Yeah, went to the auction. I had a plan. And I just went down there and just banged it out. I was moving cars. It got me back on my feet.

And plus, what happens is when you're down and out, when the water's this close to your chin? That's when you either swim or drown.

But you know what? It's crazy, but as sick as it was, it was one of the most beautiful times in my life. Because it showed people's love.

That's love. Well, then maybe it's not love. Whatever the word is, love for humanity.

NORA BAUSO A student

"We solve problems." My dad just always said that phrase to me. Anytime he does say it, he always starts with, "What have I told you since you were little? We solve problems?" I think he just wanted me as an adult to have that mindset of being a problem solver, not letting my emotions get in the way, or evaluating my emotions in a way that's effective. Get to the core of the problem. Although he might argue that

I'm not, I'm very driven by problem solving as an adult now. Here's the issue. We're going to get to it and it'll be solved.

When I started college, I was very much like, *Oh, I'm a New Yorker.* You know, like that's very much an identity. It definitely gives you a sense of pride. I was kind of the outlier. At college it was funny to see people who have grown up in the pampered suburban lifestyle. And then they're like, "Oh, well, I'm going to be a city girl."

People would talk to me all the time, "Oh my gosh. After college let's move in together. Let's move in together in the city."

Yeah, we're not doing that. That's for sure. There is a certain skill set that you have to have.

As a child growing up in New York, I lived a lot more lives than most eighteen-year-olds. I was talking to my friends a while ago. They were all from the Midwest and one of them sighed and she's like, "Nora, you have done so many things in the same amount of time that I feel like I've done nothing." And I was like, "Huh, I never thought of it that way." And that is a product of my surroundings, of New York.

One time I was physically picked up by one of those Times Square Elmos, except it was a Cookie Monster. He physically picked me up. And instead of doing anything, my mom videotaped it. She thought it was hilarious. Once I woke up and there was a woman, a neighbor, sleeping in my room. This was after a guy had been shot outside of our house. No one was injured, but I couldn't go to dance class that day because our house was a crime scene. Again, sentences you don't hear many ten-year-old girls saying. And then there was Sandy.

After Sandy, the weirdest thing to me always was the amount of family photos that were in the street. They had been picked up from people's basements and the current carried them. I found random family photos for a full year after. They'd be stuck in the bushes. You'd see it, but you wouldn't really register it: little faces staring up at you. You don't recognize them. They don't belong to you. For a full year afterwards, I'd be just walking and see them on the street, see them sticking out of a bush. That was very strange to me.

That's the thing about New York—the diversity of the experience. I think as a child, I struggled with that a lot, because I just wanted to be like everybody else. But then I realized, it's okay to not be what the expectation is. It's made me resilient. I don't get knocked down very easily.

8

Life Is a Parade

MICHAEL BUZZARD A Salvation Army bell ringer

Everybody's got their heads down. Everybody's got their headphones on. You can't look anywhere without seeing tablets, iPhones, and Beats headphones. So nobody's gonna notice if you're standing there singing or ringing the bell. If they can cancel you out, it knocks out the mighty bell with the hundred-year-tradition.

So, a couple years ago there were a couple of cadets that were at Penn Station. They're kinda jovial guys. They started dancing around. It caught attention and people liked it. Keep in mind, the beautiful part about New York City, you have a constant flow of visitors, of new people. A place like Penn Station is one of the busiest entranceways in the world.

Every hour there are ten thousand different people coming through. And most of them are visiting. It's holiday season, you're a block away from the windows at Macy's. People are coming to see that. They come up the escalator and they come out and what's the first thing they see? If they see two dancing, crazy, outta-their-minds guys—even if it's bad dancing, which most of the time it is—they're going to stop. It's a show. They just got their first New York show and they didn't have to pay a dime. And they stop and they listen and then they give their thanks.

So that's what it morphed into. The other cadets started seeing it and other people started seeing it and it kinda just went from there. We started bringing out MP3 players and amps. Everybody gets their own little routine and finds their niche and goes. It's amazing, it really is. It's like seeing the Rockettes, just all in blue and not talented and with their legs covered in three different layers 'cause it's cold.

WE LEAVE AT 5:00 OR 5:30. Get into the city, by six o'clock we're set up. It's all the morning commuters. It's not even dawn yet. The sun's not up yet. It's a lot of focused people, and in front of Penn Station you have the newspaper people. The free papers. So it's, *Good morning–good* *morning–good morning–get your paper–get your paper–good morning–good morning, how's it going? How's it going? How's it going?* It's this all morning. Focus straight ahead. I gotta get to work. We would get donations, mind you. Usually it was just put in and then go.

'Cause you know they're headed to Wall Street or whatever. That would go until about nine, ten o'clock. Then we'll get a break and there were not many people there. Then you start to get your ones that don't have 9 to 5s. That's right around lunchtime, now you're starting to get a good influx of tourists. And people that are just there for the season and coming out and stuff. They're more like big-eyed. You know, seeing the city. That's when the novelty of the army comes in.

It's New York City. And what do they see? The two dancing guys just going at it.

I realized pretty early on that first wave of people, they're so focused on work that the dancing gimmick they don't care about. *Get out of my way.*

I had a guy who had to have been big business. Every day he would drop twenty bucks in. When we made the *Wall Street Journal*, he brought us three coffees without asking. When I came back the next year, he gave me a hug. Like, *Now it's Christmas.* Never knew his name, never knew anything about him.

I wear full Salvation Army uniform and tunic and hat and, depending on how cold it is, usually long johns and a couple T-shirts underneath my uniform to stay warm. Thankfully, the lord has blessed me with a larger frame than most. So I get heated easier than others.

You wouldn't want to go to a Knicks game and see them shoot around in their warm-ups, you know? If you're coming to New York City, you're coming to Rockefeller Center to see the tree and you know the Salvation Army is going to be there because you've seen them in all the movies. You want to see that hat and that tunic and you want to see that bell. That polyester gives. So much give. It's amazing, it's absolutely amazing. If they did Salvation Army *Dancing with the Stars*, it would last half a season because people would give up.

THE WORST PART IS the forty-five-minute drive back. Because you have been dancing for eight hours straight. We're not talking a little dancing, we're talking, have you ever gone to a wedding where they play the "Electric Slide" and the "Cha Cha Slide" and "YMCA" like back to back to back? Okay, picture that on the loop for eight hours. That same energy, the physicality, because there's a new wave of people that didn't see you fifteen minutes ago. Relentless at Penn Station, and Rockefeller Center, same deal. You gotta be at that energy. They're dancing with you.

ALYSSA THERESA LOPEZ A student from Staten Island

When I tell people that I'm from Staten Island, they never say like, "Oh, that's fantastic, that's wonderful," you know? "I heard such great things. I've been there." I'll hear, "I drove through there to get to Jersey" or "I took the ferry once" or "I have a relative that lives there." But no one says anything constructive or good about Staten Island.

Sometimes I won't even tell people I'm from Staten Island.

Not keep it a secret, but I'll tell them after they know me, because they do stereotype people from Staten Island as lower-educated or narrow-minded. I don't feel like I fit into any of those categories. I will be proud to be like, "Yeah, I'm from Staten Island," but that won't be the first thing I tell people.

Staten Island is not connected by subway to any other borough— so our people are very insulated. To get to Staten Island you have to cross a really expensive bridge, or take a really long, free ferry, or a bus from Brooklyn that takes you longer than it should, quite honestly. From the top of Staten Island to Brooklyn it's like twenty to thirty minutes, but to get to where you need to go, you usually need to take a bus or another train. It's really inconvenient. There was supposed to be a subway line but then they canceled it.

It's completely different from other boroughs, more suburban, more like Queens, unlike the Bronx or Manhattan because there's way more homes than apartments. A lot of people are in the service industry. A lot of people are white compared to Manhattan, or Queens, or the Bronx, or Brooklyn for that matter, a lot of Italians and Irish people went there and thought it was a great place to settle down. We're the only place in New York that's Republican.

I do love Staten Island.

There's definitely a Staten Island culture, it's mostly an Italian culture.

The people that stay love it, and the people that don't stay hate it. But a lot of people stay. A lot of people go to the College of Staten Island, which is our community college, and will go on to get a business degree and own some business or work in the service industry, and forever complain about Staten Island traffic, but love the fact that we're not a part of Manhattan. In Manhattan everyone walks with a purpose, everyone walks with a goal in mind, where on Staten Island if you walk with a goal in mind you look a little psycho. Most people saunter.

I went to a pizza museum in Queens and they didn't have Staten Island. I was disgusted. Staten Island is home of some of the best pizza in New York. Brother's, Goodfella's, Joe & Pat's, Crispy for their pesto pie. They only make it on Fridays. It's so worth the thirty-minute free ferry ride that would get your ass over. But, honestly, none of the good pizzerias are near the ferry, as far as I know. You have to go in a little bit.

You've not had a bagel until you've had Manor Bagels when they fresh deliver them at 5:00 in the morning. There's no bagel in New York City that would be comparable to their bagels. I had a bagel with rocks in it from Harlem, okay? Rocks in it, yeah.

You can make a living, and own a house, and settle down for the American suburban dream, that's what a lot of people go for on Staten Island. Staten Island women are no different. There's a very big ideal of just getting by, making money, having enough to make do, and buy the house, and have the husband, and get your kids through school. But there's no drive to kind of change the world. I don't know if that's more pervasive in Manhattan because there's so many different people from different places that come here for a really specific purpose.

We're doing the best we can. That's the mantra of Staten Island: *We're doing the best we can.* We got good stuff. The pizza is good, the bagels are good. Don't fucking change it. There's no real innovation coming out of it, there's no people going there and trying to start something new, there's no start-up companies that are starting there because it's so far to get there that who the fuck wants to have a company in Staten Island? No one. No one is going to have a company in Staten Island where it takes forever to get to.

You have to realize that there's certain factors that limit Staten Island. That's where all the people that are ambitious get the fuck out. They leave, they go do other things, me included. I'm just one of the people that want to go back and change shit.

SCOTT WIENER A pizza guide

I just always liked pizza. In college I was always the Guy Who Likes Pizza. At every party I would bring pizza. If my friend had a barbecue, I'd show up with leftover pizza and grill it. Now I only know the city by the pizzerias. You tell me what intersection you're at, I know the pizzerias. I don't know where anything is except for pizzerias.

For people on the pizza tour, I bring survival kits to go with their pizza journals: palette cleansers, candies, breath mints, Wet-Naps, the whole thing. And I bring an infrared thermometer, so we can take temperatures of ovens.

On tours, we do only cheese pizzas. Sometimes people may think, *There's nothing on it—how do I know how good it is?* Well, how do you know how good the pizza really is if you're masking it with other things? It takes them a little bit to get over that, but once they see the elegance and simplicity, it's a different ball game.

That's why the whole thing is exciting. There's so much more context necessary than just saying, "Where's the best pizza in the city?"

The one closest to your apartment. That's the answer. Then people say, "But say you're on death row. Where do you go?" And then it's like, "Actually, to be honest, if I'm on death row, I might want to go to a place that's really crappy so I want to die." You know what I mean? Everybody wants to discover a new place, and they want to be like, *Oh, I know this secret place.* Or they want to know that the guy who does pizza tours likes their favorite place. I get that.

Somebody called me today and said, "Oh, I only want to spend an hour. Want to go around and check out some pizza stuff?" I was, "You don't want me. I will give you a list of pizzerias. You don't need me. You just want to eat pizza. I don't want to take you to eat pizza. I want to take you to learn about pizza."

OKAY, FIRST THINGS FIRST, we got a little excess flour happening on the crust. So when they stretched it, they stretched it in a bed of flour, and they didn't really dust it off, which means you might get a little bitterness on the crust. Whatever, maybe it works. On top we see this dance. This is very much a sort of Midwestern-looking pizza or something that's not necessarily New York–style because of its size and because the crust is not quite super poufy. In New York you get a lot of Neapolitan pizzas, which this is not at all trying to be. The soppressata is pepperoni basically. It's a higher-end pepperoni. It looks really good. These raw bits of fennel fronds are really cool.

This pizza is totally different from anything else in this neighborhood. It's like a very well-made Midwestern pizza. It's really the thickness of the crust is the thickness of, I hate to say it, but Domino's. The quality of the pizza is without a doubt far beyond that. The give that the crust has is not New York–y. I bet it's a winter wheat flour.

A New York crust is a little bit more dry. When you bend it in half, it doesn't snap on the bottom. There's a larger crumb structure, cell structure. This is a little dense of a cell structure. There's oil in this. Not a ton of yeast. It's hard to really put words to it, but you know it when you see it. You know a New York slice when you see it.

Slice shops are small. There's no room for tables, which is why they serve pizza by the slice. They don't want you to hang around, they have limited space. You go to Joe's on Carmine, which can't be more than 500 square feet, 600 square feet. They feed you a slice. There's no TV, barely a radio, no Wi-Fi. There's no newspapers. You're in, and you're out. That's what they want. That's what a New York pizza is—get in, get out, fast on the go.

Dough, cheese, sauce, oven. If you want to own a pizzeria, you have to buy an oven. That's almost it. It's so crazy, and it's so complex—because of its simplicity. If you only have three things going on, what if one of them is a mess? Then the whole thing is a mess.

I always hear this story from people. They're like, "Oh, yeah, when I first went to college, my roommate was from New Jersey and he said, 'Let's get a couple pies. Let's share a pie.'" They were shocked when a pizza arrived. They're like, "Oh! That's a pizza."

Look, "pizza" is an extra syllable. "Give me two large pizzas." New Yorkers don't have time. "Give me two large pies?"

Done.

EDMUND THOMAS

A Macy's Thanksgiving Day Parade balloon captain

I've been obsessed with Macy's parade since I was five years old. I watched it every year growing up. The balloons—it's great when you're five, or six, or seven years old. The parade would come on NBC at 9 a.m., and we always cooked on Thanksgiving, so it was that perfect scene: the turkey's in the oven, and I'm in my pajamas watching the parade. That's kind of how it began. So I always watched it as a kid, watched it in high school, and then when I moved here for school, I went. I've been at every parade in one way, shape, or form, except one year. I was either on the street or on the sidewalk until I got the job at Macy's.

They were looking for a product copywriter, so that's how I came in and interviewed to be a product copywriter. And literally on my first day there, at lunch I went to the office and said, "How do I become a balloon handler? This is my favorite thing, I've watched all my life, every year I love this parade. How can I be a balloon handler?"

I think it might have been just because I'm tall, but they said, "Sure, you can be a balloon handler if you want. How would you feel about being a balloon captain?" The handler is just the guys that are carrying the ropes. I didn't know there was anything else you could do with the balloons, I thought that was the job.

There's flight management, which includes the pilot for the big balloons. The pilot's the one who is walking backwards down the street with the whistle, telling the balloon to come forward, slow down, stop, move left, move right, go up, let the rope out, bring the rope down.

There's a Pilot A, who has a wind meter and who's a block or two ahead, so they can say, "Alright, we're coming up on a gust up here, at this cross street, so just watch when you get to this cross street, the winds are 20 mph." 'Cause if the wind is coming this way, 20 mph, then we're going to want to move the balloon towards the wind, so when you get into the wind it tilts it this way. And there's a Pilot B, who trails the balloon, and is more like an eyes and ears position. And then there's a captain, who oversees all of the handlers. There's a Captain A and B, so that there's one on each side of the balloon.

The big balloons have 60, 70 different lines, and about 90 handlers. They put more handlers than they need because people don't show up. Everyone gets excited and wants to be in the parade, until the alarm goes off at 4 a.m. on Thanksgiving. Then they're like, *I don't need this anymore.* So the pilots manage the balloon, and the captains manage the handlers.

"Sure, I want to be a captain," I said.

ON PARADE MORNING, there's people lining the streets, there's bands in front of you and behind you, and the handlers themselves are really excited. There's just a lot going on for people to lose focus, especially the handlers. The one thing we tell everyone is always look forward, don't look off to the side. Watch the pilot. The pilot is the one who's saying slow down, stop, go, all that kind of stuff. Watch him, don't worry about anything else.

On the big balloons, I always talk like Janet Jackson. We have a headset so flight management can talk amongst each other. The pilot can say something to me even though he's thirty feet ahead of me, and then we can communicate it to the handlers. People are screaming, the marching bands drone on and on, it's hard for everyone to hear everything unless we can talk on this kind of thing.

Every year the NYPD goes along Central Park West and Central Park South to trim the trees. They make sure there's no potholes in the street. The DOT goes and repaves the parade route a week or two before, because you can't have someone tripping, or you can't have a car that's carrying a float blow out its tire.

The parade is my absolute favorite thing I do during the year. It's my favorite three hours of the entire year. And everyone knows that, so now I have friends who in October email me, what balloon are you on this year? What balloon do you have?

THERE'S A LOT OF New York traditions, but I can't think of one that's that kind of big and important. This city is tough and it's brash, and that's what New York has its reputation for. This is about fifty-foot-high Snoopys and other big balloons going down past Radio City and Central Park, and marching bands from Minnesota and Arizona marching through the streets of New York. And Broadway shows performing a number in Herald Square. It feels very un–New York, but kind of perfectly New York.

It's so different attitude-wise than the rest of the city, but it's also such a big production that it could only really be here. There's just this big, fun, lighthearted celebration of kitsch in the middle of late November, it can be gray and drizzly and the trees don't have any leaves, and there's ice, or freezing rain or sleet or whatever, but here comes Sponge-Bob turning the corner, which is kind of insane.

My sister was a handler. She said afterwards that she told our mother, "Oh, Mom, you do not know your son. The quiet guy who just sits on the couch or isn't the most social, outgoing person turns into a totally different person." 'Cause I'm doing the cheers, "SpongeBob! SquarePants!" on the parade route. She said, "He's not my brother that I've known for thirty years."

The secret to happiness would be a job or anything else in life that gave you this much happiness for more than one day a year. A daily parade. That's the kind of secret that we're all after. Whether it's personal relationships, or work, whatever, you just want to find that one thing that makes you that happy and have it every day.

9

Beneath the Streets

EMILY KRAMER A retiree

The subway. There's no other, as far as I'm concerned. People say to me I shouldn't ride the subway or this or that, because I've got some health issues. But I just don't know how else you would do it, really, unless you think the trip is all the fun. It could take you an hour and a half on the bus. Who's going to do that? I think you walk east to west if you're in Manhattan, or west to east. North and south, you get on a train.

Trust it.

I stand at the window and look. If I have to stand on the 2 or 3 train, the express, I stand facing the local. Because I'm going to have to change to the local, I want to see where it is. My family—my husband and my daughter—they get on the train without a thought. They don't think they need to know where the door is that they need to use to get off, or if they need to get off at the beginning or the end. Wherever they come into the station, they stand there like rocks. The train comes and they get it. They don't have a strategy. Of course I have a strategy. I'm not just going to waste ten minutes standing someplace that's at the total wrong end of where I want to go. It could be two blocks away. Any place I go to more than once, I have a pretty good idea of where I need to stand on the platform so I will get off near the staircase. It's what a compulsive person does.

I once worked with a guy and I asked him—he lived in Brooklyn, we were working in Manhattan—I said to him, "So, what train do you take?" He said, "The first one that comes." I looked at him. That I can't imagine doing.

I just keep moving.

SAL LEONE A subway conductor

The train operator is in his cab with the windows closed just operating his train. The conductor's the man with his head out the window. So, who do they complain to? Me. "Where's the R train? Where's . . .

I'm waiting twenty minutes." But I'm not the person who's making you late. I'm *here*.

You know, New Yorkers are funny. New Yorkers are funny. They want to get where they got to go. It's our way. This is the city that never sleeps. Twenty-four hours a day, 365 days a year. The subway system and the buses never ever shuts down. Never ever shuts down, so you can't compare it to Boston, Philadelphia, Washington, Canada, wherever.

There's nothing like it. You could ride the trains from one end of one borough to the other end of another borough for the same two dollars and fifty cents, or whatever it is now, and ride it all night long and it never shuts down. Yeah, at night you may have to wait. There's twenty minutes between trains on the midnights but you could always ride the train.

New Yorkers are very, very impatient. We've learned to live like that. We understand it, we understand how our fellow New Yorkers are, but in times of crisis I've seen New Yorkers come together. I really have. When there are people hurt on a train or a person has a heart attack. The people that are there? The people that are there in the car are helpful. New Yorkers in times of crisis do come together. But you get the people on the train behind you going, "Ah, why can't they just get the body off the train. . . ."

I worked the early AM hours, bringing the people to work. Much different than bringing people home from work. In the morning people are like, "Well, alright, if the trains are bad I'll be a little late to work." But when they're coming home, they're hungry and they want to get home to their family. They don't want to hear about the trains breaking down or signal problems or somebody fell or whatever.

I HAD MY SHARE OF incidents on the trains with people getting hurt or people getting sick, people having heart attacks, this, that, and the other thing.

One time I had some kid stabbed. They cut his face, across his neck. He was bleeding. They pulled the cord between stations. As I'm going through the cars, I'm checking the cords. I'm going through the rear of the train and one lady says to me, "You going in that last car?" So I said, "Yeah." She says to me, "You don't want to go back there." "Well, I have to dear if you want me to move the train."

When I get there I see blood on the window. I'm thinking, *Oh my God, what am I gonna find in this car?* Now my first instinct, which should've been the right instinct, was to just get the cops there. Not put myself on the line. But I'm thinking maybe there's a child in need. Maybe a woman God forbid's getting raped, getting killed. So I went in there. It was a bunch of school kids. They got into an argument. This one kid, he got cut bad and he was holding his neck and he's grabbing me, saying help me, help me. "Alright, alright. We're gonna get you help. Let me reset the cord." I relock the door, I said, "Just sit in here until we get to the station." He was cut right under his jawline. He was bleeding all over the car, all over everything.

He grabbed me, and I'm saying to him, "Okay, I will help you. But you got to let go of me and let me get you help." There was a girl with him. I don't know what kind of rag she had, a sweater or whatever it was. "Keep it pressed on there," I said. "Let me get the train into the station and when we get into the station we will get you help."

It was the Ninth Avenue station on the D line and the kid who cut him, when I unlocked the door he ran out and he ran onto the tracks so we had to watch for him. He knew that he was gonna get in trouble, so he ran onto the tracks and he must've ran out of the station. Whether he got caught or anything I don't know.

You deal with the suicides. I had three of them. People jumped in front of the trains. Usually they used to tell us be careful around the holiday times. These homeless people are depressed. They jump in front of trains. Not a pleasant thing to see. Not a pleasant thing to deal with. The train operator who deals with it more because he sees it. He's your partner and you work with him every day and he's shaken because again it's like hitting someone with your car.

I once had a lady die in my arms on the platform. I was working the western line here. I pulled into the station. One of the passengers ran up to me. It was a cold, cold March morning. Said to me, "There's a lady laying on the platform. I told the token clerk and he wouldn't do anything. He didn't call for police, he didn't get out of the booth."

So I got off the train and I went over. The woman was barely coherent and I called it in to the control center and they said to me, "Is the woman responding?" I said, "Not really. Her eyes are fluttering. She's an elderly woman, she's laying on a platform." They said, "Okay, we want you to discharge the train. Train operator will get the train out of there and we're gonna call for medical assistance then you stay with the passenger." I said, "Okay, I'll do that." Took my jacket off. Put it over her, she was shivering. It was very cold. And I stood there with her.

The next train came in, picked up those people. I stayed in contact with control and they said, "Okay, we're gonna have the trains bypass that station because we're gonna have EMS and police come." I stood with the woman. She opened her eyes once or twice and then that was it. By the time the two police officers arrived they walked up to me. They got there before EMS. One was a sergeant and one was a rookie, and they looked down and they said, "Is that your jacket?" I said, "Yeah." He goes to me, "You might as well pick it up, 'cause she's dead."

Her name was Blanche and she was an elderly woman. I'll never forget her name because things like that stick in your mind. They went through her bag to see if she had any medications. She did have heart medications and everything. Another thing that struck me was the sergeant said, "Well, Blanche, I guess you're gonna be a little late for work today." How cold can you be?

It was such a strange, strange feeling I had for like a week or two. I didn't know this woman from Adam. Our paths crossed at that time. Just happened to cross and I would've liked to let her family know that she didn't die alone. That even though I didn't know her, I was nobody, I was there with her. She didn't die alone.

OVER THE YEARS, you're breathing in all that stuff that's down there. Who knows what asbestos was down there? That steel dust? At the end of the day you blow your nose, everything's black. Clean your ears, everything's black.

You're breathing in all that steel dust. As those wheels grind on the rail and steel particles are thrown into the air. You don't see them. Perfect example is if you look at a conductor who's got a blue coat. Back then the coats will all look shiny. They had that shiny marks on them and that was this dust. The steel dust actually embedded in the coat. It was the metal grinding on metal creating metal particles and you breathe that in.

Since 9/11 every other day there's white powder on a train, the steel dust I was breathing in, the asbestos out of the stations. The tunnels? Who knows what's down there? The homeless people, the rats. You never know when a nut's gonna get on the train. You used to hear things on the radio, "There's a guy on such and such on a train with a machete." With a machete? "Oh, conductor, go check it out." Yeah, right. Okay, I'll go check it . . . What do I got? I got a key.

You deal with people getting nasty. You deal with the people getting rude. You tried to handle the situations as best you could. Sometimes the people almost come to blows with you. I used to tell them, "Listen, you can yell at me all you want. I'll sit here and take it. Go ahead. Yell at me. If it makes you feel better, g'ahead. But just keep in mind I can't control what's going on. I'm just a person here. I'm stuck on the train like you are. I'm stuck behind a train like you are. I'm not liking it." Some people say, "Yeah, but you're getting paid overtime." "You're right. I can't argue that. I am getting paid overtime if I'm late. That doesn't mean that I like what's happening. And if you feel better yelling at me, go ahead. Go ahead yell at me all you want. Curse me, yell at me. Try to leave my family out of it, but if you believe it's my fault go ahead."

I used to try to be sympathetic. Sometimes people get stupid and

New Yorkers

say the wrong thing and then you lose your cool a little bit too and some conductors got spit at. That's a degrading thing.

If they were mad they come right up. And I used to say to them, "Back up a little bit. Back up a little bit." 'Cause they would always blame you. You were the face of the transit authority and you tried, you tried so hard to keep your cool and you tried to sympathize. That was my way of doing things. "You're right, sir. You're right, ma'am. What do you want me to do?" I used to tell them, "I'm a lowly conductor. I'm sitting here like you. I'm here like you and I apologize. That's all I can do."

Scream at me all you want. I have no control over this. If there's a signal problem. If there's a water main break. If there's a dog on the tracks. If there's a person that's sick. I can't control what's going on. I can only give you the information.

What I used to try to do when the trains were stuck in the tunnels, I used to take my car number and say if you're late for work, here's the car number. Have your employer call the transit authority. We are the 8:05 D train out of Bedford Park the Bronx. We were stuck here. You have your employer call the transit authority and they will verify that the train was late. It's the best I can do. So you see people take out their pens.

I realized over the years that the confrontational way wasn't the best way to go because all you did was you got aggravated, they got aggravated. They started screaming, you started screaming, and you never accomplish nothing. So you try to just be, "I understand what you're saying, sir. I apologize. I know you must be late for work. If I could control it I would. I can't. I'm not in that position. So I understand what you're saying." And some people were still jerks. They'd curse or say something about your family. I couldn't take that family stuff. "Whoa, whoa, whoa, whoa, whoa, whoa. Let's stop it right there. I'm not saying nothing about your family. Don't do that, don't do that." "Well, you're an asshole." You're trying to be sympathetic and they're cursing you.

There was no uniform way of handling it. A friend of mine used to fight with the school kids every day. When they saw his train, they pulled the cord. I says to him, "You're fighting a losing battle. There's a hundred of these school kids to you. You fight with them. You curse them and every day they look for you." They would get into their station, pull the cord, and then most of them would run off. They would wait 'till he opened the doors in the station 'cause they knew then he'd have to walk the whole thing to reset the call. It delays the train and this was what they would do. "You're fighting a losing battle. Just go with the flow. Do the best you can."

A LOT OF PEOPLE are lonely and they like to talk to the train conductor. So, they come over, they start giving you their life story. You're like a bartender. And you try to listen and you say to yourself, "Try to deal with these people because they may be depressed. They may be lonely. They don't have people." So you tried to listen. You know, I say, "Gee, I wish this guy would get off at the next stop." But sometimes they ride a while.

You're a civil servant and you do as much as you can. You're a psychiatrist, a bartender, a protector. An ear to listen to. Sometimes a medic. It was a little disrupting for a while but you listen to their stories. It didn't really cost you anything. You got to know who to talk to. Who not to talk to. Who's a little suspicious. New Yorkers are very skeptical. They're not stupid.

You hear the stories where somebody falls on the tracks and the people jump down to help. This was in New York . . . New Yorkers in time of crisis are usually very, very good. If somebody gets hurt, has a heart attack. *If* they see it. But if it's on the train in front of them, "Can't they just take the guy off the train? I'm late for work."

I WAS IN MY OWN little world there. I used to think about different things, put myself in another place. Thank God I was never claustrophobic.

At the end, after thirty years of service, they gave me a little citation. What am I going to do with it? Wipe my ass with it, throw it away. Why didn't you say along the way, "Mr. Leone, thirty years of service, you never got in trouble, you know what? We're gonna give you another week vacation. We're gonna give you a day on the city or something." What is a piece of paper that says thank you for your help? This doesn't mean anything.

Did I make a difference? No, I probably didn't. I retired and the system's still there. But my regular passengers in the morning, I'm sure they missed me.

PROJJAL DUTTA An MTA official

I have heard it said that the MTA is the largest manifestation of the state in a benign way for its citizens in the US. There's no other thing that is run by government that is working for you and you're interacting with it every day in a basis like this. The magnitude of it is just incredible. Eight and a half million people every day. There's nowhere the state manifests itself in Americans' lives in such an obvious and as in-your-face way as the MTA.

Nothing in the Western world is anywhere close to the New York system. The London system, in terms of carrying people, in terms of everything, is a baby version. It shuts down every night, it charges you eight bucks for a ride at peak hour. It transports many fewer people. It's not in the same league. The closest systems are all in Asia. We are the largest in the Western world by numbers of people carried.

Grand Central has more people pass though it every day than live in the state of Wyoming. But unlike Wyoming, Grand Central does not have two senators. So I think the senatorial system is also very skewed against density. It's basically anti-density. It hurts public transportation in a way that it doesn't hurt many other types of infrastructure.

The hard thing is to take physical infrastructure that is one hundred years old, that has been through storms and calamities, and keep that in what we call a sober state of good repair. Let's say your great-grandfather, or whichever piece of your generational tree, was born in 1907, and he had a great coat. And you keep wearing it all the way to now. All you've only ever managed to do is on some nights patch it a little, stitch it a little. Just imagine what that coat would look like. And you wear it every day all the time. It's very frail, it's threadbare. So things can push our system over the edge very easily.

Especially in a system that runs 24/7, 365 days a year. Wheels wear out, the paint is peeling. When do you paint? There's a live rail there. You can't walk on the track bed because the steel dust can form these random connectivities to the third rail and you can get electrocuted. Because of the brake dust and the shoe dust—the shoe that rides in the third rail. It's a very gradual process, but if there's enough of a sprinkling of steel dust, it's called straight current, it finds a pathway and it electrocutes. So for even the littlest thing, you have to wait for a weekend or you have to wait for something. It's not like you can start at 11:00 p.m. on a Friday night and it can be done by 5:00 a.m. on a Monday, it's not like that.

Not only do we have to do all of these things, but we now also have to cater for flooding. People have to realize the enormity of the damage from Hurricane Sandy. It's like the Atlantic Ocean came and visited you. For three days there, your land, your home, your basement was a part of the Atlantic. You should be damn glad that you're still alive. That's the enormity of it. The Atlantic Ocean redrew its boundaries and the map changed and what we understand to be the shoreline was not the shoreline anymore, it was a new shoreline. What are you gonna do? Are you gonna shoot the shore? Who are you gonna insurrect against?

DINO NG A NYC Department of Transportation engineer

Growing up in Brooklyn, I hung out with kids who don't want to use a Chinese name. So they gave me a name, Dino, and it stuck.

New Yorkers

At the beginning at DOT, I worked for the Department of Transportation Bureau Highways. Bureau Highways is in charge of all the streets in the city of New York. So, my role in design is to reconstruct those streets. Whatever needs to be done.

Whatever you see in the street, when we do the project, we do all the stuff: surface, street lighting, traffic signals, sidewalk curb, roadway. And of course anything underneath it, the sewer, the water main. And we coordinate all our work with the private utility, electric, gas, telephone, all those people. So that's how I started with the city doing the infrastructure work. And then in 1996 this agency was formed to accelerate some of these capital concerns. It takes a long time. It still takes a long time to do something.

Each year, typically, we only have enough capital money to reconstruct approximately 30 miles of streets out of over 6,000 miles of streets in the city of New York. So, that's one half of one percent, right? So, to use that as the rule of thumb, that's every two hundred years you come back and do this.

When I go in a neighborhood, people say, "Oh, you're going to be disruptive." And so I say, "I promise you, I won't come back for two hundred years. How's that?" A lot of people have found out after we finish that the value of the neighborhood goes up. Every neighborhood that we've gone into when we've done renovation of the sewer and the water and the streets and all of that, the property value goes up, right? Yes, you have to bear with us for about two years typically on a project. But the reward's going to come at the end. You're going to have a better street. You have better services.

We have had people in commercial areas adamant about how we're going to kill the businesses and all that. And I always had the theory that the businesses that were going to be closing during the course of construction were already on the way out. But when we complete, you're going to have a much better infrastructure for future development.

When we were doing Columbus Avenue many years ago, they had

restaurants out there, an outdoor café. I never forget, I went up to DOT construction, right, they were excavating, and people were actually getting those tables outside with all the dust, sitting there watching construction and eating. I said, "Where are the businesses that went out of business because of us?" I said we were actually attracting people because this was like a sideshow, people seeing construction done.

The reality is when we need to do it, we have to do it. The infrastructure in the city of New York goes back one hundred plus years. Yes, in Roman days people built things that lasted hundreds of years. But they didn't have heavy trucks. If you go to Pompeii, you can see the ruts in the granite. They have actually a track that was cut by the wheels of the chariot. That's what happened. You can trip and fall and sue them.

But the truth of the matter is, the usage has changed through the years. Now they're building more bikeways. And greenways and we're building bioswales now to take care of the stormwater. Engineering is not a static thing. You have to be proactive in looking ahead to see what's coming. You can't just say, well, today's use is this and I'm going to build for that. You have to take a look at what the future's going to bring. Because you're not going to get funding to rebuild it again. So you have to foresee how the world's going to go.

One of the things that I've been advocating for is a difficult task. If you expect global-warming sea rises, the forecast for this region is it's going to be in the neighborhood of around thirty inches. The city of New York has what they call legal grades. In other words, all the streets have certain grades, street elevation that's been established previously. Nearly all the sewers in the city of New York for the most part, I wouldn't say one hundred percent but maybe ninety-nine percent, are gravity. Same thing with the water. It's not pumped, it's all gravity.

In order for the sewer to drain, you have to have a pitch on the pipe. They worked from the outlet, which is near the shoreline. You have to use outfall that goes to the river. You have to build right above the tide. So that's your starting point. And then you work backward. So they established this elevation. But remember, if the sea rises by thirty inches, they're going to be under water, right? So I said, look, you have to reestablish these elevations. Bring them higher so people that get flooded may not get flooded anymore. That's reestablishing new legal grades based on the forecast of the sea rises. It's a monumental task. It may take twenty years to do.

If you believe the elevation is going to go up by thirty inches, you take a look at the current high-tide elevation, you add thirty inches to it. Then you work backward hydraulically, to see what elevation the streets should be at. Because each sewer must have a certain cover over it, or it's going to come out of the ground. You got to think ahead. Look at the city water tunnels. People one hundred years ago didn't plan this, where are we in the city of New York? When you don't have enough water, what happens? People go somewhere else.

I know people don't like, what's his name, Robert Moses. But all these bridges and highways, at one time back in the '40s and '50s, however you think of that, they got built. And if it wasn't for these things, we would be nowhere near where we are economically. The infrastructure establishes and drives the economy. Whether people believe it or not, it's the truth. If the trucking industry said, look, I can't get my truck to drive through here, people wouldn't establish factories.

How do you get goods into the city if you don't have a transportation network that is reasonably workable? I mean, we're kind of at the margin today. Not the greatest, but it's still working. But if you don't plan on that next future, how are those people fifty years from now, the next two generations, going to live?

So, as engineer, you always have to think that way. Yes, we have to solve today's problems. But also you need to prepare yourself for the next thing that's coming.

Would that mean we'd have to raise all the streets of New York? Yes. If we don't, we're going to be in Holland. Basically you build a dike around lower Manhattan. That may not be your solution. Because in heavy rain, what happens? If you're bound in by the levee, so to speak, look at what happened in Louisiana. The pump failed. That was the end of that. But politicians just want to have a ribbon cutting. Mayors, they only want to take credit for things while they're in office. I think they're only interested in the four years. Or eight years, whatever the term they're going to get. What I'm proposing, it's going to be one hundred years or more.

Most American families have a house for something like seven years, right? That's why they have these flexible-rate interests because they don't care. After that they move out anyway, right? I think a lot of Europeans and Asians think longer term. You have a house, the house is going to go to the next generation, next generation, next generation. I think we need to plan on the very long term.

I ALWAYS TELL my staff that this is a never-ending job. I mean, it's a profession that people outside may not understand. They may not even miss us if we go away for a year or two. But if we don't exist, I don't think the society will last for any length of time. Does the public understand what we do? We're not like architects. Architects love flamboyance. "Look at my building." Engineers don't do that. They don't say, "Look at my sewer."

It's invisible until you flush the toilet or turn on the tap. When nothing comes, that's when you say, "Oh." Right? Or after Sandy when people were out of electricity and all that, then they realize how important some of these infrastructures are.

When you're doing this work after a while, you kind of understand why things were done a certain way. You look at the old sewer systems in Manhattan, right, when they started to build. Why it is egg shaped? Do you know why it's egg shaped? Because that's how big the basin is when they're standing inside laying the brick. It's not to do with capacity, how much flow you're going to get. That's what the engineer always thinks about. No, it's you'd have to have a guy in there who's laying the brick. That's why the size of the sewer's like that. Right? Simple things.

It's amazing how the profession has taken care of a lot of these societal problems, societal needs. People don't even understand. The first water system down in lower Manhattan was because all the cholera and everything that fell in the water, tainted the water that we have.

What will the engineers of the future think when they see our work? I hope they say, Wow, these guys put some thought in what they did. And that it lasted as long as it has. Hopefully that's what it is. And, now, they will then use the latest and greatest concepts and materials and so forth and carry that for another generation. I think our duty is to make sure we contribute long-term, to make people's life better. It's difficult. It's very difficult because we don't make the final decision on many things. We just carry out what needs to be done.

I believe society needs people like me who understand the technical side, but also understand the implication if we *don't* do something. If we *don't* improve what we're building in society, I think I'm not doing my job. As a professional, I believe that is part of my job. It's not written in my job description that I have to do that, but I think I'm obligated for societal reasons. For the next generation and the generation thereafter. Hopefully other people do the same thing. I'm sure I'm not the only one. I think there's a lot of people out there similar to my position who want to encourage these things.

Who would ever recognize an engineer? In the old days they actually did. Like the Holland Tunnel; they named it after the chief engineer. Today, do they name anything after me? They don't name anything after me.

10

The Teeming Shore

Somebody recently questioned whether or not I grew up in New York City, because I grew up in Woodside, in Queens. I said, first of all, we're the heart of the Big Apple, we are the geographic center of New York City. Number two, I don't care where you're from in New York City, your world really exists over the course of a couple blocks. So, some kid from the Upper West Side, who might be a gazillionaire, who's probably born wealthier than I'll ever be, his world exists in the course of a couple of blocks, just like my world did, just like my nephews do up the street.

Woodside is not the Upper East Side, I get it. But the Upper East Side is not Woodside, and God knows it's not Sheepshead Bay or the South Bronx. But I would never say to somebody in the South Bronx, "You don't live in New York City." You know, it's crazy. But there are people who think the Upper East Side is New York City, and so then on the Upper West Side, you might say they're crazy, that's not New York City. So I don't know what is or what isn't, but if you run, you can go anywhere you want.

When I run, I get to be a part of the entirety of New York City, at least for a little bit, and see all these places. But when you come home at the end of your day, you come back to your little world and your part of New York City. Running in the city, you've got people, you're dodging workers, there are lights, constant lights. So I try to run in Central Park or in Astoria Park as much as I can, just so that you don't have to keep stopping and jogging in place and all that nonsense.

One of my rules is if I hear anybody honk or anybody scream I always throw my hands up and go, "Thank you!" Like they're my personal cheering section. Meanwhile the guy can be honking his horn because the guy didn't go fast enough at the green light. But I always throw my hands up and say, "Thank you!" They yell at me. Oh, yeah, yeah. "Run, Forrest, run." You get that all the time. Today I was standing out on a corner, and this beautiful woman walks by, she was gorgeous. And these guys in a FedEx van go *[he whistles]*, so at this point she had passed and they're looking at me and I say, "Thank you very much, guys." And the guy, the guy like ripped his head out and said, "Not you!" and I'm like, *Alright, it doesn't make you gay. Take it easy.*

You could see it on this guy's face, he had to make eye contact to tell me, "I wasn't whistling at you. Just for the record. I'll never see you again. I've already forgotten what you look like, but let's get this down. I was *not* whistling at you. I was being aggressively sexual towards that woman, not you, okay? Not you, the guy with the body of an eleven-year-old boy. With one wet side, and one protruding nipple that's really chafed."

You want some diversity? I ran through Flushing Meadows one day, and they had the big Unisphere, the globe, and probably every country in South America is represented, having a barbecue. (As somebody who's worked in the food world, I'm looking at this and thinking, *That chicken's got to be refrigerated.* But I keep my mouth shut.) As I kept running, I came across a Tibetan dance troupe, there was people playing cricket, two hipsters getting married. You go through Flushing Meadows park on a sunny day, and you will see the world.

IN 2008 I WAS DRUNK on red wine at my aunt's house. Christmas night my sister said, "If I decided to run the New York City marathon, would you do it?" So I said, "Yeah. Yeah, I'll do it." And you know, being an actor you do have a lot of time to train.

I had never run anywhere. The most I'd ever run in my life at that point was probably half a mile nonstop. So I thought, she's not going to do this. She'll forget. She was drunk too. And then, sometime in March, we were signed up for a 5K, and we didn't think we'd finish. We did. Then it was a 10K, and a half, and I'm starting to think, "Holy shit, we are running the New York City Marathon."

It was exhilarating.

You start on the Verrazzano Bridge into Brooklyn. I've got people all along the route. My brother-in-law is really good. He hops around so I see him in Brooklyn. He's a yeller and a screamer. When my sister's with him, she wears rubber gloves so she can hand out oranges, pretzels, bananas to perfect strangers who are running. They make crazy signs. A lot of people wear their names on their bib. So if it's like Stan, my sister will get in this guy Stan's face and yell out, "You are the man, Stan!" If somebody's name is William, she'll yell, "You got the will, come on William!" And then it's like a game with just like how bad a pun can you make.

So I see them in Brooklyn.

One year my ex-girlfriend said to me, "Hey, I'm going to be on the route. I'm going to be in Brooklyn. I'll see you. My boyfriend's going to be there." I was like, "Oh, alright, great." She goes, "If you don't want to stop, it's okay, I just wanted to let you know." So here I am. This is my shit. I've been training. And I'm wondering how am I going to do this. I was approaching Bishop Loughlin High School. That's where my dad went to high school. Someone was playing the *Rocky* theme song over and over and over. As I'm approaching my ex-girlfriend and her new boyfriend, I want to look like I'm going to win this thing, *Rocky* is playing. There's my dad's high school. I'm in a full-on sprint. It's mile 8, and I'm sprinting for the finish line. I stop, I suck in my gut, I'm like, "How's it going?" I met him, I shook his hand. He had a bag of pretzels, he's a nice guy. I took some pretzels. I said, "Well, I gotta run."

We run through Williamsburg, Brooklyn. It was very Hasidic and there was very few people on the streets. They would be on the street but nobody would be cheering or high-fiving. I remember there was a little girl who had her hand up for a high five and my buddy Will went to give her a high five and her mother grabbed her hand and put it down because they're not supposed to be touching.

Then you go over the Pulaski Bridge to Long Island City. My friend Anne will be down there. She'll have a Gatorade for me. She would dump it into my CamelBak. Now no CamelBaks because of Boston. You can't run with that. I have to run with the animals and get my water from a table. It's so gauche.

Then my mother will usually be in Long Island City because it's not far from the house, I can see her there. She looks completely dazed and confused. It's as if she's surprised there are all these people running through the neighborhood. And then she sees me and she doesn't really recognize me until I've passed her.

Now you go over the Queensboro Bridge, which is a really long hill. It's dark because you're running on the lower level and there's no music, there's no fans, there's nothing. It's just dead. That's where I take a McDonald's salt pack and drink some water.

If I heard somebody call it the Ed Koch bridge, I would stop, I would bring them back to the front of the bridge, and I'd say, "Look, you see where it says Queensboro Bridge?" That's such a disgrace that they would change it. I know, I have been guilty of calling it the 59th Street Bridge too, but I have never ever ever ever called it the Ed Koch bridge. That drove me nuts, because they would never rename the Manhattan Bridge or the Brooklyn Bridge.

When you get over the Queensboro Bridge you're at First Avenue in Manhattan and it's electric. It's just ripping, and you start really running as fast as you can, you want to look good. My cousins are usually there. They live in Manhattan, so I'll see them on the side of the street. You can always pick out somebody who knows you. You always see somebody who knows you and then you feel extra cool.

I'm eating pretzels, I'm eating oranges, I'm eating these goos, you know, little gels. I'm full at the end of the marathon.

You see every culture in New York City. Manhattan, when you go up First Avenue, is electric, but then you get up into the 100s to 110s it really dies out and gets quiet again. You're like, *What the fuck am I doing?* That neighborhood just doesn't come out. There will be people out there cheering but not as loud, or not as many.

You go over the Willis Avenue Bridge to the Bronx, then you come out of the Bronx over another bridge into the top of Manhattan and you come running down the west side of Manhattan through Harlem.

It's good, it's the West Side, it's alive. And then you come all the way along the west side of Central Park and you duck into Central Park and you're really close at that point. Three years ago I saw my brother Drew and I just started crying, at mile 25. He was at the Trade Center. He got out fine, thank God. I call him every year on 9/11 and I tell him, "Drew, I'm so grateful I can call you today. I don't know what I would do if I couldn't call you today." So when I looked up and saw the older version of myself, I got all weepy. At that point, you're physically shot, you're mentally shot.

My sister was running with me. I thought I was going to get like 4:45 or something, and she's saying, "You're doing it, you've got it." I've seen the video. I'm not even moving. There's a woman with a stroller, a double stroller, walking past me. So my sister says, "You totally got this!" I finished at 4:56. I was happy, I was brutalized.

Crossing the finish line, as exhilarating as it is, is also extremely sad. It's like graduation day. As much as you want it to be over, you know that you're not going to be seeing these friends now for a little while, and those friends are: your chafing ass, your CamelBak, your ripped-up nipples, your pounds and pounds of pasta that you eat and justify because "I'm running a marathon," the cheeseburgers that you eat like crazy, the beers, your friends who you run with. Your marathon friends.

I got so emotional the first year. First of all, when I crossed the finish line, I got my best friend's hand in one hand, my sister's hand in the other hand and we literally just pulled each other through, and then the next year my sister and I crossed the finish line and my mother—who can't work her TV remote control—gets the best photo of us crossing the finish line. Above us is a giant screen that has our face, so she got a picture of our backs with our hands in the air, but on the giant screen is our faces. Just a great photo.

NOW I RUN in the cemetery a lot.

Calvary. I have my grandmother and my grandfather both buried there, so I run from my house, all the way up past the school, past the church, alongside the cemetery—it's a really steep hill. And then I make a right turn underneath the BQE and then I make a right turn into the cemetery when the gates are open and then I just loop in and out through all the loops. I always stop and say hello to my grandmother and my grandfather. A beautiful view of Manhattan from there.

I run past the school where not only did my mother and father graduate from, out of the seven of us, six of us graduated from. I run past the convent where I made my communion. I run past the church where I was baptized, where I made confirmation, where I graduated from, where some of my brothers got married, my mom and dad got married, my grandparents were all funeralled and waked out of that church.

And I run past the block that my father grew up on, past the block that I grew up on, past the block that my mother grew up on. 'Cause they only grew up a block away. And then they moved about a hundred feet. And then, yeah, you know, you run past the cemetery where—I ask my mother all the time, "If I were to go tomorrow, do we have a spot for me?" And she's like, "Don't be morbid," but she's like, "Yes we do, though." My parents have never owned anything. They've never bought a house, they don't own anything, but they own many plots of cemetery land, so we're good there.

I run past the apartment that I shared with some of my brothers, where my brothers first finished and moved out of the house and got an apartment, and I moved in. So I run past one of my old houses. I get close to the high school—I taught high school for a couple of years, I get very close to that high school when I run that way as well. And then, you know, when you're running across Queens Boulevard and you look to your right, the Empire State Building is right there.

The neighborhood does change, which I have no problem with. Nothing stays the same. And when people say, "Oh, but it's changed," and they give you that wink, I know what they mean. They're saying it's darker than it was when I grew up there. I met a lady the other day, seventy miles away at a cooking demonstration. She says, "Oh, what part of Queens?" And I said, "Woodside." And she says, "Oh, I grew up in Woodside." I said, "Oh, great, blah blah blah," and she goes right into it. That lean-in, and she's like, "But it's changed." That secret handshake? I'm not a part of. I don't want to be a part of.

So, we have a ton of new Americans who live in Woodside, right? People always say, "They don't know our language. They don't want our culture." And I say, "Well, maybe they don't. But their kids probably will." And they're like, "Well, when my ancestors came here, they learned the language." Well, your ancestors were Irish, you idiot, so they spoke the language, but they still stayed with their guys. They still hung out with the Irish guys and started Irish clubs and only Irish things.

I know Italian guys whose parents came here who still don't speak English or, if they do, very, very little. Greeks who came here many years ago who really don't speak a lot of—. For me, I think it comes down to the fact that, yeah, they might be Greek or Italian or this or that, but they're white. Whereas I think a big part of it is that, well, "They look closer to me." And I say, well, don't worry about it. First of all, things are gonna change. Second of all, maybe the new people who came here when they were thirty-five years old are probably more loyal to their home country. I get it. Maybe they don't want to speak the language. Maybe they don't know the language, but their kids will. And that's how America, I think, goes on, is that we take in people, and that through our bad television shows and fast food, you eventually do become Americanized.

Someone's parents come from another country, and you see after X amount of years the cultural divide that happens between them and their own children. As years go by, their children start to give back to their parents, and their parents down the road start picking up the American stuff from their children. I think that's America. I think that's the beautiful part of America.

In a generation the Hondurans or Colombians will be like, "Oh,

Woodside, it's just not the same." It will change. Now, I wish that we had more thriving businesses here. I think eventually we will. We're in a turnover right now.

That's the first thing you saw, when you come through the harbor, was that. "Bring us your tired, your poor, your huddled masses yearning to breathe free."

And now it's like, "Last one in shut the door."

In my little world here, I try to embrace it as much as I can. I try to shop over at Rico Pan Bakery because they've got the best goddamn empanadas I've ever had in my life. I have a supermarket by my house, I'm the only person in there who speaks English, but they have fish swimming around, live, in front of me. Their prices are great. We communicate through smiles.

The fabric of America, the things that make us this country, we're stripping them away. The idea of like, "Let's make America great again"... well, then, we should be more welcoming, because that is what made us great in the first place. You know, we should stand up and say to tyrants around the world, "If you mistreat your ethnic minorities, your religious minorities, you're okay here." That's what New York, and especially New York, has always been about.

That's why people hate New York. That's why people from around the country hate New York. Oh, it's so fucking... You know, people say to me, "Oh, New York, it's like a foreign country." Yeah. We've always been. That's the deal. It blows my mind that that word can be denigrated, you know? What is bad about sanctuary?

You know, come to New York. I'm on a train the other day, and I look around, and I see all these different colors and all these different shapes, styles, fashions, whatever. I love it. That is New York. That's my city.

NASIM ALMUNTASER A bodega employee

I'm a Yemeni-American, bred and born in Brooklyn, New York. My father, he was actually a school leader at Yemen, but when he came to America, his degrees couldn't transfer. He came here for the American dream—which is, you know, for his children to get the American dream, to be educated, to do things that he wasn't able to do. He never had that opportunity to get a college degree and work in other kinds of institutions and get to explore what America is about. His transition was so fast and overwhelming. The bodega, it was the quickest thing.

We have two in downtown Brooklyn—many years ago it was really poor and now it's very high class. And we have two in Brighton—a very busy neighborhood. Brighton Beach never is quiet. I've been working in the bodegas assisting my parents in all four of them across New York City for the past ten years.

I've been assisting lately at Brighton Beach, which is a predominantly Russian, Ukrainian, and Uzbek community. At the moment I've been taking cashier responsibility because of my language and I'm a people's person and I'm very outgoing. I try to help people to the best of my capacity. We have plenty of consistent customers. We hold stuff if there's a customer that likes one thing. In terms of our most consistent customers, we get so it's like we forget they're our customers. They turn into some sort of very, very close friend. Our conversations tend to get deep, right? Certain things that you won't tell someone that you don't know. We tend to open up to our customers too. So it's reciprocal, bringing some sort of community within the store.

PEOPLE IN NEW YORK CITY are very materialistic. I mean, Brighton Beach, it's all money, money, money. If you look at other countries, people actually communicate with each other. But a place like Brighton Beach? It's really good in terms of business, but in terms of social life, it's hard. People are always running by, walking by each other and you, and if you say *hi, how are you?* or start a dialogue with someone, that's one of the most awkward things you can do. But we try to do that in the store. You know, to build some sort of community.

Owning a bodega is not just being a businessman, right? I think it has to do something with the arts or something, being like morally and socially responsible and knowing who your audience is and knowing who your customer is, knowing your community. Being patient, a listener, a leader, being helpful, courteous, courageous, and taking risks. Risks in terms of your neighborhood. Especially for those that have been owning bodegas for like twenty years. They've seen the neighborhood go from poor to rich or rich to poor, and your items, the things that you sell, reflect that.

If you have a poor neighborhood, your prices tend to drop or tend to be very different. Poor people like certain things. If it's predominantly African American, the kind of produce you sell would try to lean towards their culture. Because you need to be open, an open-minded person, you need to be open to the community change, the culture change, and make sure that your shop reflects that.

If you were to ask people about Muslim holidays like Eid or Ramadan, a lot of them would not even know what those holidays are. People see a lot of stores selling things that come from that culture, like the candy and treats that we sell. A lot of people say, *What is this? I've never seen this before. Why is this coming out during this time of the season?* So it's reciprocal learning. I think the products also have some sort of voice too.

Before you enter in, you see a huge display of fruits and vegetables. So usually on the right side we have vegetables, potatoes, broccoli, and onions. As you get towards the door, you see apples, strawberries, cucumbers. And then on the other side is the remaining produce like peaches, blueberries, and avocados. I mean it's not the traditional Russian food, right? But in terms of fruits and vegetables, we try to implement a little bit of our neighborhood's culture. So we have Russian yogurt, Russian desserts, Russian ice cream, and we'll mix it up with other traditions, like the Arabic food, baklava, and treats.

Some of them are Spanish too, 'cause we do have Spanish populations. It's not like the Russian community comes into the store and buys only the Russian produce. Some of them look at the Spanish food that we have and they're like, *Oh, that's a good thing. Let me try that.*

I'VE NEVER COME to work with such fear and anxiety until the coronavirus came along.

We've been really worried about the two bodegas in Brighton Beach, because some of our employees do have masks and some of them don't. They would just wear a bandana. Some don't wear one at all. We're just really risking our lives. I don't want to take this home either.

I've had several customers come to me and tell me one of the most drastic things that had happened in their life—a person passed away. People dying from coronavirus. I have a few of my friends that have gone from coronavirus. I think it's about being a listener too, which is what builds that community. Sharing with people what's going on in your life because it's not just you giving. Customers bring something to the business besides the business.

Now that we're one of the very few stores that are open twenty-four hours, I noticed not just people running away from each other and being germaphobic but people actually coming out and asking, *How are you? Do you need any help?* In every crisis—hurricane, tornadoes, any crisis—people tend to come together. I hope that one of the main lessons that these times are teaching us is to stay connected and hold on to the fabric.

Around March when they were talking about it, it wasn't taken as seriously because no one was really sure if it was true, the virus. But then towards April is when we started taking proper precautions as we try to learn from our customers. Our customers and our community teach us at the same time.

Our customers, we try not to touch their stuff as much as we can. So if they're paying by credit card, debit card, food stamps, we try to have them do it themselves. But unfortunately we have to weigh stuff. We have to touch the stuff. It's overwhelming. The gloves and the masks—it was like an extra layer on us. It's like wearing a winter coat in the summertime.

A lot of customers feel very uncomfortable with us touching their items, weighing them, after we've touched money. I try my best to change my gloves as much times as I can. But the amount of times I change basically reflects how many I have. I can't change them every hour if I don't have a lot. If I don't have any, I can only change them twice a day.

Sometimes I think coronavirus is within my hands. Or sometimes it's in the register. And that irks me so much because part of that comes with the disrespect customers give to us when they give us cash. Many of them, prior to this virus, would hand us cash. Now they just throw it at the counter. Literally, they throw it. Sometimes I'm fetching, like it's some sort of baseball. I'm like, *So do they have the virus and they're not admitting the fact? Or they're doing that because they think we're dangerous?*

What did they touch? What did they come in with? What just came out of their house? Where was this dollar bill last placed? We can talk financially, we can talk personally, we can talk socially, we can talk from all these different ends. But the main fear is, where has this dollar bill last been placed?

IT'S LIKE SURVIVAL of the fittest. Everyone is on unemployment, prices are skyrocketing high. A lot of things we don't even have, we can't get because markets are closed and those that we can get—there's a huge inflation, in terms of the prices gone real high.

Some people, when I tell them to put a mask on, you know where the mask is? It's in their pocket. So they just pull it out of their pocket. I'm like, So what's the point of you carrying it with you? It's meant to be put on your face.

These people, I would always ask them, *How are your grandparents doing?* They would tell me things about their grandparents. I would remember them as if they were my family. And now no one wants to have conversations anymore. Let's talk less and get home quick. It's so dead.

Obama once said that a change is brought about because ordinary people do extraordinary things, right? And I think at this moment we are the ordinary people. And we are doing extraordinary things.

CAMILA ORTIZ, an immigrant from El Salvador; **YESENIA MEJIA**, a house cleaner; and **MARTA FLORES**, an ultrasound technician

---

CAMILA ORTIZ: Inside of our house there was a small opening to the sky, and because it's El Salvador, and it's hot, plants grew underneath the opening, and they were green and lush with big leaves. For a five-year-old, it was a secret garden inside of the house. One year, for my birthday, my father brought home two cats. One was black and one was white and we named them Blanco and Negro. That same year he bought me a globe—at least in my mind it's the same year. When we decided to leave El Salvador, the most important thing to me was this globe. Were we going to bring it with us? How were we going to bring it with us? What would happen to the globe? And what would happen to this world that I knew as a child—running around my grandparents' house, being outdoors and free? I remember the hairs on the upper lip of the woman who sometimes cared for me, and her soft voice. I can hear her voice right now, its tender sound.

This is where we are, my father said when he showed me the globe. I remember being shown where we were going. I was fascinated by the way the globe turned. It was an opening into the world, this whole planet, this object that hinted at the lives of all these other people, all seen through a child's imagination. I don't think I fully understood what it was, but I started to imagine the journey with the help of my parents. This is where we are. This is the world. This is where we're going.

But I didn't truly understand. I left the globe behind when we went to the airport. We'd asked the woman who cared for me to come with us. She was all set, ready to go. She wanted to come to the United States to work. At the last minute it was too much, she couldn't do it. She said it had to do with her ear. She couldn't travel on the airplane because of the pressure, but it was because she was scared, she couldn't leave her family, she didn't speak English, and in retrospect she wouldn't have done well in New York, she was too anxious. My sister and I had been given dolls when we were born. We loved these dolls. The woman who cared for me came to drop us off at the airport, and I remember watching her cry. I felt so confused, and I thought, *I need to give her my doll so that she remembers me.* My sister couldn't believe it. *Why are you giving away your favorite doll?* I handed it to her and said, "You keep this." I wanted her to have it. Twenty-five years later, somehow we got back in touch and I went to the village where she lived. Her granddaughter was playing with the doll. It had lived a whole different life in El Salvador.

When we arrived in New York, my cousin greeted me at the airport. She was six, a year older than me. I got into my first checkered cab, and had to sit on the extra pull-down seat, facing my cousin. Aida started playing Miss Mary Mack with me. It was July Fourth, 1980, though I didn't know the significance of the day, and I remember looking away from her, out the window at these enormous buildings and feeling so overwhelmed, so I played hand-clapping games with my cousin but I was drawn, again and again, to look out the window. I felt tiny, I don't remember my parents in all this, or my sister, just my cousin, six years old, in the car, touching my hands, and looking at me. I'm sure she was examining me; she was curious. I've always thought of her as being so cool. This was her element, her city, she was a born New Yorker, she was the first human I felt connected to in New York. And all around me were these immense buildings. I bounced into the city on one of those pull-down seats. My mother used to dress us in matching dresses. I'm sure we had braids in our hair.

We went to live with my aunt on 65th Street and West End Avenue, where all those Trump buildings are now. It was fine, but back then it was a different kind of neighborhood, more isolated, and the Upper West Side was dirtier. We all lived in her apartment. At the same time, a woman, Yesenia, had come to New York. She was living in Miami working for my cousin for a bit but she came to stay in the apartment on the Upper West. My grandfather had helped her get into the country. She'd left behind her two daughters in her small hometown on the border of Honduras. They were close to the ages of my sister and me.

All I remember of Tia Cecile's apartment was this hallway. It felt dark and unknown, nothing like my secret garden. One moment stands out. My sister and my cousins went to do something else. They disappeared from sight. All of a sudden I was alone.

It's so strange. It's difficult to reinhabit the mind of a child. But the sense memory has never left me. This moment has come back to me over the years—at times where there's been an instance of abandonment, a friend choosing not to speak to me. It's a childlike response, a desperation, this sense of abandonment, when I trace back that memory, every single time, I see the apartment. All of a sudden I realized my parents weren't there. They were gone.

I found my way to the bathroom, went in, closed the door and locked it. The light was off. And I started crying, then sobbing, I was terrified. My parents had left me. They'd abandoned me, and I was never going to see them again. I sat in the corner, weeping and sobbing. It is only one moment, insignificant in the city, even in the life of the city on that particular day, I hadn't been separated from them for a week, or a month. But this moment has been with me my entire life. It always feels so present. I see myself sitting there, with New York outside, all those buildings I had seen from the cab. I would be alone in the immensity, in a place I couldn't comprehend. I was terrified. Who can say what separation does to a child?

Then something happened. I became aware of the world around me, the world outside the door. Finally, I heard the sound of Yesenia outside the door. She came closer. *Mi hijita, mi hijita*, she said through the door, my little daughter, my baby. Her accent was pure Salvadoran. I always think that about her. She coaxed me out. She held me for a long time. And then I remember being on her back. She gave me a piggyback ride down the hall, I was safe, and I distinctly remember being able to touch the ceiling with my hands as we walked.

Somehow Yesenia ended up coming to live with us. She shared a room with my sister and me. She loved me and still does. She taught me about love, about spirit, about kindness.

There she was, comforting me, this child, while her own daughters were back in El Salvador. She never knew what they were doing, she wouldn't be able to comfort them when they were alone. I can't imagine what that was like for her.

It's still tangible. That moment, I feel it in my throat.

YESENIA MEJIA: I lived outside of Candelaria de la Frontera when I was little. I left there at the age of nine when the woman who raised me, my mother, put me to work. I didn't go to school. I only made it to the second grade.

I lived in the countryside. So they sent me to the city. The woman I worked for was a good person. The house was one square block in Santa Ana. I would water the plants, sweep the garden, mop the surrounding area. My mother would go there to see me every fifteen days. They paid me two colónes per month. That would be about 25 cents. My mother didn't have a house. She didn't have anywhere to live. Sometimes she'd live with her sister or her brother. She would keep one colón and leave me one.

I was nine years old. I left when I was twenty. But that's where I learned everything: to wash, cook, set a dining table, make beds. Ironing, because there was no machine. I learned how to sew there as well.

Everyone woke up at 5 a.m. I worked, all day. There was no schedule there. They gave me a uniform, striped, with an apron. I would go to the market, to the beach. They sent me to San Salvador to buy the decorations to put on the dresses.

When I was young I would say, when I have kids, they won't have to go through what I went through. I had Lorena at twenty years, and Marta at twenty-six. Since I didn't have enough money for food, I had to leave them with my mother, and I would go to work. When I came to the US, I entered legally, of course. My daughters came illegally.

I always entered legally. I first went to Miami. It was another world. We went to Disney World. When I saw how beautiful it was, I began to cry, because I thought my daughters would never see that. The beauty. We had never seen anything like Mickey Mouse or all of those characters. They would come out from under the ground and start dancing.

My daughters would go to the public phone in Candelaria. They would call collect, and I would pay it. They would answer whatever I would ask. Remember, they were quite young. Lorena, I think, understood. The younger one didn't.

I was in the US two or three years. But then everyone returned. I did too. Since I liked business so much, I bought a stand at the market. I bought a house with the money that I had earned. I took $2,000 and put it as a down payment on the house.

I liked business a lot. But I couldn't do it there. I had to go to the United States, because there was no money. What happened was, Camila's nanny, she didn't want to come. That's when I came.

Her grandmother, she interviewed me. She said, "So you want to go over there? First, you've got to sign this paper." Like a contract, that I had to stay for five years. And I said, "We're not in Christopher Columbus times."

I didn't want to leave my daughters again. But there was no work.

I had to emigrate again. The younger one didn't mind as much. But the other one . . . She was sad, but they were going to be okay, because I had a store there. The older one took over the store from me.

They sold shampoo, deodorant, sodas, potatoes. And when she'd write to me, she would say, "Mom, thank God you are there, because the sales . . ." Nothing was selling.

Before I came to New York, I didn't know that snow existed. I thought it was a lie. I was sleeping in the middle of the night. Camila's mother said, "Yesenia, wake up. It's snowing." And I was in disbelief. I saw that it was true.

I would see it in movies. In the cartoons, especially. So I thought that wasn't something that was real. When we got there to 72nd, the 2 and the 3, I was shaking like crazy, because I was terrified of Black people. Because in movies, all Black people are villains. They're always putting on gloves, and I saw them doing it here.

The trains were old. They made a lot of noise. Camila and her sister slept in Aunt Ceci's house.

And none of the kids liked Camila—they made her cry. I would defend her. I remember the braids that I would do for her when she went to El Salvador. I learned that from a woman who had them. When Camila would go to El Salvador, she had her braids. People had never seen anything like that.

They all slept in the living room. I don't even remember where I slept.

I HAD SUNDAYS OFF. I would go to the lodge. It's a temple where you meditate. I felt alone at first. I never met any other Salvadorans. Just the family I worked for.

With my daughters, we would write to each other, or speak on the telephone. But in that era, my brother had a telephone, so my daughters were expecting my call. Once a week. I missed out on their lives. I missed a lot. My goal was always for them to study in school, because this is the country of opportunity. I couldn't have that opportunity, because I was already grown when I arrived, and I came to work. Also, I don't speak English. I never learned English. Never.

Instead of coming here to learn, I began to work. I would do the housework, the cooking—all of it. They never got upset with me, but Lorena did get ill because she was caring for her younger sister. The guerrillas were there. They would drop off murdered people right in front of our house. Perhaps they knew that she was the only one there, because she was left alone.

It was the guerrillas from the '80s in El Salvador. They killed—what do you call him—a bishop. Lorena got ill because the guerrillas were rounding up all of the nine-year-old children, and Marta was nine years old. So Lorena would tell Marta that when they came, you had to open the door for them, because if you didn't, they would machine-gun the door and take her away.

Lorena said, "I'll go with them." But she knew what would happen. If she had gone, the guerrillas would rape and kill her, because she was sixteen years old at the time. She would get headaches. Fever. My objective was for them to come here. They charged me $6,000 for each one. I had to pay $12,000. It took four years.

Oh, honey, I'm going to tell you something. We're not supposed to let others see those problems when we have them. My brother or my son can die, but if I'm with the family I work for, I put on a happy face, even though I may be crying inside.

I would cry at night, I would cry in the day.

The process began in the Rosicrucian Lodge. I met someone who told me that his aunt brought people from over there. They'd bring them legally, but with false passports. So he told me that he'd charge me $6,000 per daughter. I had to give him $6,000 up front, and when they were delivered to Kennedy airport, I'd have to pay $6,000 more.

To save the $6,000 I always did cleaning. I cleaned offices. I worked for a psychologist. All cleaning. Just cleaning. Four years. And then I saved $20,000. Because I would only have used clothes, things that were given to me.

I remember the day, everything that happened. They told me that they'd be leaving there at 9 a.m. And at 3 p.m., they were going to be here. I wasn't connecting with Lorena directly. The one who was in contact with her was the woman who was going to bring her.

They were going to arrive the same day.

I had to trust. I had to.

They went through immigration in Miami at the time. Poor Lorena. Her passport photo was of the lady's daughter. It wasn't Lorena's photo. Because her mouth was crooked, poor Lorena had to twist her mouth.

Marta was acting nervous from the lights. It's not so much the lights, but the fear they caused. They cut her hair to match the photo. And the girl from the photo had light eyes, just like Marta. So when she was with this person from immigration, Marta began crying. They asked, "Why is this girl crying?"

And the woman who was bringing them over said, "It's because we're going to New York to our sister, who has died. She loves her very much."

I don't broach that subject with her. We don't speak of the entry because it makes me feel bad for what they had to go through.

We were scared. We knew that it wasn't legal. We waited for them at the baggage claim area. When they arrived, I greeted them, and Camila's mother did too. We got their luggage. They said, I have to give the woman the other $6,000.

She was the wife of a diplomat. The woman and I went to the bathroom to give her the money. We had to count it, and people kept coming in. You find a way. She stood like this, and I stood like this, and we counted.

Then my daughters came walking down the stairs. Oh, honey. Lorena has always been a bit standoffish. She is not too affectionate. But the younger one is. We embraced. We were not supposed to make too much of a fuss. Because they weren't supposed to be my daughters. It had to be almost like we didn't know each other. They had cut their hair to match the photos. Lorena was already sixteen years old.

We stayed up talking all night. There in the living room, where we spent the night. And the next day, I went to work.

MARTA FLORES: I grew up with my aunt and my grandmother in El Salvador. I knew my mom was working in the US. She used to send money for the people that were taking care of us. We used to write little short letters, always the same thing over and over. *I miss you, I love you, I can't wait to see you,* things like that. It wasn't big conversations. When I came, I hadn't seen her for two years.

When we came here, my sister and I went to meet the person who was going to bring us. My sister was supposed to be her daughter and I was supposed to be a friend of the family. I had very long hair. The person in the passport had short hair, so they had to cut my hair. Before we landed, they gave us a pill so that we wouldn't be so nervous. When we came through immigration, they asked a few questions to the lady, because we were under age.

I didn't know any English. I didn't even know that *hi* meant, you know, hello. Coming to New York, I came to an apartment. I had a television, I had a tub. For a twelve-year-old, that was great. But then I went from going from home to school, back home, school, home, school, home, like that; it was nothing like going outside to play like in El Salvador. I went to a school that was close to my mother's job, not to my house. So I didn't have any friends.

I didn't get upset with my mom and lash out at her for leaving us, nothing like that. I understood. She never forgot us. I heard about so many other immigrants that come to the US and they forget about their children in their country and they left them to be raised by the grandparents over there. My sister and I were lucky that my mom never decided to just get married and have a family without us. She worked during the day and she worked during the night and I was always with my sister. My mom used to come in at one, maybe two, three o'clock in the morning, sleep for a little bit, and then go back out to work.

I asked my mom that all the time: *Why did you come to New York? Why not, you know, Texas or California where it's nice and warm? Why here?* She went where the job was. I strongly believe that the people that come here, they come to work, to provide for the families. I really hate when I hear people saying, "Oh, you know, they're taking the American people's jobs." Nobody wants to work in the fields. I don't think one of those white Americans is going to want to work planting corn or whatever. In New York you see it. In Brooklyn, around my neighborhood, there are always on the corners a lot of men waiting to be picked up to be given work. Can you imagine waking up in the morning, grabbing your bag—hot, snow, cold—just being on a corner waiting all day for someone to approach you? Maybe there's twenty men there and the car comes in and takes two.

If you work hard, you can accomplish, if not yourself, your kids, your children can accomplish. I tell my daughters that. My oldest daughter, she tells me, "Oh, I think I'm going to study what you're doing." And I say, *No, you're going to be what my boss does. That's where you have to aim. I did better than my mom. You're going to do better than me and your kids are gonna do better than you.*

My daughter wrote an essay for college, the essay you have to write when you send the application. She wrote it about my mom, about her coming here, things that she had been hearing from me when I'd speak to other people, things that she had heard from our talks. She wrote about what my mom went through in the civil war in El Salvador, about when we used to be taken out of buses because the guerrillas would shoot at them, about seeing people on the streets beheaded on our way to school. And she wrote about how recently my mom went to sell her house in the city of San Salvador, saying the last link that connects her to El Salvador is broken now.

I told my mom, and she was so happy that her granddaughter wrote an essay based on her life. I felt sad and happy at the same time because I never thought that she would be interested. But my daughter has a gift for writing. Her teachers always told me they see it for themselves whenever she writes—it's like they actually see what she writes, like it's happening to them. She wrote this beautiful essay that she kept on fixing. Every school needed a different amount of words. So she kept on adding for some schools and taking out for others.

I was afraid she might not get into a school. So I made her apply to so many different universities. She got accepted into every single one. Then it was like, where do you go?

11

Pandemic City

AMY HUGHES, a nurse at a Manhattan hospital; **DAN BAUSO**, her ex-husband; and **SIOBHAN CLIFFORD**, a nurse

Dan Bauso eventually got rid of the Nissan Quest that we'd driven around in, and bought another minivan. There was the same chaos in the back—court briefs and pizza boxes. He'd started working more in the Queens County Family Court as a family court attorney, and he reported even as the court started weighing whether or not to shut the building down as the coronavirus cases in New York began to rise.

AMY HUGHES: That Sunday night, Dan called. I was going on a reunion call of people who I used to work with in the ICU, but I thought, *Let me give him a call back first.* I hadn't touched base with him in a while and I wanted to see what was going on. So I called. When he said he had lost his taste and smell and everything, I was like, *Oh.* It went from a relaxing Sunday evening to no sleep that night at all. I was hypervigilant.

On the phone I said, "Listen, I know your history and I know you, so I really think you should just go in." I was trying to be pushy but casual. "I really think you should go get yourself checked out." He said he'd had two virtual doctor visits, but I told him, "Yeah, but they don't know you like I know you. So I think you should do it. At worst they would take a look at you and send you home." That's what I could only hope for.

He was like, "Alright. I'm gonna get myself ready. I'm going to go." I gave him about an hour and a half and I called him back and said, "So what's the news?" And he was like, "I haven't left yet." I didn't want to, but then I had a flare of anger. I said, "I really think you should go. I'm worried about your oxygenation." He was kind of low to begin with. And when he walked, his oxygen dropped even lower.

After that first phone call, I was physically shaking—because of the proximity, the close connection. I just wanted everything to be okay. I wanted to get him to someplace safe where somebody could take care of him, because I knew I couldn't.

I knew he was positive even before they had tested him.

DAN BAUSO: We left Kew Gardens, I don't know, maybe about 10:30 p.m.? Around 10:35 we walked down and the van was right there. There's silence, nobody on the street. I didn't have a lot of smell or taste, but I could feel. And I'm feeling the coldness and the dampness, you know? I remember in literature, for whatever reason, that cold is death, and dampness, and dankness. That's in our literature. That's where death is, in the tranquil. So that feeling hit me. The coldness of things.

Now, I'm not a Long Island guy, but LIJ is on the border. In fact, some of it is in Queens, so you couldn't really fault me. My mom, when she had a stroke, she convalesced at LIJ for a year and they did wonders with her. We've always had good feelings about LIJ.

So we get in the car, not a word is spoken, very quiet. I'm losing breath and I have a fever, and I'm getting some chills. My wife Kate was very motivated. She brings the GPS, and I tell her, just get to the Grand Central Parkway, I'll tell you where to go from there. A ride out to Long Island Jewish Hospital should take about thirty-five, forty minutes. We got there in fifteen. The starkness and the emptiness of everything around me was noticeable. There was nobody on the road, nobody on the highways. It was very eerie for a New Yorker who's used to the frenetic nonstop pace of life.

Then we pull into the LIJ, which is this huge complex, and we don't see anybody, there's more emptiness. It's a large hospital, been around for whatever, sixty years, it's from the 1950s. They've got a geriatric wing, a children's wing, it's huge. There is this vast parking lot. But nobody's there, there's no cars in the lot. This is strange. I said, "Go up to the front. I guess we'll see." I was nervous that since nobody was there they weren't going to take me.

At the front where the entrance is, there's two people, almost like guards. I was thinking they were lions or dogs at the gates of fucking hell. There are these two ambulances and they're parked on the sidewalk parallel to the hospital, so that the back of one comes up to the door entrance and then there's the door entrance unobstructed, and then the front of the other comes up to the other door entrance. And their lights are on, which is another ominous thing. No sirens, but their lights are on. I would later find out that they were there so people wouldn't bum-rush the hospital. They didn't want you to run in.

We pull up and someone comes out, fully hooded with a hospital hat and the gown, goggles, mask. It was almost like a specter. She says, all business, "COVID?" And we say yes. She looks at Kate and says, "Both?" Kate says, "No, my husband in the back." "Alright," she says. "He gets out; you got to go."

SIOBHAN CLIFFORD: The tidal wave of destruction brought by the COVID virus was fast and furious. The staff I work with had no idea what was going to be expected of us until we received an email asking about our nursing strength. I've been a nurse for over thirty years and have worked in many different departments. I did not feel prepared to work in an ICU but I wanted to help in the best way I could.

You come in the morning and they send you to where they need you. That was really hard. We do our own IVs and blood, which most nurses in the hospital don't do. Most of us were going in to see patients and drawing their blood or putting in an IV, but they were so sick they couldn't even take a sip of water. So then you're giving them water and you're sitting them up and washing them. Every room had to be on isolation. Every door was closed.

They had doubled up beds in rooms that never had them. Every floor was converted, except for forty beds that had people who just happened to be in the hospital but were too sick to get out. We were shifting people out as fast as possible. We were having people come in for their appendix who we were sending home within an hour. Doing the surgery, we're like, "You're fine. Just go home." Broken leg, broken arm; we'd do the surgery and within an hour we had them out of the hospital. We're like, "Go home. It's safer for you to be there."

Every nurse was overloaded on the floor. You'd have to make sure you had the protective equipment, which was in short supply in the beginning, and you didn't want to be in the room that long because we were afraid to get contaminated. Then you go in and some of these patients hadn't spoken to anybody and they were just in the room by themselves. The TVs weren't turned on. The windows, the blinds were closed because most of them had headaches. The lights were hurting them and they were just sitting in the pitch black alone for eight hours, sixteen hours, or twenty-four hours with no one to communicate with.

DAN BAUSO: So I walk into the waiting room and there's—I don't even know if they're nurses, they may just be attendants. They're all masked up and hooded. They give me a mask immediately. They tell me to sit down and give me a clipboard to fill out. I fill it out and give it back to them. I look around. There had to be thirty people sitting in that area, which was a lot. The first thing I recognized: everybody was limp. You know, you go to the emergency room, and some jackass is screaming all night 'cause he's got glass stuck up his ass or something. Here it was dead silence. It was extraordinary how quiet it was and how lethargic people were.

And then, as I heard the names being called, it was Singh and Khan and Peshawar. I couldn't make people out because they all had masks on. But it seemed to me that there was a number of local residents, Southeast Asians, New Yorkers, Americans: the neighborhood was representative of new New York.

In that area of Nassau, this is what's considered a border neighborhood, it's New Queens. I grew up in Old Queens. Old Queens, Woodside, you been around, you've seen those neighborhoods. They look like Manhattan or Brooklyn. They're old. They're close to the city. The working man lived there for all those years. This is way out. The edge of Queens on the Nassau border was farmland and swampland until the '50s. These neighborhoods have more of a Long Island feel to them, more of a suburban feel. Bigger houses, bigger yards, tree-lined blocks, more of a plan. Not many apartment buildings. Very nice, calm, quiet streets. The typical white ethnicities lived out there—Irish, Italian, German, Jewish, Catholic—but they've all gone. This neighborhood has attracted a lot of Indians. Well-to-do, not like working class, like Jackson Heights. This is where the Indian doctors and the Pakistani accountants live.

So everybody was COVID. They'd taken my oxygen level, they'd taken my vitals, they'd given me a mask, I'd filled the information out. I got some bad baseline stuff. I got some problems: I'm heavy, I got high sugar, I got hypertension, I had an A-fib in the heart, all that kind of shit. I had the fever and the shortness of breath, but it wasn't pronounced. I didn't know what this thing was doing inside of me, but so be it. I'm like, maybe they'll give me oxygen and I go home. There was no fear factor. I had had two virtual doctor appointments over the weekend. I gave them my symptoms and they were pooh-poohing it, you know? And I was like, ah, it's 100.3, it's not that big a fever.

The only thing I thought was wrong with me was the oxygen at this point.

I was alert. I was watching. They were questioning other people before me and there was this lethargy. They had to dumb it down to ask questions. I had a fever, but it's not raging, and I got the oxygen problem. And my oxygen was 92, which isn't terrible. It's not the best; it should be 96, 97. They didn't give me anything, so I'm like, what's going on? I heard them talk a couple of times, people came out, they're like, *Hey, he's got an A-fib, he's got hypertension. We're going to bring him in.*

And then a couple of times she said, "Someone's going to help you, someone's going to help you soon. We're just . . . It's very busy." I said, *Nah, it's fine. I'm fine.* I was almost like defiant like I wanted everybody to know, I'm okay, fine.

I called Amy early on in the waiting room. I was in, I'm gonna be okay. That was it. And she went to bed, everything. I was like, I'm fine.

I waited five hours.

A guy comes out at like 4:30 in the morning and says, *Bauso.* I'd been dozing. I say, *Oh, pardon,* and he's got a gurney. So I get in the gurney and they take me through . . . I mean, it's like nothing I've ever seen before. It's just people everywhere. They're just on gurneys, they're on chairs, they've got blankets over them. A couple of guys might've been dead because there were blankets over their fucking faces. I couldn't tell, and I wasn't asking any questions. But everybody's masked, everybody.

As the guy wheeled me on the floor, he had to move three or four bodies. They were alive. And again, no screaming, nobody's in there with a knife wound, nobody's in there with, you know, "I was playing Wiffle ball with my kids, and the Wiffle-ball bat got stuck up my ass." There was nothing comical going on. There was just all these lethargic, limp people. Many Southeast Asians, like who were in the waiting room with me. But it was diverse. There was old people, there was young people, there was Black people, and there was white people. Nobody was talking.

At like 5:00 a.m., there was a flurry of activity. Different nurses and PAs were coming by. I was like a NASCAR pit change. They took my blood, they took my temperature, took my blood pressure. Then the one guy goes, "Alright, you got a fever, 103." They give me a Tylenol.

The guy says, "Let's do your oxygen." It was holding steady at 93, that's a little low. "Alright, here's the big thing," he says to me. "We're going to take you for a walk, ten feet, ten feet back. Let's see what you got." I do ten feet, ten feet back. And the oxygen is 81 and dropping. This guy says, "Whoa, whoa, whoa, no, no, no, no. You're not going anywhere." I asked if he was going to give me oxygen and he's like, "Yeah, we're going to give you oxygen. Level four saturation. Not a lot. You're not desperate, but we're going to give you a level four and see how that is. And you don't need the mask." They give me the nasal cannula. It's the little clear plastic tube that goes around your ears and into your nose. So he does that.

I said, "Can I take this home?" He's like, "Well, we don't prescribe oxygen. We don't do that." I said, "My mom used to get it." He's like, "Yeah, well maybe, but we don't do it. You got to stay until you're better now." Alright, so just get used to it. You're going to be fine. I said, "Okay. I'm good." I had the Tylenol. They took the blood. Then they came in and took the chest X-ray, and then the nurse comes in and says, "Well, listen, we're not going to wait." The nose swab for the COVID, right? They did that. At one point I joked to the guy, I said, "Hey, you gonna rotate my tires and change my oil?" He's like, "You're funny. At least you're talking. Look, you don't know. This is fucking mayhem."

Then they gave me hydroxychloroquine, the controversial malaria drug. They gave me that and they took my blood. The nurse said, "You got good veins. Your blood pressure's good. A little high on the fever. And your oxygen, we gotta watch that and we're going to see about the COVID now that you're in." He said, "You're admitted. We just don't know where we're going to get you a room."

SIOBHAN CLIFFORD: I don't have a chance to find out their names. They're so sick you're really not even finding out anything about them. It's usually pages long of information the admitting nurse is getting. They brought it down to one page because it's too hard for these patients even to breathe. I'm trying to read their ID bands, you're lucky if you get that. I know nothing about these people.

You don't even know if they speak English. I can go in there and be like, do they know what I'm saying? Do they understand me? You say hello and they're not responding, but are they not responding because they're just so sick or do we need an interpreter phone to come in here with us? The universal: give them a glass of water. Everybody's accepting that.

I wish I didn't have to do this. I think it's going to affect all the nurses I work with for the rest of their lives. The amount of dead people they've seen, the amount of bodies they've had to wrap, the amount of people dying alone. You don't want to do it. You feel scared walking in the door, but we have to do it. But I'm a New Yorker, we're rough and tough and that's our personalities and that's kind of the way we even do nursing.

We're not afraid to do what you got to do and we do jump into it. Like when 9/11 happened, how the firemen and cops ran towards it. The same situation—we're all afraid, but we're not thinking of staying home and not doing it. You just go. The difference is with 9/11, once it happened, it happened. Where this . . . I feel it's harder, because you don't know when it's going to get you. I'm in my fifties, most of my friends are in their forties and fifties. We realize that we're not going to live forever. That this can bring us down as much as the next person. When you're in your twenties you don't ever think that, you're just going to run in there and you're not afraid or anything. We are afraid. But we're still doing it. And we don't know who: is it going to be a patient that brings us down? Is it going to be just walking in the hospital? So you're just so afraid of getting sick and ending up in that spot, but we continue doing it. It's, go back and you do it again when we're called to do it.

The world will never be the same. For the people who've gone through it will never be the same. There's no way. A few people have already said, are they offering counseling? Once this is done we're going to be right back going to work and saying just get on with life? I don't think people will be able to do it that easy. I've had nurses come into work, just start up crying or coming off shift, they start up crying, traumatized, and I've never seen people as upset as we have been.

The last time I worked, I was in with sixteen COVID patients. So sixteen times I had the chance of getting exposed and I'm like, *Why am I being put into this predicament?* But then you push that down, you say I'm here to help because that could be me or my mother or father at his bedside.

Last week I just happened to work with this nurse, I hadn't seen her in eight years and then we were put together. So on a twelve-hour shift we worked together and we were talking about how the COVID is, we feel, like the boogeyman. I think that's definitely an Irish thing. Growing up from my neighborhood, we'd always say that the boogeyman was coming to get you and you'd be afraid to go to sleep. You're afraid. We're opening the door of the patient's room and we're like, is this the boogeyman that's going to get us? Is this the time I'm going to get sick? So you're so afraid every time you're walking into the hospital and every bedside that you approach that this monster's going to get you, and you'll be the next one sick. It's like this unknown entity out there is ready to attack you and we don't know what it looks like, where it is, where it's hiding, but it can get you, so you're just afraid all the time.

DAN BAUSO: The oxygen was replenishing me. I sent out a text to my friends. We'd been chatting, there's like nine guys on this chain. We were on to the COVID, everybody's talking about COVID. We were chatting with each other. So I took a picture of my wristband and I said, "Listen, fellas, all jokes aside. The reality is I may have the virus and I'm in LIJ right now." They're all like, *Whoa, are you fucking serious?* And then one of my friends says, "Wait a minute, LIJ? My sister works there. What's your room number right now?" I told him not to bother her, but in my heart I'm like, *I want her here to cut through the bullshit and let me know what's really going on.* So I told him what room I was in and he's like, *She will whip you into shape, Bauso!*

Meanwhile the nurse had given me a bucket. "We don't want you walking anywhere. You gotta pee, pee in the bucket, ring the bell and we'll come and get it." I'd lost my appetite the day before, I couldn't eat anything, but I could drink. The water was refreshing. So I was shotgunning pitchers of water. I just kept drinking water and peeing it right through and everything.

I was exhausted. So I somehow curl my fat ass into the gurney with the oxygen and I fall asleep for about fifty minutes uninterrupted, maybe an hour.

When I get up, it's about six. I think the oxygen saved me. I think it was replenishing everything, my blood, my organs, everything. 'Cause I woke up feeling refreshed and the fever had broken. They came in and took my vitals, no fever, my oxygen's good. But I'm getting aided oxygen so I can't really hang on that other than to just say, *fine, just keep getting a good number.* I know they can't send me home just 'cause I'm good now after an hour. I know it's going to be maybe a day or two, but I really don't know much. Nobody's come to me. I'm thinking maybe it's not even COVID. Your head starts thinking a lot of different things. I still can't taste or smell so good.

The only sound in the emergency room was the very sweet sounds of nurses coming up to me, reassuring me, "You're looking good, you're going to be fine." I sent a message to the lawyers because I felt that obligation; I was in court with people and now I may have it. So I tell our head, I tell her, *Don't raise the alarm, I don't want to talk to a million people, but I'm in the hospital. I don't know what's going on, but I feel fine. I don't want anybody worried about me. I'm going to be okay. But you need to tell the personnel out and OCA because I was in that courthouse for a week. I'm trying to be a good citizen here. I got to let them know. You got to broadcast it.*

So that brought on like fifty million nice emails and nice texts: *Oh, Dan, we love ya. Blah, blah, blah.*

I do a family one, same thing. I'm like, *I'm doing great, nobody's got to worry. I just want everybody to know* . . . And my sister loses her shit, of course, but that's just who she is. So I go that route. I hit my friends. It's about seven o'clock, they're up now and everybody's signing in. You can only read so many "Oh, we're praying for you" messages. After a while you don't want to see that anymore. So now these guys are breaking my balls. *How many pallbearers are we going to need? Who's walking Nora down the aisle? Tell Kate to get her Tinder account up and running* . . .

The nurse does my vitals every three hours. Seven's turning into eight. Eight turning into nine. Nine is turning into noon. Then a meal comes, I can't eat it. The second meal comes, I can't eat and I'm like, what the fuck is going on. I'm not sleeping again on this gurney. Hours go by. Finally, at 10:00 p.m.—I got in there at 4:30 in the morning—they finally say, "We got a room for you." Thank God I got to get into bed. But they're like, "Yeah, we got a room for you, but you got to hold on." They're so overwhelmed, it took them three hours for transport. I didn't get to the room 'till 1:00 a.m., and the room they take me to is a birthing suite on the new wing of the hospital. The nurse was like, you'll see a doctor tomorrow. I'm texting with these guys and I'm like, "I'm in a birthing suite. They're hedging their bets. They don't know if I have the COVID or I'm going to give birth."

And then I went to sleep.

SIOBHAN CLIFFORD: When I went in to my patients, I'd try to spend an extra ten minutes just talking to them, helping them understand. Most of them were really short of breath. Everyone was afraid, that's the first thing you would see. You'd walk into the rooms and the fear was in their eyes. Everyone was just absolutely petrified. A lot of them were wearing oxygen. If it was a nasal cannula, that meant they were doing okay. If they had on a breather, which is the mask over their face with the bag, that meant that they were really having difficulty breathing. So, that's the step before being put on the ventilator. They would just be trying to catch their breath and coughing or being afraid to cough. A lot of them were scrunched on the bed, afraid to move.

I'm this tough New York nurse that would come in to them and be like, "You have to sit up. Sit up, get up, try to move around. You have to sit on the side of the bed, you have to cough, you have to get up." If they were too sick, they would just not even move, almost like they were catatonic, but they weren't.

I would start at eight o'clock in the morning and their breakfast was sitting there for an hour and a half outside the door, ice cold. It's as simple as, *Can I heat this up? I'll make your food hot or just make you a hot cup of tea, hot cup of water.* I'd try to get them to drink. They were so appreciative that I gave them fresh water in the morning. One man—he was really doing poorly, he was struggling the whole day. I went in the evening to do finger sticks. I was doing the diabetics and he was lying prone. If they were really sick they would lay them on their belly to try to help them with the breathing. And I went in and I was talking to him and he's panting away and I was just saying, "I'm here to do your finger stick and how you doing and you feeling okay?" And he's really struggling. He's like, "I'm feeling good." I'm thinking to myself, *How is this man feeling good?* He's barely able to breathe. And I'm like, "Oh, good, you're feeling better." And he said, "I feel better because you're with me." It broke my heart. I'm thinking, *Oh my gosh, this poor man . . .* "Do you have a phone? Can I try to call your family for you?" He's like, "I didn't bring my phone with me, I've been alone since Sunday." It was a Wednesday I was talking to him. By the time I left the room, they were getting ready to put him on a ventilator to help him with his breathing. That's usually a poor sign. I don't even know what happened with him, but I gave him that five or ten minutes just to talk to, so that he wasn't alone.

One of my friends, she was being sent into the rooms of patients who were doing poorly or being made ready to be put on the ventilator. She was given an iPad to call family members so they could see their family members for the last time via FaceTime. So if they got their phone number, they would call and she'd just hold the phone. People were saying their goodbyes that way. It was just so hard. Their families are saying, "Can you please tell them that we love them?" And they're putting the iPad next to their face so they can have their last goodbyes, even if the patient was out of it, just so they heard their voice.

DAN BAUSO: Now here's where the story starts. In the birthing center room I got to sleep, but not too much. I was awake, I was asleep, I was awake. It wasn't a good sleep, but I probably got to about eight o'clock in the morning. I'm waking up and this apparition comes through the door. Even with the hood and all of the costume, I can tell it's my friend's sister. She's like, "Dan!" Later on she said I didn't look so good when she first saw me, but she just said, "It's crazy here. You got in just in time." She was telling me it was 450 cases, now there's 500. The hospital only has 600 beds. When I left there was 720 cases. She said I was right at the start of the fucking wave.

She was like, "We're all COVID nurses, this shit's nuts. We're overwhelmed. People don't realize. But don't worry. I got you." The day nurse walked in, and she tells her, "We grew up together. Vitals are good." But she's like, "Yeah, Dan, this is a crazy thing. It's taking all kinds of forms and shapes. Wait 'till you hear from the doctors." And then she said, "Lungs, lungs, lungs. It's all about the lungs."

She got this idea of what's called an incentive spirometer. It's a breathing machine. You've seen it, you know, you suck the air in and there's a little ping pong ball or disk you elevate, you hold up for three seconds and that's a good sign, a sign of strong lungs. And if you do it ten times or whatever for five minutes, you're really in a good way. She told me she'd get one and bring it back before lunch.

Around noon, the doctors come in. Two doctors with masks on. It was hard to hear them, but they were very concise. "My friend," said one of them, "let's get down to business. You may feel fine, but let me tell you what's going on. You're positive for COVID. You have a smaller pneumonia on your right lung, on the top of your right lung. You've got COVID. We don't know a lot about this disease. It's really stumping us. But we do know some things. You probably had it eight to ten days. This is the time it's going to make its move on your lungs. Let me do your lungs."

So he does the thing with the stethoscope and he's like, "You sound good." I told him again that I felt fine and he's like, "You may be but this thing is in you and it could be regrouping and we have a million cases where it regroups and it's not pretty. It goes quick. And you get fever, vomiting, chills, and diarrhea. It happens pretty quickly. Not like a minute after each other, but like within an hour and a half. This could happen to you."

"You got a pill for me? You got a shot for me?" He's like, "No, we gave you everything we got." I said, "Whoa. What the fuck am I supposed to do?" This was the first time I was getting nervous. And then the other doctor chimes in. As calm and assassin-like as the first doctor was, she was the opposite. She's like, "You're too big, you're too big." It's actually kind of funny, she was making a belly with her hands. She brought her hands together to make a big "O" around her stomach 'cause she was slender. I'm looking at the other guy like, *What the fuck is going on here?* She sobered me up.

She points out the window and says, "Look out the window." At the other building catty-corner across. That's ICU. "We take you there, we put you on a ventilator. You're not going to do good. That's not good for you." I'm like, "Okay. What am I supposed to do here? Just wait for this thing to kill me?" The first doctor says, "No, no, no." He took over again. "Your lungs are good. Can you walk?" So I get up and walk. They do a check of the oxygen, 96. 96 it stayed. Very good. Then she's like, "Could you cough?" I start coughing, deep coughs, 'cause you've got to break the mucus up. They're afraid of the pneumonia. "Very good." But then she says, "Can you breathe deep?" I can breathe deep, but she's doing it in a way that I can't do it. She's doing it from her diaphragm. I don't have muscular control to do this shit. I'm a lump, you know. And she starts breathing from her diaphragm, from her fucking waist. She's like, "No, like this." And as she says this, my friend's sister walks in with the incentive spirometer and the doctor says, "That's even better. Can you do that?" I said, "Let me see." Oh, like a fucking home run. I would win at a carnival if this was a carnival game, I'm fucking sucking in, I'm keeping it up. She asks me to do it ten times. No problem. "Oh, very good." Then the first doctor takes over again and says, "So here's what you're going to do. You're going to keep getting the medicine. We're going to keep you on the hydroxychloroquine. If you don't have a fever, that's good. So no Tylenol." And then they changed face and said, "No fluids."

I'm like, what, no fluids? "We got new data. The new data is if your lungs are moist it likes that. Keep your lungs dry." I'm like, what the fuck? I could have two ounces an hour. Two ounces of fucking water an hour. Jesus Christ. But this is what they say. This is what I gotta do.

So he says, "Every hour, in the first five minutes, walk around. Second five minutes, cough. Third five minutes, do the incentive spirometer. We'll see you tomorrow." I'm thinking, *What, are they going to leave me here like this?*

My friend's sister says, "We just had a meeting. What they told you about the liquid? They talked about that. Also, if you've got to lay down, lay on your stomach . . ." I can't. My stomach's too big. Like I could lay on my stomach if you needed me to do it, like a planking-type exercise. But I can't sleep on my stomach. I can't. I sleep on my side. I made sure I sleep on my side. She's like, "Alright, sleep on your side. At least it's half your stomach." She said, "Which lung?" So she went and read the chart again. Now she had the whole chart. She was amazing. "It's your right lung, so don't sleep on your right side, 'cause then your body will be collapsing on the right lung and it might be spreading the inflammation. If you've gotta sleep on your side, sleep on your left side."

When she leaves I'm like, *I'll call Amy.* This was the only time I was scared. I told Amy what had happened. It was a bad moment. Amy's like, "Oh, okay." Real matter of fact. "Okay, you got a pneumonia. Well, that makes sense." She could tell I was distant. And this was the only time I cried. I just kept thinking of Nora and I . . . It wasn't a big bawl, I just like, you know, choked up in the throat. And Amy—it's the fucking Irish boardinghouse mother with the broom, that's who she is. Her approach is, *I'll nurse you back to health if I have to kill you.* She's just like, "Listen to me. So you think of her and you listen to me and you don't fuck around. You understand?" She wouldn't let me be sad. She got me angry. We solve problems.

"Listen, just do what you gotta do every hour. Nobody knows, Dan." It was a little sobering. I'm like, alright, alright. I'm going to do it. Amy said, "If there's a symptom, you can call me first. Call your nurse, you call your nurse. If she doesn't come right away, you call me. I'll tell you what to do if there's something that needs to be done."

When my friend's sister came back at lunch she told me about the mayhem. She said, "Dan, we're walking over bodies. It's really bad. I've got to close doors on these people and they're screaming, *Just stay with me.*"

Thank God I had this phone and I kept charging it, you know. And then she's like, "And I'll try to get to you tonight. I thought I could get to you more." I said to her, "You've done so much, you don't even know." But let me tell you, I was a good patient. I didn't need anything. I wasn't eating. I wasn't complaining for food.

The doctor had also said to look for vomiting, fever, chills, coughing, or diarrhea. He said, "You got to get the nurse right away if you get any new symptoms. Other than that, they'll check your vitals, do these little stupid pet tricks that we want you to do and we'll see you tomorrow. We know this, people who have good immune systems are beating it." And I looked at him and I said, "Doc, I know I'm not in good shape health-wise and I got to lose weight. But I never get sick. I don't wear a coat in the New York winter. I don't get colds, sore throats, fevers." And I remember him looking at me saying, "Good, that's good."

And then he walked away.

AMY HUGHES: It's funny how people are like, *I could never do what you do.* It's just very natural for me. From when I was four or five years old, it's something that I always wanted to do. And I always consider myself lucky because I actually love what I do. I've been doing it for now thirty-two years. Sometimes I can get miserable about the situation, but I absolutely love what I do.

I am in such a specialized hospital. Not only are we trying to take care of the patients that are COVID-positive, we're trying to keep our own health-care workers safe. A lot of redeployment is going on and it makes you almost feel like you're in wartime, where people would say, *I'm being deployed to here* or *I'm going to the front lines.* ... When you hear that, you know you're going to be taking care of very sick patients, seeing a lot of things that you've never experienced before. So it's a whole new world for nurses. Everybody asked me how I was feeling as it was ramping up. I said, *I'm appropriately nervous.* There's reason to be nervous.

Sleep hasn't been good for any of the people I work with. We all talk about it. I'm having strange dreams. Even while you're dreaming, you're still trying to move forward and figure out how I can help. How can I do something? I remember being in the dream, with people all around me, and saying, *We have to figure this out.* I'm trying to mobilize everything, trying to get everything working, even while dreaming. Then I wake up.

Being a mom and being a nurse, you're able to wake up and be as aware of your surroundings as possible. You feel like you're always on. Somebody will always need you. In the dream you're fighting so much to try and work it out. You wake up in a kind of confusion. Where am I? You don't know where you are because you're so entrenched in the dream. You're thinking that you are fighting at the time. Then you wake and you're like, *Okay, it's all okay.*

Not only are you overwhelmed, but you still have to go back in the next day. We're getting updates in the hospital every day, sometimes twice a day, about what we should be doing, what we can't do. They're trying to give everybody as much information as they can. Okay, now we know this, so we have to do it *this* way. We're learning as we're going.

I get up about 5:30, six o'clock. Get dressed and get ready and my partner's here and it's a funny thing: the time when you need hugs and kisses the most is the time when you can't even give them to the person you're living with. You have to keep away from everybody as much as possible. You don't know what you're going to be facing as the day goes on. So it's a big sigh when you wake up. You're like, *Okay.* And you get on your way.

Driving into the city can normally take over an hour. Now it takes me thirty-five minutes, because there's nobody on the road. You do see some people, and as a health-care professional you want to roll down your windows and start screaming, *Go put a mask on!* It's very eerie. It seems like a continuous Sunday morning, a quiet Sunday holiday in the city where not a lot of people are around. There's not a lot of movement going on. One of my favorite books was *The Stand* by Stephen King. There's so many times where it reminds me of that, where there's just the survivors around.

At work, you hear about certain people, almost like a roll call. You know, this person is positive, that person's positive. Their appointment's canceled. And then you're worried. I found out last week one of the colleagues I was working with had tested positive. There is a lot of paranoia about your own health and safety. You wake up with a dry throat because you had the heat on and you're like, *Is this it? Do I have it?* The diligence that you put towards taking care of your patient, you have to turn it on yourself now to make sure that you're okay to go in every day.

I eat at my desk. I bring lunch in. You want to order out, but you don't. I've just been keeping to myself and trying to eat by myself. I've even heard some nurses will go eat in their car. You don't want to infect anybody or catch anything. You almost feel like self-isolating yourself as much as you can at work. It is such an antithesis of what nurses have to do. We want to go and help people. Anybody who is sick could potentially get you sick and you could potentially get somebody else sick. So you have to take a step back and then, you know, try and direct as much as you can from a distance.

It's a gut punch every time. As a nurse, your first thing is the power of healing, the power of touch, how you can connect with somebody. And this is taken away. When we interact with our patients, you have to put on the gown, gloves, mask, double mask, eye coverings . . . You have to do that to go in to see the patient. You can't be in there as long as you want to be in there. You want to reassure somebody and yet you have to make sure that you're keeping yourself safe. It's such a hard thing to do. As a cancer nurse, I've had to hold people's hands so much. And now you can't.

DAN BAUSO: I think this is where I disappeared. I just was like, *I can't.* I'm all alone and I start to have this philosophical moment of thinking, *This thing may come and kill me.* I wasn't happy about all the lethargic zombies I was seeing at every turn, but I didn't feel like that. So I wasn't empathizing with them. I was like, *You're fucked. I'm not.* And now the doctor had basically told me, you know, this could be you in half an hour. He gave me a mental image of the virus swimming around in me, making up its mind. It doesn't know if it wants to take on the fight and go after you, but if it does, it could ravage you. This is what they leave me with and now I start thinking, *Holy fuck.*

I got scared on the phone with Amy because I was thinking of my kid. Then she yelled at me, and I didn't get scared anymore. I did the fifteen minutes of the doctor's tricks and I sat down and I got angry. I said to myself, *This is not the way I was supposed to go.* I started thinking about who's going to figure out my practice; I'm owed so much money, I have open accounts, I've got clients that need papers filed. My kid, I just finished paying off her tuition. I don't have the nest egg for her. I don't have the wedding for her. This dance is not supposed to end for me.

This is not supposed to be me. I get it—I'm going to go eventually, I'm not fighting fate. So I'm talking to God a little bit. I'm like, *I know I gotta go.* We all gotta go. And I know we can't necessarily control it— but I need to have one more time at the bar. I need to be at Uncle Nick's and have his tomato sauce one more time. I get it, it's coming. But not like this. You know how many people haven't seen me in months, just because that's the way we get in our lives? It's nobody's fault; that's the way adult life is. You get wrapped up in work and you don't go out. You don't see people. You see them at the next christening or the next wake.

So first there was this anger, but I got off that quick. I was thinking, *C'mon, Danny, you got to stop it now. You've got to come up with a fucking plan.* 'Cause that's been my whole life. I've been through adversity. I'm not trying to say I'm the most rags-to-riches story ever. But I had some tough times.

So I made a plan of people I had to call. Nicky, thank you. You're the business. You've got to talk to this lawyer. My files are in my office. You got to lay out for the funeral. You get a benefit going, right? And then there were the women—Kate, Amy, my daughter, and my sister. I had to tell them I loved them and how they were the best things that ever happened to me. The last call was going to be Nora. She was going to get two calls. On the first one I was still going to be upbeat, optimistic. It was like, *Listen, I might've got a tough pitch to hit here, honey. I'm going to try to hit it. I just want you to know that I love you no matter what happens. They've still got faith, so you got to keep the faith . . .* You know, I was going to say some tough things. *I'm on your shoulder. You're going to have a million dads if I'm not there. You're going to dance with all these guys at your wedding and it's going to be my dance . . .* It was just streaming out of me, you know.

And then I was going to give Nora the second phone call. I was going to tell her, *Listen sweetie, you're going to hang up, I'm going to call you right back, but I don't want you to pick it up.* And the purpose of that was so that she could have my voice, you know. This is who I am. I'm a memorial type of guy. I'm a remembrance of times past. I'm Woodside, I'm New York, I'm the Boys' Brigade, I'm fucking Saint Sebastian's. I'm all those things. That's who I am.

I'm not looking to be on a dollar bill, but I don't want to be wiped off the face of this earth without being heard from. I don't mean for the whole world, but for *my* world. My world, my city's got to have one more fucking dance with me. That's how I'm thinking. My crowd, my friends, my people, one more night where we scream and yell and dance. When you get called on the carpet and you know this is your life, you gotta be who you are. That's how I fight. That's how I reduce this thing. I had to put it on my terms, on my level.

So now I've got the plan. I've got all the people I want to call. I wrote it down. And then I say, *I'm not calling anybody, 'cause I'm not scared. I'm checking out.* Now I'm dealing with this. The last all the troops heard was, *I'm fine*, and I'm gonna leave it at that until I've got to make these calls. The doc had said it wasn't going to be like I sneeze and I fall over. He said it was going to be a progression. Maybe quick, maybe an hour and a half. The fever will intensify over an hour. The vomiting will start. So the minute I get a fever, I'm making the calls. I'll have time. So I get up and I do the exercises again. I walk, I cough, I blow into the machine. I have no problems with anything. No symptoms.

Now I'm getting angry again. I'm getting pissed. They always say it's okay to talk to yourself, just don't talk back—because that means you're crazy. That's bullshit. Everybody has voices in their head—their internal voices, that comfort them and move them, right? That voice in your head, that's you leading yourself to a place, and I needed to get there. My unconscious or whatever you want to call it, my animus, my spirit. My conscious voice talking out loud was saying, *I can't believe this shit. I can't believe I gotta be here like this, all alone—in a fucking birthing suite? What the fuck?* And then the voice, the anchor voice inside of me, that raises things, engages things, the spirit, the animus, says, *Hey fuck-o, you're not alone.*

And I'm like, *What?* I'm having this conversation with myself. *You're not alone. You're here in the chair. This fucking bug is inside of you.* I'm like, *That's right. You motherfucker, show yourself. Show yourself!* Then I put the chair in front of me, and I started talking to the virus. It was maybe five, six o'clock in the afternoon. It was right on the hour when I came up with this. I walk, I cough, I do the machine, I sit down. Then I said, *Alright, get over here, fuck-o. Who the fuck do you think you are? You're going to come and do this? You don't want to take me down, bro. Move on. You got off on the wrong train station.*

I've got all that swagger, I feel like De Niro for a second. You know, like in *Goodfellas*. This is who we are. That's part of being a New Yorker. I mean, I know we're blowhards and peacocks, we all got that swag and we all fucking talk that yak and everything else, whatever neigh-

New Yorkers

borhood you're in, whatever ethnicity. We're all characters, we're fast talkers, we're hustlers. And it's coming out of me. I'm not talking with it, I'm not having a conversation with it, asking it to please spare me. I'm like, *Motherfucker, show your face! You don't know who I am. Bro, I'm from Woodside.* I kept saying that at first. *I'm from fucking Woodside! You got off on the wrong stop, bro. Get back on the 7 train. You don't want this shit. You don't know what I'm like.* And then this morphed into, *You want to know me? You think this is going to be an easy job? You get to know me.*

I used to say this when I was younger, *I'm Patsy's son.* And I thought of who surrounded me, the strong women, my mother working two jobs, cleaning, working 'till midnight. We'd call mom after dinner at my aunt and uncle's, so she was happy because we were well cared for. She was doing what she needed to do. That strength. I don't know why I went there. I went there. And I thought of my friends. We got a crowd, we got my homeboys. It's endemic to the boroughs. This is too big a city to go out there alone, one of eight million, so you always got a crowd, you go out with your crowd, you know.

I said to it, *You can't carry me. You made a mistake. You got to go. Beat it.*

I told it about New York. For some reason, I stayed in the 1970s and '80s, which was my adolescence into my late teen years. *The Lords of Flatbush.* That's what New York had. *The Warriors*—it was a joke in a sense, the way they made it—but that's the way New York was. I kept this going for maybe an hour. At some point I kept saying, *Come know me now. Let's see who it is you know.*

I started showing it pictures of things. I started googling things. I had a picture of Saint Sebastian's, a picture of Donovan's. For some reason, I went to David Letterman, showed it Letterman when he was the craziest. There's some crazy guests, New York guests, that he had on that people don't remember: Brother Theodore, Calvin Trillin, Quentin Crisp, and these Village freaks. Brother Theodore was the first clip I watched. He was this Village icon, a maniac, a German guy who would put on one-man shows and he was insane. That's who Letterman was the first several years. For whatever reason I was staying in those years. I was telling the virus all of this. I'm like, *This is who I was.*

Hours go by. And then I got into sports. I did every team that I loved. I did the Rangers. They were always a day late and a dollar short and they couldn't beat the Islanders, but I had to go to the Cup. McTavish is doing the last 1.5 seconds and Sam Rosen is calling it. "And this one will last a lifetime! No more curses. This is unbelievable." The place is going fucking crazy. You know, I'm skating past it now. I'm like, *Messier, Messier,* I'm screaming at the chair. All the while I'm like, *You can't keep up with this, you can't keep up with me.* I said, *I'm a kid here. I'm a kid. You can't keep up with me. You don't know what I'm about.*

Then I did the Mets—the Mookie Wilson / Bill Buckner play in 1986, the year they won the World Series. One hour started with it. When I had to do my five minutes of walking, I didn't just walk; *I was Mookie.* Swinging the bat and running past the chair in that birthing suite as the scene played, and I was going along with Vin Scully in my head. The famous Scully call is very sequential: it's five things that Scully says, and each one rises in crescendo on the call. "Little roller up along first." That's one. "Behind the bag." That's two. "It gets through Buckner!" That's three. "Here comes Knight!" That's four. "And the Mets win it!" And then he goes silent and he lets the crowd take over. So I'm doing it, but I'm adding a sixth line. I'm swinging like Mookie and I'm running past it and I'm going, "Little roller up along first . . . Behind the bag . . . It gets by Buckner . . . Here comes Knight . . . And the Mets win! *Fuck you!*" I'm giving the virus the "fuck you." I must have done that for an hour. That fucking virus was holding its head like Buckner.

I love this city. I don't think there's any city in the world I would rather be in, you know? I'm like that E. B. White article, "Here Is New York." He said it best. It's like a patchwork quilt of small towns stitched together, but it makes up the whole. And I love the whole. I've worked in every borough, but you know that 7 train always takes me home.

And I suspect people are like that from all over. You're from the Bronx? You're very proud you're from the Bronx and whatever ethnicity or nationality, I think everybody thinks of Manhattan as the City and we all own that. We all have a piece of that. The towers are all ours. The Empire State Building is ours. Radio City's ours. It's everybody's. But you take the train out, you take the bridge and the tunnel out and you go to your borough. The sun rises and sets on your borough.

So I'm showing it pictures, I'm dancing, I'm singing, I'm Mookie. I had maybe three, four hours of sports. I was getting tired, not symptomatic, but I was doing this late into the night. It was like two or three in the morning. And I remember saying, *I ain't going anywhere. This city ain't going anywhere. Look at me. You think I'm sleeping? I ain't sleeping, bro. I'm the fucking man.*

I remember saying, *You're not getting it. You dumb motherfucker. Start to get it, bro. This isn't happening.* It's three in the morning. I don't even have a fucking sniffle. *My family's here, my family's got my back, they're with me right now.* I was like, *They know me. You don't know me.*

And then for the last song—this has to be about four in the morning—Steve Winwood just showed up. "Back in the High Life Again." This became the theme song. I played it the next two hours. I just kept playing it. I played it 'till my head was gonna pop. And that's what I said. It's like the symptoms weren't coming and I just felt like every hour and I'm like, *I'm going to be back in the high life again.* He sings about the doors opening up again.

I just kept singing it. I kept singing it to the chair. This must have been about three, four, five in the morning. I never slept. I refused to sleep on my stomach, or my side, even though they said I could. I was afraid to go to sleep. I felt that doing this kept it at bay, like I was beating it up. If I fell asleep it would make its move. I know it's a silly thought. But it's just what I thought, you know? So I didn't go to bed and I just kept saying, *We'll be back in the high life again.*

And then I stopped. I don't know why. Probably because I just was tired and you can only act so long. About five in the morning I stopped.

SIOBHAN CLIFFORD: A friend of mine was given the job of working with the morgue, calling family members up to tell them their family members had passed away. They might have been dead for two days, three days. They were just getting notified then. There was no time even to call the family members. No one was allowed in the hospital, no visitation, no one was there. So everyone died alone, which is absolutely heartbreaking. Even if you weren't on a vent.

When a patient passes away from COVID, once the body is picked up by a funeral parlor, they have to be closed-coffin. They're not allowed to open the coffin again. So family members were not able to say goodbye. Didn't see their family member die if they were their mother, father, brother, husband, or wife. And then when they went to the funeral parlor, they weren't seeing their body either. It had to be closed, so there's no closure. There are no goodbyes.

DAN BAUSO: The next day, I had no symptoms. Tuesday, no symptoms. By Wednesday I'm through it. I'm just a little nervous. Wednesday's uneventful, I even paid for the TV, watched TV Wednesday night. I mean, this is crazy. So then the oxygen. Get up Thursday morning, I could eat a little Thursday. I had cereal. Cereal and some food. Still not so much. I probably lost twenty pounds. The last day I got a great nurse named Edwin. And he gets the 411 that I'm probably going home.

The doors around me were locked. When they would open the doors, you would hear the moans, you know? My friend's sister would tell me this after. She didn't want to scare me, but she's like, "Dan, nobody was going home. I didn't want you to know that." I was glad she didn't tell me. I stayed upbeat the whole time. Edwin knew there was a good chance I was going home, so he was all over me. He made sure. I had to give blood for cultures. They needed my blood walking out the door. They took my blood. Edwin took the oxygen off me at noon, 3:30 comes back. We walk. 96 to start, 96 to end, no oxygen. He's like, "Oh, bro, you're great. We got to give you a blood culture and then you're going home." He gets me ready. Everybody's happy. So Edwin comes to get me. I put on my sweatpants and I hear a bell ringing.

A bell rings like a PA bell, and a voice comes on and says, "We're happy to announce we are sending a healthy patient home to relax and get even more better," or something like that. And everybody in the hallway, the nurses, the orderlies, the transport guys—I can hear it 'cause my door is open now I'm leaving—everybody's clapping. You could hear it out the window. Everybody across the way. The whole hospital's clapping.

Edwin comes in. He's like, *You ready?* "What the fuck is going on?" And he says, "That's for you. Bro, we need it. We need good news." I said, "I've been here since Sunday. I haven't heard that bell once." He said, "Dan, you're the first guy that's going home this week." That hit me. I sat down and said, "Edwin, give me a minute. I gotta take a breath here." Since the brawl with the virus, this was now almost a day and a half later. I'm more than ready to go home. I could have walked out of there, but protocol is they put me in a wheelchair. Edwin was so good, he's like, "Listen, here's your medications and your discharge."

I got a mask on. Kate was waiting outside.

SIOBHAN CLIFFORD: At my cousin's hospital they play, overhead, "Here Comes the Sun." That goes on the intercom so everybody knows there's another COVID patient going home.

Everybody leaving gets clapped and everyone cheers that we have somebody leaving, which is a really good feeling because normally you are only hearing STAT, code blue, anesthesia STAT bedside. I was working I think Tuesday and Thursday, it probably went off at least every half hour, maybe every fifteen minutes, sometimes either every five or ten minutes for the full twelve-hour shift. That's what you heard calling overhead. And everyone from the cleaning people to the doctors knows that means one more person is in distress. It really got to you. Code blue is patient not breathing. Anesthesia STAT means that they have to rush to the bedside to intubate a patient. Emotionally it's just really, really draining.

So that's the reason why they started doing the bells and the songs—for the staff to know that there are people going home, people are improving. Just to give you a sense of positivity in your job.

AMY HUGHES: A girlfriend of mine lives on the Upper East Side and every night she posts on Instagram about the seven o'clock clapping. So, I was dropping something off at hers and it was just about almost seven o'clock. Where I live, in the Rockaways, it's very wide open, so I don't know if people are doing it as much, but in her neighborhood, right outside her window, she gets it a lot. I said, I think I'm going to stay for it.

At seven o'clock, everybody starts clapping and screaming and banging drums. It's deafening. She's right by 85th Street, and there's a little bit of a downward hill there and then it goes up again, so you feel like you're at the bottom of a bowl and you're listening to it all around you. That's what I did. It was amazing. I was standing there, turning in a circle, taking it all in. With my mask over my face, but a big smile on my face.

There was one person banging a garbage can top. It was so loud, it was startling. It had been so quiet and then all of a sudden came this thunderous sound. And as the cars are coming over the hill, down First Avenue, they were all honking their horns too. Everybody's participating in it. People were hollering. There was one woman clapping clapping clapping. She's like *Woooo!* every five seconds or so. And you think it would stop, but she kept on doing it for the whole minute. I got out of the car, right on First Avenue, and I was listening. It really . . . It meant a lot. When it died down there was somebody who was in a lower window and I said, *Thank you.* And she said, *No, thank you.*

I was getting choked up, I was starting to tear up. A nurse never goes into nursing for the accolades or for the back pats or anything like that. I've worked in the ER, or urgent care—which is our emergency room. You take care of these patients, you do what you can to help them at the moment, and they move on. That's what you want. It's always a joke when patients say, *Don't get me wrong, but I hope I don't see you again.* I don't get offended by that at all. I hope I don't see them again either.

Afterwards, I got back in my car and I was like, *Well, that just made my week.* I just needed that. And it was . . . perfect. It was very flattering.

But a nurse would never let it go to their head.

INTERLUDE

Another Sunday
on the Street

ONE FREEZING NOVEMBER EVENING, after I'd spent nearly a year of Sundays with Joe at the Welcome Table on 16th Street, I invited him back to my apartment for the first time. The temperature had dropped, and I didn't like saying goodbye at the end of the afternoon. Joe stood next to me, bent over, on Sixth Avenue. The crowd passed. It seemed like the same people on repeat: sunglasses, new jeans, rustling bags. He refused at first, then accepted, then we haggled over how best to get to my apartment. Joe had a suitcase with him, and a stuffed bag.

"We'll get a cab," I said. "It's a celebration."

When we got to my apartment, Joe sat down at the kitchen table. I found a playlist called 60s Favorites. I poured out some chips. I poured him a glass of water. He looked around. He told me he couldn't tell much about me from the apartment because it was furnished with the possessions of other people. I lifted a magnet on the fridge and passed him the photo of a beach near where I lived. In the photo I'm lying on an expanse of sandstone reading a book.

"Look," he said. "You've got that rock beneath your head."

"Did I tell you about the rock I stick beneath my head?"

"Yes, you did," he said.

"You remember the rock?"

"I remember everything. Is *that*," he asked me while pointing at the photograph, "the mainland you can see across the water?"

"No," I said, "it's another island."

I pulled a plastic bag full of carrots out of the fridge. They were misshapen and dirty, so I washed them, started peeling.

As he sat at the table, I cooked the carrots and onions. I stirred up chicken broth in the big plastic cup.

"Why did you come back to New York?"

"I was a coward," he said.

His aunt was sick. He left Pittsburgh anyway. Whenever he used to return to Pittsburgh, she had been his welcoming presence. She had taken the place of his mother. She'd swat his head, reprimand him for this New York business. New York wasn't where he belonged.

"I committed New York–icide," Joe said.

I poured him a bowl of the soup from the blender.

"It's hot," he said.

"It is."

"There's a bit of kick to this."

"I put in two tablespoons of curry powder."

"You got me to eat curry? You curried me?"

"Do you want some rice?"

"I'm an American," he said. "I eat potatoes."

We ate the soup, slurping away.

"This is good," he said. "You believe that?"

BY JANUARY A ROUTINE had formed. On Sundays we took a cab from 16th Street and Sixth Avenue. On the journey we talked about possible eye appointments, or at least the potential of an eye appointment, and sometimes just the benefits of getting rid of the glaucoma.

On some visits, I sat with Joe before going to bed. The room was lit with little more than the peripheral glow of the city. From my window I could just barely see the faint lights of the Empire State Building uptown. I'd become fixated on the lights of the tower. How were they hung? Who put them there? Shouldn't I speak to the person who stood out there in the wind and lit up the city? Shouldn't I speak to everyone? Just that week I'd gone from the home of an eighty-something on Roosevelt Island to Washington Heights to wander along the boardwalk with a young Russian who'd moved back in with her mother. It was both overwhelming and exhilarating. I would trace my map and invoke the day's set of new names: Norwood, Allerton, Pomonok, Auburndale, Floral Park, and Bellaire. There were always more neighborhoods to visit, more people to talk to.

"I had a good day today, Craig. You know that?" he'd often say. He said it quietly. Then he started his evening preparations. He stuck a pair of jeans under the mattress of the day bed in my front room before he went to sleep and said, "That's what they call the Joe press."

One evening I made pork chops and put on some music from his era while I chopped vegetables.

"All this music happened when I was in Vietnam," he said from his usual seat at the table. "You remember that movie *Good Morning, Vietnam*?"

I said I did.

"On the lines," he continued, "in your perimeter, you had three strands of barbed wire, right? You got razor wire, concertina, and barbed wire. And you would see red cans tied on them, with a couple pebbles in each can. The can's going to rattle if they touch the wire, like twenty feet away. We'd just light it up. Up in Khe Sanh, you'd see North Vietnamese, dead or dying, hanging in the wire, and you'd see rats on their hind legs jumping up for people's cheeks. Gnawing at them, hanging in the air, with their teeth sunk in the cheek, chewing."

I stopped cutting the carrots and said something about how he really knew how to get the dinner conversation going. But I didn't want to hurt him, so I added that he had such strong memories of this time.

"Yeah," he said, "how come?"

"Because it's right there."

"It doesn't go far, does it?"

I asked if he paid the same sort of attention to the landscape around him, the blocks he knew heading east from Park Avenue and 23rd Street. It was his territory, after all.

"You're busting my chops," he said.

"I'm serious."

"You're serious?"

"What did you call it? It was a military term for those streets."

"A-O-R," he said.

"What does AOR stand for?"

"Area of . . ." Joe paused.

"Responsibility?"

"Yeah, you hit it. 23rd is the northern perimeter. 23rd, from Third to Park. South, it goes to 22nd. One block. But it will go from 22nd and

Park down to, say, Third Avenue. So really, it's a block this way, three blocks that way. That's my spot."

By now, I'd been with him many nights on his "verandah," at the entrance to the waxing center. I'd seen him in the different seasons, wrapped from head to toe.

"There's a guy," Joe said, "head maintenance man for the hotel. He holds for me—it's a mattress encased in plastic. That place, the waxing center, closes at nine o'clock. So they're gone. They have that ramp going up, you know? And the railings—I put my cardboard on there. I don't want people looking in there. First, I'd put plastic on the ground. Then I would put cardboard. Then I would put the mattress down," he said.

I asked him about some of the sounds.

"I guess I block them out," he said. "I know when it's four o'clock because delivery trucks start coming. That place is next door to me. They come and pick their garbage up. So I hear the garbage truck pulling in. That will wake me up. And once I'm up, I'm up. I'm not going back to bed."

"Do you lay awake for a long time?"

"Sometimes two hours I'll lay there."

"Thinking about what?"

There was a pause. I cut the vegetables.

"My situation," Joe said. "I'm not being facetious or smart with you, but what else do you think I'd think about? My position. My fate, or lack of. Lack of fate." I looked over and saw him spread his fingers out on the table.

I asked him what he heard people saying as they walked past, if he ever heard their voices. "You hear everything," he said. "People say, 'Aren't you worried, staying by yourself? You're not a young kid anymore.' I tell them the truth: *No, I don't even think about it.* I don't lay there with a knife or a pipe or something. My *mouth* sometimes . . . Somebody will walk past and I hear, 'Oh, we oughta.' I'll say, *Yeah, why don't you? Why don't you do it?* Most times, the people with the guy that opened his mouth will razz him. 'He ain't going for what you're selling.' Like they're on my side, you know? So the guy that runs his mouth, he'll shut up. That works in my favor. To me, if you lay there and don't say anything, you're making yourself a target. But if they see there's somebody there, they'll think twice."

Once he'd been lying there when someone said, "Is that even a person?"

He said he doesn't like to make eye contact with people.

"Why not?"

"Cause it's embarrassing, Craig. Come on. Living on the streets? I'm not part of society. . . . Craig, come on. I don't feel I should have to explain that to you, 'cause I feel you know it."

"That kills me," I said.

"What *kills you*?" he replied. "That I would say that? It's true."

"You're not outside of my society. You're part of my life."

"And I appreciate that, but Craig, I'm not part of their lives. I'm just a part of New York. I'm a piece of paper on the street. That's all. Believe me. That's all I am."

We sat in silence for a moment. "You have people that want to sit down with me. I feel—in some way, even if it's a woman—violated. Just because I'm on the street doesn't mean I'm a bum. She's just gonna sit down on the edge of my bed? And once she's down, she asks me, *Do I mind?* What am I supposed to say? I'm not ignorant. I don't get smart with them or nothing. But then they give you the 'I see you almost every night when I come home from work. My heart goes out to you.' Craig, I get hardened to that. I used to believe that. Not anymore. I tell them, *Thank you.* I tell them what they wanna hear. Hopefully they'll leave. I don't know, I could talk to you 'till I'm blue in the face and I couldn't explain one evening out there. It makes me feel bad when you say you *feel* for me. There's something in me. I don't want anybody to have that type of feeling for me."

I told him I couldn't help it, and he said, "I know, I know, you think everybody's like you."

"Please believe me," he said. "Another thing that plays a big role in it is where I come from. People aren't like this everywhere. Especially where I'm from. They're decent people. Streets are clean." He said there was someone on Park Avenue last night screaming thirty feet away from him. That put him on point, so he had to sit up all night to see if there was a threat.

"You always describe Pittsburgh as being welcoming," I said. "And what's New York?"

"There's no comparison," he said. "It's like another galaxy. It's that different. Uncaring, cold, cruel, all of those."

"God, Joe," I said. "Why are you here?"

"If I really thought about it, I'd probably give you a different reason every time you ask me that question." He did. When I'd ask him why he came, there was always that moment: He was folding laundry. His business had failed. He walked out. An old army buddy had said, *Come up here for a while, get away.* "That's the worst decision I ever made in my life."

GRADUALLY I HAD a Sunday roommate. I didn't always rearrange the couch after Joe's visit. The white mattress lay exposed. When he stayed, he often disappeared downstairs and returned with a coffee. On Sunday night he drank half the coffee and left the other half on the kitchen table. I didn't hear him use the microwave in the morning. He always left the blanket folded at the foot of the daybed.

One day I took home a Zabar's bag full of donated bagels and lox and cream cheese. Joe was starting to keep more of his belongings at the apartment. I motioned toward the stack of his bags in the corner. It had grown larger. There was even a hockey bag with a name tag bearing the name "Lorne Michaels," which surely had to be a different Lorne. Each weekend it seemed Joe brought another bag, and I would say, *You've got to do something about those*, knowing nothing would happen.

Some days it was like having a child. I cooked a pork chop for him.

I worried about him when late October rains wracked the neighborhood. Some days I'd instruct him. I explained to him the definition of cover songs. Some days he was more like a chiding father, the way he said "The Canadian" when I'd pissed him off. One day he described those five shades of green he saw in Vietnam. Some Sundays he was determined to leave. On other Sundays, it seemed he had always been in New York and would outlast us all. Sometimes I felt great love for him. Once when I stopped by when he was asleep, I saw his face given over to the cold on Park and 23rd Street. I'd crouched beside him that night, cramped and angry at my inability to force some sort of change. There were times I was protective. Then there were times he was like any friend, although more generous, always offering his latest gift. Did I need a stringy iPhone charger the color of fresh spinach? Did I need a Deloitte water bottle? Did I need a one-earpiece headphone? Here was a Huawei cell-phone case. Here was a map of downtown Helsinki. Would that come in handy? Here were dress shirts—and they're clean, Joe assured me, just a little wrinkled.

After I urged him, Joe condensed some of the bags stacked near my door. I told him he had to get rid of a bag, any bag. I was finding it difficult to deal with them. When I left the apartment the next morning, light reflected from the buildings on East Broadway. I made it out in time to see the garbage man picking up an empty bag. He tossed Lorne Michaels into the truck.

Part
Three

12

The Golden Door

During my next visit to the Panorama of the City of New York, the curator and I are out walking on the Panorama itself while wearing protective cloth booties. The museum is changing exhibits and sanding the walls, so dust has migrated and we leave the occasional footprint. The city, Louise says, looks benign. It's a constantly changing story. I search and find the synagogue I can see from the window of my apartment.

You're lucky, because this is the cleanest that it's been in a long time. We can walk up the East River if you want. Just be careful where you walk. There's the Verrazzano Bridge.

I'm stepping over the Verrazzano.

Do what I do, step between the bridges. Along Roosevelt Island, the easiest thing to do is to walk on either side. Just be careful when you get to the little Roosevelt Island Bridge up there. You follow the rivers. I mean we walk on the water literally anywhere we want to go. Once in a great moon we walk on the parks because the park, the green areas, are pretty much flatter than everywhere else, and you can walk on them.

I've never moved uptown so quickly. And yet it's bigger than I thought.

It's a small city unto itself. Each one of these skyscrapers were individually made, individually constructed. The little one-story buildings that look like Monopoly houses, those were from a vacuum-formed plastic. Every other building above one story was custom-made, so that building they decided to put in separate strips for the windows, but yet the one next to it looks completely different. There are over 2,200 lights underneath, which show all of the services of the city, the municipal structures all over the place. We have somebody who puts on a little hat and goes underneath on a mechanic's seat and changes all the light bulbs.

That's Flushing Bay here, and that's Flushing.

Is that Shea Stadium or Citi Field?

That's Citi. It's been updated. Actually, both Yankee Stadium and Shea Stadium were updated. The teams both paid for or donated money to have their models made. My colleague Arnold was the one who came out and he had to gently remove the stadium itself. The diamond was literally cut out of paper and glued down. He had to gently pry out the old stadium, and then we mounted it on a piece of Sintra, which is a rigid plastic, and it's now on long-term loan to Citi Field. They have a museum there.

The Panorama is such a strange representation of New York because it feels so real, and yet most of these buildings are from 1964. That one was just built; that building is gone. It's just a fictional representation.

Does the Panorama get updated generally?

No, the museum has no funds to update. We do have a program called Adopt A Building, which means that anybody can come in and pay X amount of dollars depending on what structure they want to sponsor. It's like $100 if you want to sponsor your apartment. If you have $50,000, you can sponsor a bridge. You get a "title deed" with your name on it. Any upgrade that you see was through an outside agency or a private developer or an architectural firm that was willing to donate their maquette, their model. Right there, for example, the big green one is Citibank in Long Island City. Across the creek is the Department of Environmental Protection's digester plant, which is busy processing all your waste products. That's why it smells heavenly over there. DEP paid for that to be installed.

What if somebody nefariously wanted to pay for a building to have it removed, or to alter New York for their own reasons, or if someone said, "I don't like this building, I'll pay you $1,000 to have it taken off?" Is there a policy?

No, we wouldn't do that. The only stuff we remove is junk that falls or gets thrown onto the model. Every time we come out here, I come back out and my pockets are full of stuff. We're just constantly having to keep the lookout for what people drop by accident—cell phones, glasses—or intentionally, because kids are kids. That's part of what we do. I actually keep some of the kooky things that I find and I incorporate them into my own artwork.

It looks very dusty over here in the Bronx.

I don't know why. I think they stopped cleaning here for some reason. It's a never-ending battle.

Everything is brittle, and over time the glue dries up, so there are many, many loose pieces everywhere out here. You see all this shrubbery? When this was all first put down and then upgraded in 1992, it would have looked like actual architectural shrubbery, but over time it dries up and it just disintegrates. All these park areas would have been a vibrant green, and they would have been plush with trees and bushes and simulations of green things. That's something that kind of goes first.

One person on our staff once knocked over the Statue of Liberty, which is right there. It looks tiny in the harbor; it's only one and three-quarters inches tall. I don't know how she knocked it over. Then she knocked the spire off of the Empire State Building, I believe. She shall remain nameless.

[We head downtown.]

This is all new here, Brooklyn Bridge Park. That was quite a job. The model makers came in and, under our supervision, they carefully removed the existing pieces and then put that in place. I have the box of the parts up in storage.

I've paused here with my foot between Brooklyn and Manhattan Bridge. Even just looking at the Twin Towers, it does give you a little tremor every time. We kept the towers, that was a conscious decision. After 9/11, our director and our board felt that we couldn't take them down. The idea was to keep them up until the new building went up. But does the new building feel organic? Does it feel part of the landscape? At least here, on this version of New York, the Twin Towers are still there. In some ways, it's like a willful revisionist history. When people come, they key on them immediately. It's very emotional. A lot of people are shocked when they see them, and then a lot of people are also relieved. You get two different camps.

I think everyone has to come to terms with it in their own way. For me, it's not as acute as it was, but it was certainly huge. I mean, I didn't get over it. How do you represent a city that's both always moving forward, always changing and growing?

You don't get tempted to reach into these little dusty streets?

I do want to pluck them, but my pockets would be full of dust.

A guy I talked to, who replaces cornices in buildings, he does a lot of repair work. He was saying that in some of the material you can see the fingerprints of the workers who put it in, you know, in the 1920s or '30s. There's the same kind of feeling here where you can see this craftsmanship.

Don't knock over the Statue of Liberty. This is Battery Park City. That's new.

Look at the piers. This is all so old, seeing these big boats docked here.

I mean, that is so '60s. Actually, we're missing some of the big boats. We try not to use the Panorama for commercial purposes, but years ago there was a shoe and handbag designer who did get permission to use this as a backdrop for an ad. They placed high heels and handbags gently on midtown, which was cool. The boats kind of walk away.

We had a mishap during a recent filming: somebody stepped backwards onto the George Washington Bridge. If he had stepped on one of the Twin Towers, it would have been just terrible. Luckily he stepped on the middle, and they had it completely restored and repainted, and we just installed it yesterday.

It looks beautiful.

It's shiny, spanking new.

Uh oh, I think I just stepped on New Jersey.

Don't worry, you can actually.

You can step on Jersey?

I'm stepping on Jersey right now, see?

GLADYS DeJESUS MITCHELL A retired 911 dispatcher

All my life people have said, *Gladys, there's something about your voice.* I don't know what it is, that's just the way I speak. They say I talk like I'm singing. And that would be people who don't even know that I sang.

It was the spring semester of my junior year at NYU when I started working at 911. My mother worked for the police department and she told me that there was a position open at 911. I don't think she thought I would even think about applying, 'cause I was in school. But at the time I wasn't working, I didn't have any money. I was depending on my mother, who was a single parent, so I decided to go for the job. I didn't tell her at the time when I got the job. I left school thinking I would just take a six-month leave. I was twenty. It was 1982.

I ended up working for 911 for many years.

I didn't know what I was walking into. I had no idea. I thought 911 just consisted of, you know, answering the phone. I didn't realize how detailed it was, and how stressful it was and still is. We have requirements just like police officers when they're in the academy. We have to go through an extensive training. We have to learn the vocabulary that the police officers have to learn. We have to learn the technology, the equipment that is used to do the job.

You have the 911 operator and then you have the dispatcher. When the public calls 911 the operator handles those calls. They take the information. They notify whatever other agencies have to come into play in regards to a specific call. The operator makes those notifications for the ambulance, fire department. You have to be very calm. You have to be patient. You are trained to get the information you need from the person. Every call that you receive, you don't question it. You take everything at face value. It's not up to me to get a call and say, *I don't think they're telling me the truth.* That's not my place. I am there to retrieve as much information from the caller as I can.

You have to make sure that the information you're getting is correct and is as precise as possible. You have to be understanding. You have to be patient. You have to be calm. You have to have a pleasant speaking voice. You have to be respectful because you want the person to feel comfortable enough with you to give you whatever it is that you're asking for.

Everyone begins as an operator. After that you train to become a dispatcher, the one who is in communication with the police in the field. I was an operator about four years before I became a dispatcher. You have to learn a whole different system. You have to learn a different technological system. You have to learn a whole new language, which is coding and that is very intense. And that takes maybe a month, six weeks of training. There are so many codes that I think back and, oh my goodness, you gotta be young to do that. There is no way that I could remember now what I remembered then.

I was the police dispatcher who mobilized the entire World Trade Center area on September 11, the entire Ground Zero. I call myself a forgotten hero, because no one knows who I am. Not that I've ever wanted any type of recognition for that or the spotlight on me. No. But the fact remains that we are the truly forgotten heroes. The police and the fire department and the doctors and the nurses and all the essential workers—they're being assisted in every way possible. People are supporting them. But what about us? Because honestly if we were not there to do our job, everything would come to a standstill. We are truly the lifeline to the city because if you can't call 911, how do you get help? You have to go through 911 to get to the ambulance, the fire department. You can't get to any of those departments without coming to us.

The voices of the people needing the help, they need to be heard. And the people that are giving them the help, they need to be heard also.

THERE ARE VERY FEW TIMES where we may get a call about something happy—*my wife just went into labor,* you know, a joyous occasion. Most of our calls are about tragedy. A robbery, a stabbing, a killing, a violent dispute. And that is what's so stressful. First of all, because from one call to the next you don't know what you're going to get. You got stress on stress. You got our side of stress and the caller's side of stress. Someone that's going through an incident, a situation, not only are they going through the situation but they are stressed out because they need help like yesterday. So they call us because we're the line to this help that they need. When they call us, we have our own stresses. We know you need help and we are now in the position that we have to get you this help by any means necessary, so we cannot *display* our emotions, our stresses. We have to remain calm. But once the call is completed we go through our own moments of trauma, right? For what we've experienced. We've experienced it through the call and people may think that, *Oh, that was just the call.* No. We *feel it* as though we are there with the person.

You can't help but to feel it that way. If you get a call from someone you know and they are going through a moment of some type of stress, don't you begin to internalize that also? You get excited. You become apprehensive. You want to help the person and you really can't because you're on the other end of the phone. You're not even there, so you're trying to think of what you could do from your end to help the person. That's what we go through. This is back to back to back to back. The person that calls us, they're going through that stress. Yes, but then they hang up and they get help. We hang up and another one drops right in. So we really don't even get a chance. We don't get the opportunity to loosen and take a deep breath and inhale and catch our breath for the next . . . whatever it may be.

When a 911 call was about to end, I'd say, "You take care of yourself and help is on its way." And they would say to me all the time, "Miss, thank you so much. Thank you so much for your help." Sometimes they would say, "Could you please just stay on the phone?" And I'd be like, "If I stay on the phone with you, the next person that needs help, I won't be able to get them that help."

So I'd tell them to wait five minutes, and if help hasn't arrived to call me right back. I mean, it was a little fib there because sometimes you don't get the same person. But I said, "Okay? Promise me you'll call back. Five minutes." And they'd say, "Okay, I will." And that would ease them into hanging up. I had to prepare myself for the next call.

The only time I would never hang up on a person is if they were suicidal, if they were threatening to take their life. That's a call I would never hang up on. *Never.* You just let them talk. By the time they finished talking, they calm themselves down or you help to calm them down. You ask them, *Would you like some help?* Some say yes, some say no. But when they say no, you have to send someone whether they want it or not. Because the police, when they get there, they will know how to handle it, you know? And if they tell me no, and the police knock, and they said, *Miss, you lied. You lied. You told me you wasn't going to send nobody here.* And I'd say, *I told you that I wouldn't send anybody there while we were talking. But as time went on, I needed to get you some help because you sounded like you're calm, now. You've calmed down. So, you know, now is the time to maybe get some help and let somebody help you through this.* They would open the door, you know.

I loved my job.

WHEN YOU'RE A 911 OPERATOR, we're broken up in different boroughs. We're all in the same place, but you may work in the Bronx this day, or Brooklyn that day, or Queens another day. But most of the times you may be assigned to work in the same borough, you know, every day. If you get used to a borough and they see that you do good in the borough, they may assign you every day to that borough. So you become accustomed to and knowledgeable of the borough.

When I first started, I was dispatching mostly in the Bronx. After a few years, Brooklyn was the borough that I was mostly assigned to. It was very rare that I wasn't assigned to the borough of Brooklyn. So that was where I usually worked.

When you dispatch a borough, they're broken down into sections. So in Brooklyn you might have twenty precincts, let's say, and each dispatcher is assigned a precinct. That's how it works. In Brooklyn I was assigned most of the time to the most dangerous area, which was the 73 and 75 precincts.

They were just voices. I never said, *Oh, they sound white, Black, Hispanic, Chinese, Russian*, you know. Only if I heard that they had a problem expressing themselves, I would ask them, *Do you speak another language?* And then they would say to me, *Oh, yes, I speak, I speak Spanish* or *I speak Russian*, and then I'd ask them, *Would you like an interpreter? Would that be a better way for you to let me know?* And then I would connect them to the interpreter.

Not only am I getting my calls, but then, you know, my coworkers around me, I could hear their calls. So I always knew what was going on around me, if it was a high-crime-level day or if it was a nice quiet day. We could always tell by the number of calls we received. We knew what number call we were up to. That's how we were able to keep track of if it was a quiet day, a slow day, a non-criminal-act type of day. A high number could be, let's say, maybe 1500. Maybe 1300, maybe a thousand.

You know how police officers and the fire department, they have that brother and sisterhood? That's what we have. But nobody knows that, nobody knows. No one even thinks to ask us. But we have a brother and a sisterhood. And we love the people we work with.

You get to know each other even though you don't know each other face-to-face. You speak to each other every day, and they depend on me with their life. I have their lives in my hands every day that I sit to dispatch.

If they didn't hear my voice one day, they would say, *Where's central? Where is she?* They would ask for me 'cause they would say it's that voice. There's something about your voice.

THE DAY OF SEPTEMBER 11 we were having a ceremony, which we had every year to honor the 911 workers. They give us certificates for those who don't take no days off, nothing grand, but they would make it kind of grand because the police commissioner and the mayor and all the dignitaries would come. Every year we would have a ceremony. And that particular year I was supposed to sing a song. Of all the years! That day, September 11, 2001, they had asked me to sing a song. I was going to sing the national anthem and then I was going to sing a song called "The Way We Were" to honor my coworkers who had passed away.

I had never sung for any ceremony at the job. But that particular day I was scheduled to sing. So I was not working, but my supervisor told me, *Oh, Gladys, someone was supposed to start at nine o'clock. Can you just take a few calls?* I was like, *Sure, no problem.* I sat down. First call I got, a man said, *I'm a lawyer, I'm in a high-rise building, and I just saw . . . I don't know if that was a commercial plane or a jetliner. It just went into the World Trade Tower.* And I said, *Oh my goodness*—just to myself, 'cause you never speak this out loud—I said, *Oh my goodness, we got an alcoholic on the phone early in the morning.* I thought that in my head. We're supposed to take everything at face value. Then, right after he said that to me and that thought went across my mind, all hell broke loose.

The calls just started coming in back to back to back. I heard the other operators. The second call I took, a man said, *Miss, my wife is trapped in a building. I'll give you a million dollars if you please just get her out safely.* And I told him, *Don't worry about it. We'll get her out, don't worry about it. We'll get her out.* To this day, I don't know if she made it. I think about her all the time.

And after that call the principal—we've got different levels of supervisory positions—the head, which is the principal, came over to me and she said, "Ms. Mitchell, I need you to come with me right now." She took me into the Manhattan dispatching room. She said, I need you to sit here and handle this. And to this day I always wonder, why me? Why was I chosen to do that? My life was never the same after that.

What I went through that day in dispatching . . . All those lives—I heard them losing their life. I heard it all. I heard the buildings falling. I heard the people screaming. I heard the bodies hitting the pavement. I heard the officers begging for their lives. That's when you feel helpless. You can't help them because the building's falling on them and you can't even let them know that that's what's happened.

Almost twenty years later, we have a new tragedy that has hit us and what are we gonna do with what we learned before? Because they were telling us, *Oh, it's okay. It's okay.* And I'm telling you, I'm having like a flashback, *Oh, everything is okay.* You know, they were telling us, *Don't worry about it, the air is safe, you can come around, don't worry.*

We all are resilient. The human being has been born with a strength to make it through whatever it is. We all have that inner strength. In New York, we have been through so much as a whole that, you know, we're not going to give up. We pick ourselves up, dust ourselves off, and handle whatever the next thing is that's going to come our way. But I'm still affected physically, emotionally, psychologically. I have five illnesses associated with September 11th. I want people to know that everything that people are going through with COVID—that's going to last them for a lifetime.

PETE MEEHAN A cop

People want to know, but they don't want to know. People think they want to know, but they don't want to know.

There are conversations that I can't have with people that weren't there. I could talk about it, but it's not the same. It doesn't relate. There's no meaning to me, to talk about it to people who weren't there. You can't talk about abstract art with a person who's never seen it.

It's weird. The one thing I've always told everybody is that I just remember when the dust settled. It was just rubble. I didn't see a desk. I saw a lot of paper. But I didn't see a desk. I didn't see a chair. I didn't see a filing cabinet. Hundreds of floors, two buildings, plus other buildings.

I have pictures of myself. You had the one and the two, three, four, five, all those different buildings. One of the outer buildings, I forget which one it was, which in another city would have been the tallest building, and it was like a shrimp in the complex. And I'm standing in front of it, mostly collapsed, nothing but rubble. Where are all the desks? Where are all the bodies? Where is everything?

It was just rubble. It was glass, steel, and concrete. And vehicles that were demolished in and around. I was standing on a vehicle that was demolished and a fire truck too. It was a mystery as we dug shit up, stuff started coming. And then the quiet calm afterwards. And the smell. And the smoke. The smoke was terrible. Not being able to breathe, the physical aspects of being in it. Initially being there. Psychologically, just enduring.

The physical effects were very very real. And I had a mask on, a really big mask too, by the way. It didn't prevent everything.

You have guys now who are in their nineties and they're dying, and they're talking for the first time about Saipan: talking about island hopping in the Pacific, Midway, talking about a shipmate drowning, sixty-something years later for the first time. It's the same kind of thing. It's going to be for life. That's life. I don't think there's any psychological therapy or any type of medication or anything that's going to cure anything. It's a part of the human condition. You can alleviate things, but it's never going to cure it.

Psychologically I think I'm very good with it because I've spoken about it in the proper settings. I haven't let it consume me. With other people, it's consumed them, and they don't talk about it. It will eat you from the inside out, and I never allowed that to happen. Even from the beginning. I knew from the beginning it was horrific. We had a lot of post-traumatic stress right after.

I remember that Thursday. Everyone freaking out, the thirteenth. And we knew it. We knew what we had witnessed was going to fuck us up.

How do people talk to me about 9/11? I get every question in the world. Answer the question. None of your fucking business—you know that helps a lot too. What does brain matter taste like? Then we'll fucking talk. How do you feel about skull fragments in your shoes and picking them out? Then we'll talk. But if you can't talk about that, we don't talk about that. We'll talk about this. But you want to talk. We can't because you're in the brotherhood or you're not, and not to disrespect anybody, but you wouldn't get it. You wouldn't get it. You'd have nightmares. You'd get fucking nightmares.

I've told a few people things, and they can't fucking handle it. They'll walk out on me. They can't do it. Or you show people pictures of some of the things and they'll go, "Oh my God, don't show me that."

You asked.

I was in the Bronx. We were teaching a class that day of how to deal with crowds, so I had fifty cops with me. It was me and one other sergeant. And we're standing there, and cops are from all over the city, all different places.

I put fifty guys on a bus. We commandeered a bus. Fifty cops. I sent them down. What the fuck did I just do? That was my call. I just sent fifty guys to their death. You know? Thank God they all lived.

There was another boss, we had a physical fight in front of the bus on who was going to go on the bus. And he goes, "I'm fucking retiring in a month. I've been a sergeant longer than you. Let's get the other fucking vehicle down there." He won. I lost. He went down.

I remember that moment stopping time. What the fuck did I just do? And they went willingly, willingly.

"Boss, we got to get on the bus. Boss, boss, we got to get on the bus."

I also realized at that time, that people were willing to follow me to a certain death. If there was another boss, "Fuck you. Fuck that." You would have gotten the "fuck that"s. But not that day.

I used to have a lot of the typical cop dreams like you're pulling the trigger, you're pulling the trigger, you're pulling the trigger, you're pulling the trigger and the gun never goes bang and never even clicks back. It's like a trigger that's a mile long. And the other one when you pull the trigger, no fucking round, it tumbles out of the ballast. That's a typical cop dream. Or you're fighting with somebody, or you're falling.

I'm not one to point at dreams, actually. I love dreaming, so even if I have a crazy one I love it because I can analyze it when I get up.

I just love it. I think dreams are great. I love dreaming: good, bad, and indifferent. Send me to dreams 'cause dreams don't scare me. It's a good thing. I don't have the nightmares.

If you handle your stress well, don't drink too much, don't take pills, and all of that shit. You'll sleep fine.

Cops, firemen, people that were down there. People that I know. In public situations, the guys get very agitated. They can't talk about it. Any time it comes up, they just cannot handle talking about it. One on one we can talk about it all day long. There's that common bond of you were there. You experienced. You know what it's like. But it's a very emotional feeling. It's very hard to actually handle at times. Very hard to deal with. You can't digest it sometimes. It really affects you, especially in a public situation. A lot of guys avoid stuff. A lot of guys have not gone down to the World Trade Center museum. They've not gone to the World Trade Center site, Freedom Tower. Because they know what it's going to bring up. It's going to hurt.

My friend and I spoke about it many times. We knew. Right afterwards, we were like, this shit's going to kill us. Someday, it's going to kill us. You know? It might be when we're fifty, sixty, seventy, eighty. Some even in our thirties. A lot of people walk around with that. They feel like they have that unexploded bomb in their body that's just going to explode one day. That's the toxins from the World Trade Center. The ailments it's brought on. Or future ailments they're going to find. A lot of people walk around with that fear, waiting for the other shoe to drop.

With me, it's already dropped. I don't have to worry about that anymore. It's already happened. I've gotten a terminal illness with it. I've had cancer also with it. I've had terrible upper respiratory issues with it. Things of that nature.

The neurological stuff kicked in. I seem to be one of the first people that's been severely affected by it. I can't let it bother me. It's a part of my life. That shoe dropped.

Everyone else is walking around waiting for that other shoe to drop. It might never. But that's a horrible feeling. There are other people that dwell on it. Because they see me. They're like, oh shit. That could be me.

It was so bad. That cloud. That toxic cloud that hung around. The fires that burned for months. Months. Burning. The amount of body parts and the amount of chemicals and the amount of man-made materials that were in that building, just burning, pulverized, atomized, just in the atmosphere. You'd go home and the shit would be in the locker room. It would be on your clothes. It would be in your shoes. I remember I had to bring my car down to the site because we had no cars at work, so I took my own car. For months, when I opened my gas cap, this milky substance was coming out. It was in the bends and folds in my car. It would rain and there would be a milky white substance coming out of my gas cap. It was always in that little crease.

We knew we were all contaminated. To what extent? No one knew. We knew that this was not good. It was definitely not good. Although we didn't feel anything. It had the potential to really be a problem.

I was very sick. But I fought through everything I could. I fought through this as long as I could. I'm still fighting. But it's tough: asthma-like symptoms. Wheezing. Out of nowhere. It's not food induced. It's just out of nowhere induced. Heartburn on an atomic level. You couldn't imagine how that debilitates you. COPD. RADS, which is a reactive area disease issue. Horrible things. If I wasn't in good shape, I would have been dead already.

I've been with other guys that have not experienced that yet. They may someday. Hopefully not. It's like someone who was shot. They have a bullet in their body that you can't remove. It could just one day hit your heart or your lung and you're dead. Maybe. It's a horrible feeling to walk around with.

It could have been going on for five or six years. About three or four years ago I started noticing just some generalized weakness. I just thought it was age or maybe I wasn't exercising right. Eating right.

It slowly progressed. The World Trade Center has not acknowledged the neurological issues yet. But Winthrop University just did a study recently. I was in the study. They told me I was the worst they've seen with a neurological condition. That's what I've been told. From looking at everyone else, definitely. I was definitely the worst. But the scientists there have proven the toxins affect the nerves in the body. The neuritis and the neuropathy has been proven. It's just a matter of time before the World Trade Center has it listed as a condition. It will happen.

It sucks. I'm so weak, I can't even shave. I don't have enough strength to shave. I go to a barber.

I hate having to live like this. But what do you do? Do I sit in bed? Take pills and drink all day? Or do I get the fuck out of bed and live my life? I do the latter. I'm not a good drinker anyway, so I wouldn't be able to drink all day.

My environmental specialist, he speaks all over the world. He's helped me out with a lot of stuff. He's gotten me to the right places. He can't figure it out. Neurologists can't figure me out.

I'm a physical specimen of what 9/11 can do to somebody. Going from somebody who was, at forty-five years old, in phenomenal shape, better shape than most the people half my age. Three years later I need help getting dressed.

In addition to all my respiratory issues, in addition to getting cancer. Basically I got dealt the shit sandwich. Or I got hit by a shitstorm for the most part.

If you experienced 9/11, you're married to it and there's no divorcing it. So you either make the best of it, or you let it ruin you. Myself and my buddies, we refuse to let it ruin us. You cannot let it ruin you. It happened.

You have these flashback moments but they're not nightmare flashbacks. Sometimes they're horrific and sometimes just nostalgic. I understand the psychology of that so it doesn't freak me out, it doesn't bother me, it's just part of life. If anyone was involved in a traumatic incident, a horrific car accident where someone died, they are going to remember that the rest of their lives. But it doesn't stop you from doing what you need to do. It can be debilitating, for people. It's never been for me, and I don't think it has to my friends. That's the cop nature. And the firemen. We soldier on.

You know what it's like? It's like bringing someone to your dinner table, to Thanksgiving with your whole family there. Bringing in an outsider and now you're going to talk about some horrific event your family went through. It's the way it is. Not that you're not going to have that discussion. They're not going to understand. You can't, it's impossible.

It comes at the weirdest times. Recently there was a documentary on one of the rescue dogs that was there from an outside organization. The dog's still alive, and they brought him back to New York to give him his birthday party. Some big lab. He was old and everything.

I remembered one of the moments I was on the pile and I looked up and I saw this dog, and the dog didn't look right. It wasn't an NYPD dog, it was an outside agency dog.

I asked the handler, "What's the matter?" He goes, "The dog's depressed, it keeps getting hits. Digging up and finding a finger or a foot. He's finding body parts. He's getting so depressed because he's not finding a body. He's getting so many hits, he's overwhelmed with his senses."

I remember laying on the pile, hugging this dog, kissing the dog, and crying, telling the dog it's going to be okay.

I remember that moment like it was yesterday.

It wasn't a flashback, it was just a vivid moment. The dogs were nonstop working. They don't know when to not work. They work until they can't work anymore.

I remember seeing the dogs and petting them and laying with them. I'm in one of the biggest disasters that the city has ever seen—

there's been bigger disasters, but I've been in one of the biggest we've seen in a long time—and I'm laying on the pile with a dog, crying and kissing it and telling it it's going to be okay. I'm worrying about a dog.

There wasn't a thought or a speculation or a glance on the pile. People were just stepping over me, just walking around me. That was normal. It's okay. Everyone was feeling that way. I just felt so bad for these dogs. This dog, you could see it was distressed. Not depressed, distressed. When I laid down with it, it kind of calmed down.

I grabbed it and I hugged it and kissed it. *It's going to be okay.* It just calmed down and I calmed down.

I was looking for my partner who died, who we never found.

That was one of those moments. I relive them like that. But it's okay. It's not a bad thing. That's a good thing because that's never forgetting.

Those moments are not uncommon.

It's going to be a part of your life forever. If you suppress it, it's going to fucking eat you up from inside. I'll never allow that because I'm not ashamed of my emotions, and I never want to be. I know guys that just suppress it. It doesn't work, it doesn't work, and World War II is the perfect example of it. You've got these guys in their nineties now, saying, "I wish I would've never done that." I never thought about that, I just wasn't the kind of person to suppress it. I always feel it. That dog. That was a defining moment at Ground Zero for me.

JUSTIN GONZALEZ A security guard at the Statue of Liberty

Some people are nervous and then they'll try to rush through everything. Some people are just regular calm. Some people get annoyed. "Why do we have to go through security? This is just the Statue of Liberty." Or some people ask, "When did the security start?"

And I say, "Basically, they started doing strict security after 9/11." "Oh, okay." And then after that they don't say anything.

We're guarding the symbol of freedom for the United States. I rarely thought about that. Because for three years I was just like, *work, go home, work, go home.* I was so stressed out. I see 20,000 faces a day and say the same thing to everybody. And it's like, I just want to go home, sit on the couch, go to sleep, and then the next day do the same thing again. It's now that I'm really realizing the severity of the job and that we can't take the job for granted.

A lot of people come and give you that blank face because they don't understand English. So it's like, "Belt, watch, wallet, cell phone, camera, keys, coins."

And they're like, "Okay, I don't understand that." Some people say, "Do you speak Spanish?"

"Yeah, I speak Spanish. Okay. *Todo en la cubeta, cinturón, reloj, billetera, llaves, monedas, celular.*"

Which would be, "Everything in the bucket, watch, wallet, keys, coins, and cell phone."

Or some people that come from Brazil, Portuguese, is, "Okay, *cartera*," which is the same thing, *moedas* and *cinto*, which is belt. *Relogio*, which is watch.

And then you have a few from China. Then it's like *pídài*, which is belt; *shǒubiǎo*, which is watch; *qiánbāo*, which is wallet.

And then Italian: *portafoglio*, wallet; *orologio*, which is watch; and then *cintura*, which is belt.

I started trying to figure out how could I help move people, but at the same time not have us both be confused. Some people try to figure out what you're saying. You keep telling them the same thing. They still don't understand you. They get kind of upset. So then it's like you either keep talking or try to figure out what language they speak. Or just try to use sign language. I can see the world in one day, even though I don't get to travel.

I get to have some incentive to learn new languages. A lot of people say, "Why I'm going to learn a language for? All I need to is English."

I want to learn how to say "belts" in like Arabic or Korean or something.

Their face lights up. They're like, "Really?" You could speak Chinese or you could speak Portuguese. Then they want to have like a whole conversation with you. So wait, wait, wait, wait. I don't understand everything. I just understand a little bit. I just understand these words and then after that if you want to teach me a word. Can you tell me how to say this or that?

We can talk about watches, wallets, keys, coins, all day long. But after that, I don't know.

Arabic—that would be crazy. I think one day a family came from Israel and they were talking Hebrew and everything and I said, "Well, how do you say 'belts' in Hebrew?" And it almost sounds like *agua*, but it's *chagorah*.

Yeah, that's how you say it and you have to ... When I said it, I didn't really say it with the R. It's like you have to use that R. *Chagorah*. I said, "Okay, *chagorah*. Thank you." That's how I remember. Connect *agua* with *chagorah* and that's "belts" in Hebrew. The thing is I use these things to make my job more interesting because it's like, okay, I could always say the same thing every day in English. Why not learn how to say the same things in multiple different languages?

I feel like I'm the United Nations sometimes. I do. I keep that up. I should one day go visit the United Nations. It's like what we have at the statue.

I've never been to the UN. I always wanted to go there. But it's just like you learn in school that New York is a melting pot from the beginning. It's like this is a melting pot right here. Every single day. Sweden, Russia, Croatia, Italy. Sometimes it's overwhelming, but that's the job. This is why you came.

Even if I'm having a bad day, I know I can make it a good day if I want it to be because I should always try to interact with other people, try to see if I can make other people happy. I just say, "Belt, watch, wallet," in Italian or something. And then they're like, "*Oh, bravo, molto bene.*"

SOMETIMES I'LL EITHER work in Battery Park, in the tent, or I'll work right on the island. It's like I'm going to go to lunch at the Statue of Liberty.

People take that for granted. You don't really think about it because it's just your job. Not a lot of people can do what we do and not a lot of people get to see what we see. The view from the island to the city is really spectacular.

When you're on the island, they don't allow any food or beverages inside the statue because it gets messy. People will leave bottles around or they'll spill soda. A lot of people get annoyed about that. They'll be like, "But they let it on the boat."

Well, there's stricter rules to go inside of the statue. And not a lot of people get to go inside of the statue, so they try to keep it as clean as they can.

I've been to the crown once. They were doing construction, they had to close for a while. So when they were doing construction, I went all the way up.

I haven't seen anybody like tear up or cry or anything. But a lot of people get just happy. They'll say, "Wow, I'm at the statue, oh my God," in different languages.

It's the face of the United States. Sometimes you think about it and other times you don't, but nowadays it always comes to my mind. It's like when you go to China, the Great Wall of China. Or if you go to Brazil, the statue of Jesus.

When you go on the boat, they always give you the history. How immigrants used to be so happy when they saw the Statue of Liberty, they would cheer. They would be dancing, they would be singing. Like, "Oh, we made it to America. Now we're free. Now we can start a new life." Still to this day people see the Statue of Liberty and they're happy, they're cheering.

Some people, I see it in their face. It's like a face of accomplishment, I guess, when they get off the boat.

When I work on the island, I'm like, "I'm going to see the green lady today." I say, "Oh, that's my work wife." She's pretty serious. She's serious every day. She's like, "That's it. I have my book. I have my torch. I'm going to stand here and say hi."

She's very friendly. Very kind. Even though her arms are set, her arms are really open. She's open to everybody. She's here.

That's my work wife. If it wasn't because of her, I don't get paid. We have a very good relationship for five years, five years strong. In *Planet of the Apes*, *Cloverfield*. Yeah. *X-Men*, the first movie. *Day After Tomorrow*. She gets destroyed? I'm just like, "Wow."

A month, two months back, we had a bomb threat at the statue. I was on the island at the time. Usually they tell us if you're on the island, if something happens, you clear the tent.

We tell everybody to step outside and then we have a crazy line and then we all come back inside, everything's taken care of. But this time we cleared everybody out, we waited for the cop's okay. And we never got our okay. We were like, "Okay, really?"

We all got nervous. I got a little bit nervous.

We ended up having to evacuate the island. This was the first time, out of all the years that anybody's working at the statue, that we had to evacuate the island. After we evacuated the island, I see on CNN, *boom*, it's Liberty Island that gets evacuated for a potential bomb threat.

At that moment I understood the severity of the job. Anything can happen. We always have to be alert. We're guarding the symbol of freedom.

We see so many faces. We make sure everyone gets screened, we make sure we see everything and know what everything is in everyone's bag. It's like, *boom*, this is a cell phone. This is the purse, this is some keys, this is some coins, this is some food in there, some soda cans. This is makeup.

The weirdest thing I've ever seen? A lady, she went to a sex store and had a dildo in her bag. I'm like, alright. I told my coworker, "Can you check this?" They opened the bag and the lady just started laughing.

She was like, "Oh my God."

Yeah, she was just laughing, she was joking about it the whole time. I said, "Okay, next? Next person." I didn't even know what to say. "Alright, lady. Have a fun day."

IN THE BEGINNING, I took my job for granted. Now I'm seeing the wonders of my job, but also the seriousness. And also the symbolism of what I'm protecting and what this represents. And how many people come here all the time just to see the statue and just to feel that sense of freedom that everyone feels here in the United States that nobody really thinks about too much. Because it's like, "Oh, I was born here and then I get to do this and that and this and this and that."

And no one's going to say, "Oh, you can't do that." No, this is my freedom. I could do this. I could go over here and pray to whoever I want to pray to or speak or write down what I want to write down.

Sometimes when I put money in the MetroCard machine and then I get coins back, some of the gold coins have the Statue of Liberty right on the back of them. "Oh yeah. I work there."

13

Winning and Losing

Recycling saved my life. It took my mind off the practice of people judging me for having nowhere to stay or because of my body, how it looked. It focused my energy. In the beginning it was also about money. When the time went on it became more of a release. It was something I could use to refocus all that crazy energy.

When you recycle you've got to know where you can get rid of the stuff. Because you can get all you want. The problem is once you get it, do you have enough time to get it to where you've got to get it to? And will they take all that you have?

You're learning about where to go, what place gives you the least hassle. Is it downtown, midtown, or uptown? Where can you get rid of the most stuff? 86th Street, as long as their machine is working, I can take all I want. Ten, twenty, thirty dollars' worth. You don't never have to deal with the store employees at all. Mysteriously, their machines break down from time to time. So you've got to wait until the manager comes.

Other places I'm waiting, other places I'm begging. I've got Duane Reade employees telling me there's no room, but there's room if a white guy brings in the exact same bag. Other places say come back later. *Come back in an hour. Come back at 4. Come back at 6. Come back when the Mets have won the World Series . . .*

I go to 14th Street, they give me a hassle and tell me they cannot take my cans. You're a twenty-four-hour store. How can you make excuses like that? You've got to make room for it. If one store can do it and one cannot, what's going on? I can be an ass about that, but it's going to be my headache. It's not going to be their headache. I might frustrate them but eventually it's going to be my headache because I'm going to get locked up.

I see old people out there now. Old women and men. There's this old guy right where I live at. Every time I see him I stop him and talk to him. "Hey, how you doing? I see you're making that money." He's like, "Yes, man, I've got to do what I've got to do." I'm pretty sure that some days he do not want to do that. I think he would rather be sitting back relaxing.

But it gives you some power. It gives you power that you have control over. You decide how much, how little. That's something that's a great motivator. I would say for anybody if you get too high on the horse: do some recycling. Because it's also a humbling experience.

It's the ultimate oxymoron. It makes you strong but it makes you humble at the same time. Especially if you're living on the streets. I used to walk from 34th to the Battery, two times a day. That's a lot of damn walking. I'd start from the West Side, walk over toward Sixth Avenue. Always staying on the West Side but working over. Sometimes I come through Tribeca, sometimes I'm coming through SoHo. But always ending up back in the same place, the Battery. At the end of the day I was so tired. Blurred vision. My feet are somebody else's. I didn't have a place back then. I was so tired I'd go to somebody's house and crash.

Once I was recycling the Upper East Side. I looked through a dumpster, somebody had thrown away all these blocks of meat. Hams and roast beef and cheese. I take it out, put it in my cart, and somebody was very upset when they came out there. I got somebody's stash. I come walking out with a broken-down baby carriage full up with meat.

Now you've got crews coming from other boroughs with vans. I know guys that bought vans, sent kids to school, paid the mortgage from recycling. You've got old white people, old Chinese people, working hard, you've got people who shouldn't be out there, who should be enjoying retirement. You've got people arguing over a can, a single can of Diet Coke, you've got people showing up early to get those bags before they're ripped. You've got poor people and people with good shoes. You've got people where you're like, *What has New York done to you that you're collecting cans?* You've got one guy—it looks like it's his hobby. You've got people who believe in territory. You've got people who will just slide in when you're not looking. You got women wearing face masks looking at you from across the street, like, *Don't you dare think of walking over here.* You've got cans full of ash, cans full of dust, cans full of shit, cans full of the *wrong soda.*

I wear gloves because you've got needles, you've got edges, you've got people who've thrown out their whole lives because New York wasn't for them, you've got dry garbage and you've got wet, you've got days when it seems like no one in the city wants to drink a bottle of water, and summer days when it's like a fountain of water bottles, like those garbage cans have a mind of themselves.

I've seen wealth. I go right through the middle of it, right past Trinity, Wall Street. They've got their job, I've got mine.

I WOULD PROBABLY SAY there are three to four degrees of homelessness.

For one thing, they just recently, in the last ten to twenty years, gave it a label. Before it was, "Oh, well, they got no place to stay so sleep on the couch." Then the economics started happening and people started losing their places, then more people ended up either in shelters or on the streets.

From my experience, a lot of people, they'd rather work. It's pride. If I don't look homeless, then I'm not homeless. If I'm working, keeping busy, then I'm okay. Even though I'm moving from place to place, I'm okay.

Some people I know, they get enough money to get a room. They might have a room three days out the week, then the other four days they got to find somewhere else to stay. I even went through that at one point.

You raise up enough money. There's places in Chinatown where they got these little rooms, chicken-wire ceilings. It's so small you can touch both walls and that's it. Just one little cot, something that looks like a nightstand and normally it's like $15–$20 a day. It used to be cheaper. Most of the time you come in at night, get up, leave in the morning.

If you're trying to find work, you can't carry too much. I mean, duh, you can't carry all your luggage with you when you're going to a job interview. So either you find somebody trustworthy to hold on to your stuff, or pay extra money for storage. They used to have organizations that would hold stuff for you, but a lot of those are gone. Hopefully you'll find somebody trustworthy. That didn't work out too good for me.

I would leave my stuff with people. The next day I see them walking around wearing my stuff. I started saying, "You know what, if I don't need it, don't carry it." So I kept it down to the bare basics. Couple pair of pants, couple of shirts, one pair of sneakers, one pair of shoes, keep it really simple. You get some people they don't want to get rid of their belongings so you see them with a backpack like fifty pounds, whatever they can stuff in it, or a shopping cart. It goes to that extreme.

I would try not to be too late because sometimes you get that thing where, "Oh, well, if you ain't here at a certain time my door's locked." You can't get in. I've had that happen to me where I've got locked out and had to sleep in the hallway and then listen at the door. Hopefully I'd catch somebody leaving out so I can get in, get some rest.

And then there's other people's mess. Depending on where you're at, I've been in family houses, but I've also been in shooting galleries. Sleep with everything under my arms.

I've lived with people that had chains around their refrigerator, no lie, man. They had heavy chains and a lock on it. "When I go to sleep I lock my refrigerator and I take my key with me. So unless you've got a bag of chips or something, you ain't eating nothing until I get up in the morning."

I was always thinking, what's going to happen where I'm going to have to get up out of here, either because I want to or because I need to. There's stress on me sometimes, that's why you find a lot of people would rather go to the streets because it's not as safe, but it's a hell of a lot more independence.

A lot of homeless used to sleep in the park, and then whatever crime would happen they would associate it with the homeless, so that was like no sleeping in the parks after sundown. If I'm outside the park and there's a bench, you can't arrest me because I'm not in the park technically. I used to use that to help me get by.

For me, sitting up is the worst part because when you sit up you don't get good circulation. Like with drop-in centers, most drop-in centers you sleep in chairs, and I had doctors tell me this, you got a lot of fluid in your legs. My legs just swole up, no circulation. He's like, no, you need to lay down. I started saying okay, well, maybe I need to find somewhere else. I would leave places and get cardboard and find a nice little spot, try to catch a few hours sleep just to take care of my legs.

Couches are great, pull-out couches are the best. Recliners aren't bad. The floor is okay, chairs are the worst. I've sat at tables, I've sat in chairs. Even a chair like this it's like after three or four hours, you gotta get comfortable and it's hell. The next day you wake up, well, when you come to, it's horrible. You're tired, your body's sore.

I'd be so frustrated sometimes I'd come in intoxicated, like totally out of it, and it would leave me vulnerable for people stealing my stuff.

Even after you pay somebody for staying with them, there's always another surtax. There's always a tax. For whatever. Oh, you're breathing my air, oh, you're drinking my water, oh, you're taking up my space, oh, your storage. So people would add on. Unless you had somebody really reliable, most of the time it was better off just staying in the streets. It was too complicated. It drags too much out of you.

I'd have to wait around until somebody show up, that's a tough one. That's especially tough when you're working, trying to get some decent sleep.

So that's why I think in my case, and people like me, most of us prefer to live in the streets, on the streets because other than the streets you don't worry about too much more.

I might not be able to use the bathroom, I might not get no good drinking water, but other than that, I'm okay.

One time I was working at a restaurant in lower Manhattan and I'd get off in the evening. The winter's always the worst, summertime you can sleep on a bench, whatever, but the wintertime it's the dead of the winter and I gotta change clothes. People decide they want to hang out. "Oh, I was sleeping, I'm sorry I didn't hear you."

"Why not just give me a key?"

"Oh, no, I don't want nobody with a key."

Because if you give somebody a key then that takes away some of your power. Some people are really into this power trip. You do as I say or I'm going to put you out, it's always threats.

Van Dyke, Brownsville, Tilden. I made my rounds in Brownsville, whole bunch of projects. I've slept on the staircase and on the roof.

Try to stay off the roof because if you get caught on the roof sometimes you might have to fight for your life, with a person trying to throw you off. I've had a person try to throw me off a roof once.

For some reason they felt they didn't like me.

I was on the roof and they said something to me. Then they turned to me and they tried to rob me and I didn't have anything. "Oh, I should throw you off the roof." And they grabbed me and tussled me.

They were a little bigger than me, but what they didn't know was I was stronger than they were. They were bigger, but I was stronger. We tussled and actually I got him down and gave him a good shot. If I'm going off this roof, you're going too.

Then there's the stairwells. Piss, shit, just dirty, dingy, sometimes you go to a staircase there's people having sex, doing drugs. Back then the police didn't patrol the projects as much. They really just didn't give a shit. After 12:00, 1:00 to 2:00 in the morning was the quietest time.

That's when I'd set up, 1:00 to 2:00 in the morning, because most people settle in so it's safe, nice and quiet. I always tried to find a clean spot especially near the rooftop. I'd clean out the area and put down cardboard and make sure I got a nice presentable spot, and when I'm ready to leave I clean up my area.

The winter it's better to be down lower, because of the heat.

Summertime higher up. In the winter you want to be more towards the middle 'cause the heat comes up. Yeah, it's just being in the right spot.

Depending on my circumstances, I'd have extra clothes, sweaters. I'd get a piece of cardboard or newspaper, whatever was handy, but I didn't want to lay out on the cold concrete, I wanted to put something under me. Take my shoes off, tie 'em together, put 'em under my pillow that I made, if you don't somebody might steal your shoes. That happened to me once too, but that was outside, Stuyvesant Park. Got very tired, took my shoes off, somebody stole them, and I walked around barefoot. Who steals a man's shoes?

I'm walking around barefooted. I went to this church, they gave me an old pair. I was so angry. If I would have found that person, I'd have caught a charge. They would charge me with attempted murder. Never again will I take my shoes off.

It was never really about sleeping, but mostly about getting some kind of rest. Especially if I'm dealing with hallways and situations like that. If I was really, really tired I would lay down, but most of the time I would sit up, turn my back to a corner so nothing's coming behind me.

That's why some of us would sleep during the day, after being up all night, because at night I'm making my money, I'm doing my recycling. In the afternoon I go to the library, or I go somewhere where I can take a quick forty winks where I know people are around me, and I don't gotta worry about nobody stabbing me or throwing something on me.

Rest is a commodity. To rest—that's one of life's top tens, no, actually the top three. Even with the drop-in centers, as horrible as they may be, at least during the daytime you could sleep. They don't just kick you out. Most of them don't. You sit in the chair, your ass might hurt, but at least you can doze off.

You're so much on guard. Your body's so tense it can take days to unwind. You're always shuffled around. You're always being moved here or there or you're constantly moving for protection. Always trying to find a better spot. It can stay with you mentally.

I know people today that's been on the streets well over twenty years. They carry everything with them. They carry most of their belongings with them or they got storage and they leave it out on the people's houses.

There's people walking around just literally talking to themselves because they have nobody else to talk to. It starts with isolation. Slowly withdrawing. Then it's not taking care of themselves. Sickness comes into play. Gradually just giving up. A whole attitude change. Mild-mannered people: now they're bitter. Screaming at people and yelling. Throwing up their hands and withdrawing altogether like, "I can't deal with it." I mean, I used to have conversations with people. We'd talk about world politics and everything, then I catch them a few months later and they're out of it.

Could have been drugs, could have been just the weight of the pressure on the streets.

There's too much thinking, and too much thinking will drive you crazy. You start talking to yourself more and more and more. Now that you're conversating with yourself more and more eventually it just breaks down.

"Why am I here? Why did they do this to me? Why did I do this?" If it ain't in, it's out.

But a lot of that's how the frustration goes. It just piles up and eventually it'll just snap it. It'll break you.

Part of the problem in New York is that you can't have weapons. Police give you hell. So you gotta improvise. Pens. Some people like deodorants, sprays and stuff, which you can use. You take some deodorant and spray somebody in the eyes, that's gonna back them up. So you had to learn how to defend yourself in ways that wouldn't get you arrested. Police can't charge me if I have a pencil.

A lock. A padlock. I put one of those in a sock. I could back somebody up. I know that if I carry a knife I'm gonna get arrested.

In New York, there's this big thing about weapons. Four inches is considered legal. Illegal is more than four inches. Some people resort to razor blades. Keep razor blades handy. Screwdrivers. Some people, liquids. Bleach, other stuff. Could splash on somebody, back them up. I was fortunate when I was young, I was sent to martial arts classes. I try not to rely on it, but I'm pretty good at defensively holding a person back. I could disarm them and slow them up, 'till I had a chance to get away from the situation.

There's a lot of serious vultures. Your hearing becomes more acute. People come in a bar, you know, you're listening to the tone of people's voices. Watching how people go in their pockets and how they come out of their pockets.

It's so many sounds. Trying to block out the noise, the sirens, and the people loud talking. That's why, like for me I would never like to lay down on a bench 'cause it kept me too vulnerable. So most of the time I sat up. If I had to move I didn't have to get myself together to get away, I could just get up. And another thing too, if I'm sitting up that boosts a defensive position where in case somebody's coming on me then I can react quickly.

And just trying to keep moving.

Another thing is do the buddy system. You get down with somebody and sometimes you take shifts sleeping. I'd go to a soup kitchen and scope people out. You gotta read people, and sometimes you want to be able to read them on the fly, make a judgment: ah, I think I can mess with this person, or I think I can mess with them for a little while and keep it moving.

Once you get a person's trust, now you can start maneuvering. And that's where I was fortunate. I had people that knew me for years and so we were opened up. Their dress, you know, their hygiene. Verbally, how they speak. People that use too much profanity is usually sick in the brain, or something like that. When every other word is the F word, nah okay, maybe this person got a little bit too much going on for me.

Some of it's real simple, basic, survival. Caveman-style. Eat or get eaten, or keep running. Basic, basic survival. Yeah, real basic. You just run 'till you pass out.

Then you come to, and you start it all over again, and that's the type of cycle it is, where you work yourself 'till you get so tired that you pass out. But, saying that, mostly you're living on the edge and half the time you're sleeping with one eye open.

It's hell on your nerves. It's like a rubber band tensing, loosening up, tensing, loosening up, constantly. Each minute is a process. 'Cause the first noise I hear, I'm up. You're always on guard. You're always hyped up and waiting. It makes your reaction time so great. Your reflexes are hyped 'cause you're always thinking: defense.

I BELIEVE DREAMS can become real if you just keep working at it. When I sat on that bench I thought about cold, clean water. How I would love to be able to have it. A hot shower. Being able to sit down. I kept that going in my mind. No matter how bad it got, or how much I screwed up, I always kept that thought. I always told myself, you're gonna get a shot at this.

If you become too jealous or too angry, you lose. It takes too much out of you. You know what I'm saying? It wears you down.

Part of the thing is also, in this town, if you become too busy looking at the other people, you never get what you need. You'll never, 'cause it's like, it's costly moving, you know what I'm saying? So while you're moving on you couldn't bear to moan about that. You always gotta work. You always gotta put in work to get what you need.

LUIS SERRANO A boxer

Do you know Howard Cosell? He was announcing one of my fights and he said, "This peppy kid from Harlem can fight. Oh, no. He's a ball of fire." Oh, yeah, I would just walk in and walk out throwing punches. Every minute, every second, every round I was throwing punches. I was in that kind of shape.

I used to work in my dad's store on 103rd Street in Harlem. Back then when I was a kid we used to have street fights and the cops used to be parked right there. They used to come out of the squad car and say, "I got twenty dollars on the Spanish kid" or "I got twenty dollars on the Black kid." And it would be a street fight. That's how I started, until one day this guy saw me and he said, "Yo, I could send you to a gym to teach you how to be a fighter."

You know what my dad said about Madison Square Garden? "One day this will be your house and you should know that." He told me he'd seen thousands and thousands of fighters and out of all those maybe five stuck out above the rest. He said, "You're one of them. I feel it." My girl said she could feel it too, because I won a lot of fights I wasn't supposed to win.

I was a dirty fighter. If you were better than me and you were kicking the shit out of me, I had to get down and dirty. I hit you in the balls, elbowed you in your face. And if the referee get in I'll swing at him too, and the referee goes down everybody says, "Yeah, he's knocking *everybody* out." Because rule number one is cover yourself at all times and that goes for the referee too. So now the referee is going like, "Break," from far away because he knows I'm going to swing at him too. I'm going to swing at everybody who comes down that fucking pike.

I was sleeping on the rooftop one day when my girl came to get me and said, "Yo, what are you doing up here?" I said, "I'm reading and drinking some whiskey." That's when she told me, "Your manager, your trainer, everybody is looking for you." She's like, "You're always looking for Madison Square Garden, well, guess what? You don't have to look no more. They came looking for you."

I was undefeated, you know. That night, they called my manager and my trainer, I could hear them talking. "He's right here. Don't worry, I'll have him at the gym tomorrow. By next week he'll be signing those contracts." I couldn't believe it.

From the streets to Madison Square Garden? You don't expect that. You're just fighting and fighting and fighting. I never thought

Madison Square Garden and Atlantic City would ask for me. I was a kid. I was street fighting and I had two hundred amateur fights and I had two hundred losses. Two hundred amateur fights and two hundred losses. I was the worst fighter in the fucking world. So when I was going to turn pro, this girl I told you about said, "Yo, this is different now. You're not fighting with these kids no more. You're fighting with men so you've got to train yourself." This girl stopped going to school to take me to the gym every day because I used to fight like this. Then I started fighting like this. The difference, you throw a punch. It goes this far but when you stand sideways it goes this far. Then you cover yourself like a cat when he's playing with a mouse and the mouse says, "Oh, shit, that cat is smart." You pepper him with this one. He's paying so much attention to this one that he don't know the next time I'm going to fake him. I'm going to lift up his head with this one and I'm going to come over with the hammer.

They told me my face was going to be on the poster—and it was. That was my proudest moment. To look up at Madison Square Garden, that big screen, and see myself. I was eating a potato chip and a lady went by and I said, "Did you see that?" And she said, "That's you." I never thought I'd make it here but I did. That's why you always got to dream like it's your last dream.

Walking into Madison Square Garden that first time? Fuck it, I admit the truth. Scary. I tried to block out the sound of the crowd because there's something I had to do and I can't be wondering what everybody's yelling at me. My trainer's telling me what to do but I don't give a fuck. These guys are way better than me so I've got to rip their head off. It's the only way I'll win. I mean you want to be a winner or you want to be a half-assed fighter? You want to be a winner but in order to do all that you've got to rise up to another level you didn't think you could reach.

You're already hearing the crowd. You're behind the curtain. You're behind the doors, and your boys are rubbing you down. Your friends are like, "Come on, don't fuck up on us now. We got a lot of money riding on you." I'm like, "Alright. I'm knocking him out. I'm knocking you out. I'm knocking everybody out." When they open that curtain, you don't see people, all you see is light. You know you're in Madison Square Garden because it's the most famous arena in the world. You can't get better. I mean you can go to Vegas, you can go to Atlantic City, but there's no place better than Madison Square Garden. So when you're walking towards the ring all you see is the light coming from the ring and you know what you've got to do.

At MSG, the blood would be flowing all over the place. I used to bleed a lot, and every time they hit me you could hear the crowd, "Ohhh." Then they say, "Motherfucker, you got blood all over me." When you hit somebody and they're bleeding, the blood splatters so that people at ringside, even in the third row, they can get it on them.

Once one of them came to me the next day in my father's store, he showed me his shirt and said, "Yo, look at your blood." I said, "Sorry, dude." He said, "No, no. I'm going to keep my shirt. I'm not even going to wash it. Just sign it."

My father smiled.

ABIGAIL NOY A die-hard Mets fan

So they've had this Mrs. Met thing. Why? *Why?* Don't get me wrong, I am a massive feminist through and through. But why do you need her? I mean, you don't. Do you have a Philly Phanatic lady? What is that? The Philly Phanatic could be a woman. Why do you need that? Was there an outcry over it?

I mean, it's possible that they wanted him to have a companion, but did he express being lonely? He doesn't have a voice. You don't hear his voice. He's not saying anything to you. And I'm not saying he doesn't have autonomy because he does as a character. But why? She looks like a child. I haven't warmed to her because I think it's pointless. If it is the case that people petitioned for a lady—you are wasting your arguments. Look into maybe how much Mrs. Met is being paid compared to Mr. Met. Look into whether or not Mrs. Met can walk home from work at night compared to Mr. Met and then we'll have a talk. Thanks, baseball.

I don't like it. It trivializes things weirdly. Having two is complicated. It's unnecessary. I don't know of any others that have multiple.

Wait a second. *[Looks on her phone. Reads from the Wikipedia page for Mrs. Met. . . .]* "*Mrs. Met first appeared at games in 1975 before disappearing into obscurity.*" Probably because she got pregnant. "*She appeared with Mr. Met in a 2003 'This is Sports Center' commercial. The Mets reintroduced her in 2013.*" That's a lot of weird gaps. Her life in between? I don't know. Probably not great.

Mr. Met was like, *I don't need your income yet*, but I would imagine he lives a pretty good life. Not the guy inside the mask, I don't know about him. Him, Mr. Met himself. There is definitely something about him that is like he's a person. If you're meeting him, shaking his hand, taking a picture with him, it's like, You're kind of a guy, right? With a rich interior life. Whereas if it's like a giant bird or something, I don't know, it's just a mascot.

CHRIS CARRINO The voice of the Brooklyn Nets

I was born in the Bronx. I was thinking about going to all these other schools around the country. But my dad, who was a non-college-educated guy but a really sharp New York City guy—he said to me, "Where do you want to work when you get out of school?" When I told him I wanted to be in New York, he said, "Then why are you going to go to Boston or Indiana or upstate New York to go to school? You got to make your contacts here, establish yourself. Stay in New York. You got to be part of the fabric of the city and you'll have that advantage when you get out of school. You're already here, you're a New Yorker. You're here, you never left." It was the greatest advice he gave me.

I went to Fordham, and the first day I'm on campus I went to go visit the radio station. They had a reputation of having a really good radio station. You could sign up for workshops to get involved in the station. They had a sports workshop. They said, well, we have someone that comes up and teaches the workshops every student activity period on Tuesday, Marty Glickman. They said, "Well, you come up and Marty teaches the students. He listens to your tapes and he goes through this stuff." I knew he was an older guy doing the Jets on radio.

Marty was fantastic. First of all, he had this incredible presence about him. He commanded the room. He had this unbelievable voice. And he taught me a lot. Like, when you speak during a game, you don't yell but you have to speak as though the microphone is six feet away from you. Just as, he would say, on a Broadway stage, that you speak to the last row of the house because if the last row can't hear you, then your work is lost. And that brings out the clarity in your voice too when you use all of your voice and you speak from your diaphragm.

All this stuff I learned from Marty. He'd listen to your tape. Some guys he stopped very often. You always tried to pride yourself on how long in the game you can get into before Marty stopped the tape.

Marty's thing was all about creating a picture in someone's mind. You're the artist and you're painting a picture. His mantra was always consider the listener. You want to be present in the moment but also present enough to understand how your words are being heard. He's been gone over a decade, probably, but still, every broadcast I hear him in my head. Consider the listener.

My senior year at Fordham, I win a competition. Madison Square Garden Network had a competition to find the best college sportscaster in all the colleges in the tristate area. And every college got to submit two teams. So, I win my senior year. I got to do a Knicks game, a third quarter of a Knicks game on WFAN, I think it was at the time. Jim Karvellas was the voice of the Knicks, he was doing the games alongside Walt Frazier. . . . And so, now, I was going to the Garden that night, to do the third quarter of the game with Walt Frazier. Jim Karvellas could step aside, I was gonna do the game.

I get a call at my house, and it's Marty. And I never got a call from Marty at my house. It was the day before the game that I was doing with the Knicks. He said, "I just wanted to congratulate you, wish you good luck, and hope you do well." And he goes, "Just remember, you do the damn game like you do any damn game in your college life. It doesn't matter if you're at Madison Square Garden, or the Rose Hill Gym, the game is the game, and just do the game."

It's a living, breathing game that's going on. I'm trying to deliver the emotion of what it's like to be in my seat if you're there as a fan, watching that game. That's the three-dimensional picture that I'm trying to paint. So I'm preparing all week so I can give you information that's pertinent to what's going on. I've worked my whole life on that craft to being able to see things and describe it in a concise way that you can understand it. And then I'm bringing emotion to it. I'll give you the same line. If I said to you . . . Alright, I'll give you a line of play-by-play here. "Whitehead brings it across the mid-court line, dribbles to his right, snaps across to Bogdanovic behind the arc on the right, shoots a three, and it's good. And the Nets take a three-point lead." I'm going to give you the same line. "Whitehead, across the mid-court line, snaps it past to Bogdanovic, on the arc, for three, good! Nets take a three-point lead!" I'm not saying there's anything wrong with one or the other. But the one I gave you first was from the first quarter, and the one I gave you last was right at the end of the game. Your emotion adds to the description.

You try and find different ways to say the same thing. 'Cause a lot of times, the same thing happens over and over again, and you don't want to be repetitive. Did he bounce the ball? Did he throw a chest pass? Did he fire it? Did he lob it? Did he throw it soft? I try and do that with the shots, or the way the ball hits the rim, or anything that can be more descriptive. Did a ball clank off the rim or did it graze the rim? Did it rebound to the left, or rebound to the right? Sometimes a rebound just falls to a guy. Sometimes he rebounds it in traffic. Sometimes he snatches it out of the air. Sometimes he picks it up off the ground. So there's all different ways to describe things. That's what I try and strive for.

When you get good, you're able to anticipate a play. Especially late in the game. There were a few last night, where I could see clearly the play right now. I know what's gonna happen there, there's a clear out, the seconds are winding down, you're trying to capture yourself in that moment to make sure you calm yourself where you can describe everything, and you see every detail, you're not clouded by your emotions, but at the same time, you have to be emotional. So it's that hard balance. But when you see it, you're able to describe it quickly, and then you're on it. A lot of times too, you have to be quicker than the description because you want to be on the ball. You don't want to hear the crowd scream, and you haven't said what happened to the shot yet.

So, you know, "Kilpatrick drives, kicks it out to Lopez, here's the game, three on the way for the win, and it's good." And you get a nice "good" in, and you get it in before the crowd explodes. That's when you go, "I nailed that." You know?

You have to be emotional for both sides. You have to be excited about the game itself and deliver it in an impartial fashion—get excited for exciting plays on both sides. Because you know that in New York, you're not just talking to locals. Like when I do a Nets game, I know that most of the people listening are gonna be Nets fans, but we're on a big radio station. And a lot of people just have the game on in their car when they get in. They may just be a fan of the sport.

I may get a little more emotional when the Nets score, but I still know that I can be talking to Laker fans, Knicks fans, just a sports fan. We're all held to a high standard in New York. And as much as New Yorkers are passionate about their teams, they don't like homers so much. They like to hear the game straight. The guys who do this in New York, that's what we do.

Marty said, "The game is the thing." The only person tuning in to hear you is your mother. Everybody else is tuning in to hear the game. So that's what we have to be true to.

My on-air partner Tim said something, and I made it more New York. Bogdan Bogdanovic went into the paint, and he had gotten his step on the defender and he leaned in front of him to sort of cut him off, and Tim, my partner, goes, "Aw, he's like these . . . He's on the highway, you get past somebody, and you want to make sure . . . You want to be able to get in the lane before they can come up on your right side, so you cut 'em off a little bit." And I said, "Well, it's like driving on the Major Deegan."

When we got to Brooklyn, I started doing this. When a guy would hit a three from way out, I would pick a different section of Brooklyn and say he shot it from. "From Williamsburg he knocked that one down." You know, "From Bed-Stuy." If it wasn't too far, I'd go, "Fort Greene, that's right nearby." You know? "He hit that one from Marine Park." That was a long one. Or I'll say, "The Nets are going left to right towards the Flatbush Atlantic end of Barclays Center."

So there is a lifetime of me just knowing the city.

I think New Yorkers also know New Yorkers. Or at least know when they hear somebody talk and make references that they're one of us. Not that they're intolerant of others, but I'm a guy from New York talking basketball, they know that. I was in Shea Stadium in '86, when the Mets won the World Series. When the ball went through Buckner's legs, I was in the mezzanine. I've been in the Garden where there were 3,000 people and the Knicks sucked back in the early '80s. I was at Giants Stadium the first year it opened for a Giants game. I know the depth of this city. I've been with the Nets in New Jersey, now in Brooklyn.

A lot of Orthodox Jewish people will come up to me at games because they don't have TVs at home or kids will tell me, younger kids that are Orthodox that say, "On the weekends, when we're not allowed to use the electronics, I sneak the radio into my room and I listen."

My friend was telling me, "You should start doing bar mitzvahs because that's your fan base right there. They all listen to you because they can't watch." Well, one time I did one of those, the long three-pointer, I did the "from Williamsburg." I had a guy in the concourse, a kid, a younger Orthodox Jewish guy, "Hey, you said *Williamsburg.*

I heard you say Williamsburg, man. That's where we're from." Know your audience.

The line I'd most like to deliver is "Brooklyn has a championship." That's it. The final seconds counting down and Brooklyn, you've got a championship. When the Nets went to the finals the first time in 2001, I think I was so out of my mind, I quoted Shakespeare. I think I said something like, "If this had happened on a stage, we'd condemn it as improbable fiction, but the New Jersey Nets are going to the NBA finals."

14

Getting Out

A lot of people that live on Brighton still live like they do in Russia.

It's like 1980s Russia. During the winter if you come here everybody has these crazy fur coats, like neon green, zebra print, bright red. And any of the services around here it's like in Russia. Medical, dental. I went to the dentist here to get a cleaning and they used . . . You know how first they do the water and the instruments? They didn't use the instruments, they just did the water. And then she's like, you know in the end they polish your teeth with the mint-flavored powder? She used sand. I was like, *what*? And my mom was like, "Oh, it's the dentist." I'm like, *Are you kidding me?* This is not normal.

There's a guy that goes around Brighton Beach and builds everybody a computer. My mom hired him to build her home computer. And me, my sister, and my brother were just like, *This is the stupidest idea. You can buy a desktop for $200.* And she was like, *No, no, no, he is going to do it for me.* He told her how much it's going to cost and he ordered the parts and came over and built the computer. It works. But me, no, I wouldn't hire some guy to build a computer, I would just go to the store and buy it.

Most people that live on Brighton are older people. Like everyone's grandma lives on Brighton Beach. People come here to see their grandparents. My mom's kind of exotic here. A sixty-something-year-old woman that works, speaks English. The whole building comes to her. There was an issue with bed bugs in the building, so we got into a thing with the building's management, it was really useless. But then we got this powder. It's a special powder that kills them. You order it online, and it works. So because my mom's the only person in the building practically that speaks English and is involved in the Western world, all these people came to her for this powder. It's ridiculous. So she wrote the name down and said you can order it online, and she made them all do it because now there's no bed bugs. On our floor.

Brighton Beach is a network. Everybody works out of their house. My mom found this seamstress that works out of her house, and she brings her the stuff from Russia. Me and my sister like throwing away stuff without telling her. We've lived here for like twenty-three years, so you can imagine the condition of these things. She takes them to the seamstress, gets them remade, and then she's like, "Oh, what do you think?" And I mean sometimes it's *okay*, it's not awful. But you're not saving any money. I just told her, order stuff online, go to Century 21. You can buy a very nice discount designer dress, and new.

But it's a different mentality. There's a woman here that does facials out of her house. She has a business, she has these people come in. She's very cheap. The facial, it's a good-quality facial. But you have to go to her house. She has a machine there, a chair. And all day long she does these facials, and hand treatment too. You dip your hand in the wax, she does this all day long. She makes good money.

I don't know what product she's using. If something goes wrong . . . And then she always puts on the same Russian music. My sister goes there. She thinks it's great. For me it's a little barbaric.

It's not like in Moscow. This is more like Odessa, like a provincial town in the former Soviet Union, circa 1990. People in Russia don't really look like that anymore. They all wear Western clothes. People are in your business, they just knock on your door and want to talk to you. One time, when I first moved to Brighton Beach, somebody knocked on my door, and it was some guy in a traditional Armenian outfit with this hat made of sheepskin. He was dropping off some herbs for the woman that lives next door, and he was like, "Tell her that the Armenian stopped by, and give her these herbs." I was like, you know, what the fuck? Now I have to find this woman, give her these herbs. This wouldn't happen in Moscow. You're not going to have a person that looks like that knock on your door and give herbs to your neighbor. That's just not going to happen, you know.

I would never go out with a guy that lives here, right? Never. Not in a million years. I just wouldn't. Only if he was like me—temporarily living here for some reason. But for some reason like a good, hefty reason, like that he's trying to save up money or something. If I marry a guy that lives on Brighton Beach, I would just feel like I've failed in life.

They're not really living as part of the American society. Even the younger ones. I mean, I'm not voluntarily living here. I'm living here for the purpose of paying off as much of my student loan as possible. The dudes around here, even if they do have a decent job, they're still not really a part of American life.

Most of the people I work with are American. I speak good English. But the guys around here, they're very much living in Russia. For me, it's kind of strange, for younger people to be stuck in this. And a lot of them they haven't even been back to Russia. They've been on maybe some organized tour, but they've never lived there as adults, so they're clinging on to some memory.

Russia has moved on, and a lot of the people that live around here really haven't. They're looking towards something that doesn't exist anymore. Because when you go back to Russia now, it's a totally different place than Brighton. The way people dress too, even. When I went back to Russia, I showed pictures of some of the people from the boardwalk to my family there, and my stepmom is like, "These kind of people don't exist here anymore. You just won't see them."

[She points down the boardwalk.]

I mean, just over there, people look really pissed off. That's why when people say people in New York look pissed off, and they're wearing black, for me, I think people here are really nice, compared to Moscow. People look really pissed off and they're very rude. They'll yell at you. Whereas over here, it's kind of like a happy Soviet Union. Everyone that lives here really likes it. They don't go to Manhattan. For them, it's a big deal to go.

It's like going to another country, you know?

New Yorkers

I can't nanny forever.

These two are probably the last family I would do it with, because everyone else is really insane. Like too insane. People try to hire me. I sent my résumé and they wanted me to learn Farsi.

I don't know, I think New York has this interesting way of turning into . . . I think your attitude changes everything about it. Because it can work with you wonderfully if you cooperate, and it can be this wonderful experience: curiosity, and opportunities, and gratitude.

If you work with it. It requires that you reflect on the Vedas of Buddhism. You can't control this, it's all temporary. "Pain is inevitable. Suffering is optional." That's the one thing I remind myself of.

The inconvenience is inevitable. Suffering is totally up to you.

Because it's not here for you. New York wasn't waiting for you, Taylor Swift. It has been existing. That's the attitude that's sort of the most irritating thing. And you think it's this romantic comedy, Woody Allen experience, Broadway, whatever, that's waiting for you to give you what you want. It's not.

It's a lot more liberating to let go of any entitlement that you have about how your life should be. You let go of the entitlement when you start having a little compassion for how hard it is for everyone else.

The part of your brain that's responsible for creativity, abstract thinking, or emotional development is kind of a luxury. If you're surrounded by stress and trauma your whole life, your brain just goes, "Hey, we can't afford it. We don't have the energy to devote to thinking about things and reflecting those things." And so there's impulsivity that you see with people. If there's a lot of impulsivity and there's a lot of disregulation, there's people who are quick to anger. They probably have a trauma history or grew up in a lot of stress. It's not because they're just bad. Understanding that has made me a lot more compassionate.

I'm worried I'll lose the gratitude that comes with living in Brooklyn.

I'm scared. I'm scared to lose that. And I think it stays because it has to, like I have to exercise it in New York every day.

It happened to me in Houston. I became bratty, I became entitled, I was making a lot of money and it was really easy to do everything. You just think about yourself more. Then you're also unhappier and you're wondering, why? And you're more caught up in that stuff. Now I'm healthier than I've ever been, in terms of relating to all of that stuff. But I'm afraid it will go away if I don't have to keep it in check.

I don't think that people who are rich are inherently evil. Because it stops being hard, they stop being grateful. You stop reflecting.

I like being tested. It gives me fulfillment. There's a fullness you feel after doing something hard. Accomplishing something. You know?

I always knew that I was going to leave Houston. Both my parents left their hometown. I actually used to think it was illegal to live where your parents lived. Like you had to move.

I DON'T KNOW how much longer . . . Man, if I found out I was pregnant here it'd be like *Escape from New York*. I don't even want to have an ultrasound in the city. It's like Fukushima, like this radiation of narcissism. I'm becoming like that. I can feel it happening to me.

I'm like Jeff Goldblum in *The Fly*. I can just feel like I'm caring about things that I never thought I'd care about. Like kale smoothies and I go to barre classes. It's a rich white lady class, and it's fine and it's great and it's so good for my abs, but I'm worried that the longer I stay here, the harder it will be for me to live anywhere else. I don't know if I could go to the Container Store and Target and that be my Saturday, and a fancy one at that.

ANTWON SHAVERS A singer from Arkansas

A month has gone by since we last met and Antwon told me about his aspirations to become a singer. He says he'll be gone by this time next month. Maybe not. Maybe he'll stop working at Macy's and go to school. He's got his transcripts. It seems like most young people in New York are going to school.

New York is making me want to go back home. Not *home* home, but you know, somewhere else. Like travel somewhere else. I feel like I haven't done what I've wanted to do yet, as far as my career and trying to become a singer. It's been kind of rough.

See, right now, I'm in the process of looking for another job. Because when you're in New York, you have to have at least two or three jobs, I'm telling you, because you just cannot go with just one job.

I don't know if I do move on, I don't know. Maybe I'd go to California. Yeah. So . . . but we will see. We will see.

Maybe it's just me thinking too much. Maybe I just need to settle down and calm down and think about what I really want to do and who I need to talk to in order for me to make this move. Because right now, it's like I'm just working and working and trying to come up with plans so I can maybe go to school.

Rockaway? Oh my goodness. It's so boring there. It's cold. I'm right by the Atlantic Sea. Oh my goodness. I never thought I'll actually be staying on a beach, though. I mean, it's beautiful in a way, but I don't know . . . Maybe it's boring right now because it's cold and there's not a lot of people outside, but I did hear on Beach 96, when it becomes summertime, there be like a lot of people there. So maybe I can meet some friends while I'm there. Because I've never actually been on a beach, like walking and whatnot.

I went out in the cold weather once, but I was just walking around seeing what was around the little town, because it's a small town. And they have polices . . . all the polices, they know their area really well, so it's like they just one little town. If I was to call the police, it'd be like eight cops coming to the door. That's how bad it is. Like it'd just be that little group of police officers.

When I'm in the subway and I see these kids dancing and singing, I'm like "wow." Because I want to do it so bad. But I can't do that. What they do is they sing a song and they expect people to give them money. It'd be people with good jobs that just give them a dollar. I'm like, "I can't just do that." You know, I'm too nice. I'd be wanting to give them like at least ten dollars or twenty dollars. But a dollar—what a dollar going to do to a homeless person? You can't do that to them. I mean, it's bad already.

I love coming to Manhattan, walking around 42nd Street. Looking at the lights—I like the lights. And I like being around people. I'm a believer of it. But like, I can't be around ignorant people, you know. But there's a lot of crazy people here. I'm telling you.

One day, I was standing on the train and this man was just . . . I guess he kept staring at me. And I'm like, "Oh my God, stop staring at me." He kept staring at me, kept staring at me. Then I finally said, "Hey!" And then he started a conversation with me and I'm like, "Okay, okay." It wasn't really a conversation. It was like he just kept talking. That's how weird it is. They'll just keep talking to you even though you not listening.

TO BE HONEST with you, the most talented people are in the church. And then they break out. It's like a dove flying solo and then all the other doves come along. I want to go to a church that's known. My friends was like, "Why you can't just go to a church that's not known?" And I told them, "Well, it's because I want exposure." And I feel like if I go to a church that's known, there probably be unknown artists inside the church that can pick me right on up and I can end up doing something with them or making a duet or participating in workshops, stuff like that.

It would be nice to go to a nondenominational church just to feel the vibe and hear the choir—if I like it well enough, I'd probably join and try to get my foot in the door. Because if I'm really good, they would say something like, "This is Antwon. He's from so and so, so and so." Then that's how I got my name broadcast throughout the church, that's how I get exposed. Then there's more people there and you never know who's sitting inside the church, so it's like . . . That would be good. To be known by other people.

It's been slow paced for me. Maybe I'm just depressed, I don't know, because maybe I'm homesick. Maybe that's what it is?

I think of certain things, certain people. Like my grandmother. Because she stress me all the time about going to church. *Make sure you go to church. Make sure you do this, do that. You need to go to school and all that.* But what are y'all doing to help me here? You know, y'all should try to help me, you know. But they can't help me now because I'm a long way from home.

New York is just boring right now because I don't really know a lot of people to try to help me, but if I get myself out there then I would be able to have people out there to try to tell me where I need to be, where I should go as far as me trying to find like, you know, different types of venues, because I hear all the time that they have open-mic nights.

But I don't know where.

So what I got in mind right now is during my off days, I want to try to look up some places and see what time the open mics starts, and just go and sing a song or talk to a manager inside the club or whatnot. I try my best because when I was back in Arkansas, I used to sing for funerals and most of the people I sung for that died, I knew them. "Antwon, can you come and do this solo, do that solo?" So I had to ride around with my grandmother because she's the piano player. Ride around to different churches and sing for them.

Recently I sung for this family because they had lost their dad. I was at work and they came to Macy's to buy a suit for their dad for the funeral. I started talking to them. I was working in the area and so I seen them and they was looking for a suit and they seen me and they seen how I was dressed, and so they asked and I was like, "Okay, okay," and that's how it ended up me singing.

I sung "His Eye Is on the Sparrow" for them right there in the store. My manager was there and everything. One of them was like, "You got a beautiful voice. You're going to go places. Don't ever forget that," and *du du du du*. I was like, "Well, thank you. I was just doing this in honor of your dad."

I just sang. I felt like they was a little healed, you know. I wanted them to come out the store not all down and depressed because their daddy is gone. I wanted them to know that he's in a better place and they shouldn't have to worry because everything is going to be okay. And I been through their situation before with my grandfather, so it was kinda like the same.

What makes me stay here is me being a fighter, keeping my eyes on the prize because I didn't come here for nothing. I've been here for almost five months now.

Man, I'm so mad. I missed these auditions I was looking forward to. The Apollo—I was looking forward to it. I did get there on time. They just weren't letting other people come in to auditions because they was too lazy. They probably didn't want to invite nobody else. They was just wanting to get through it. But they could've gave me a chance.

Some man said that. Some man that work up there. You know, the receptionist that worked up there? And I was so mad. I said, "I'm not from New York. Y'all ain't going to give me no chance?" I said, "I've been waiting on this a long time."

No is no. "You know," he said, "you have to come in the fall." I said, "The fall? I be gone by then."

They don't care if you're not there. If you're not on time, it's over with. They like that here. If you miss a photo shoot, you over with. You know, that's it. You lost your money. That's it.

I'M NOT GOING BACK to Arkansas. The only time I'm going back is to go sing at my auntie's wedding and that's it. She's marrying a doctor so there's going to be a lot of people. She want me to wear black and gold, so I'm going to go up there looking right. Got the perfect outfit. And when I'm back there singing and everyone's like, "Antwon, what's

New York like?" I'm going to say it's big and rude. I'll be like, "Don't go there. Don't you go there. Don't y'all go there. I'm telling y'all, I would not come here. If y'all come here, y'all can come here to visit, that's about it, but don't come here to stay."

Nah, I'm going to say I'm doing good. You know, I'm doing good. I'm working, you know. I don't have to tell them everything. I tell them everything when I become famous.

But they know that I'm in a stable place, so you know. And I'm living with six roommates, so they know that part.

They know I'm alive, so.

I will probably tell them the Rockaways are beautiful. It's quiet. I'm by the beach and it's a lot of down-to-earth people there.

Sometimes I feel like I be missing out. Only restaurant I've been to since I've been here on 42nd Street is TGI Fridays and I had this like sweet-sour type of teriyaki chicken. It tasted pretty good, but it was twenty dollars. But I think the waiter had got his little tip in on the receipt because it was supposed to be nineteen some dollars but he had put some more money on there so I had to pay twenty something dollars for this and it didn't even cost that much. I was so mad, but I didn't say nothing. I didn't say nothing. I was just like, "Okay, maybe he needed this more than I did," so I just paid.

Like I told you the last time, every time I wake up, I feel like I'm in a movie. I'm in a subway watching everybody go through their personal issues and their personal problems, it's like I'm in a movie. You know, I meet people and I talk to them. . . and I look the other way and I see the other people and they talking about their situations, it's like a movie. It's like everybody is an actor to me. Every time I see them, it's like an actor. I'm playing in a scene or something. That's how I feel since I've been here. I feel like I'm in a movie. A documentary of me trying to make it here in New York.

I feel like it's going to be a happy ending.

15

The End of the Journey

JASON NUNES An electrician working on the Empire State Building

The management of the Empire State Building said, "We're doing the antennas. You guys qualified?"

"Absolutely, we're tower guys."

Because not every electrician goes up on that tower. It's specialized. It's all RF on that tower, radio frequency. They make probably more money from that tower than they make renting out the building. Radio stations, antennas, all on top, broadcasting, broadcasting. It's sixteen floors on that tower. Sixteen floors! It's a building on top of a building.

You've got to be qualified. I'm comms trained, I'm tower trained. They want to remove the old conduits going all the way up the tower, put new feeders in, outlets and obstruction lights, LED. Change everything out. Because it's usually bulbs. This guy had to constantly go change bulbs. I met him, he had a curly mustache, been doing the work for thirty years. Loves heights, I'll tell you that.

Basically, they wanted to clean the tower. It got congested after time. You have antennas that are obsolete, cables that are obsolete. They want to remove that, clear it up. It's real estate at the end of the day. And they want to repaint the tower because it's chipping and everything else. So it's a whole restoration. We had to go there and cut out all the old conduits, remove all that stuff.

It's surreal, it's so fucking high. Once you go up to the observation deck, the 86th floor or whatever it is. VIP is 104. You go out and there's a railing this high and you're looking—open—out off the 104. Then you go up another staircase at the dome. That's the physical dome and it's a submarine door that pops open and then you're physically on the tower. Once you get that wind... Your legs start buckling. You gotta walk around the dome and a ship ladder that's on the dome to the actual tower. Now that's sixteen stories. It starts pretty wide and then it narrows.

It's fucking scary.

You just go. To the guy with the mustache, it's nothing to him. But you're like, "Oh, man." The wind is gusting, you're like, "I'm going to blow off this thing." Then, once you're inside you're like, "I'm good. I'm good." It's so many tubes and everything. The six-inch RF copper tubes looked like steam pipes.

I got up to the sixteenth floor of the tower. Now, once you get up there it's a platform. A round platform. No railings. You come up from the middle. . . . The only thing that's above you is a twenty-five-foot antenna, with a beacon. Which we changed. And it's pegs. Pegs you actually pull down and you climb the last twenty-five feet. That's it. You come up the middle of the grating, and it's probably eight, nine feet all around. It's big, but there's no railing and you're on top . . . you're at fifteen hundred feet in the air. Wind gusting.

We did the work in January because it had to be ready for the painters in the summer. Sixty mile an hour wind. Icicles. Dude. Icicles on your jacket. Everywhere. Your hands. Cold. Cold. Hand warmers. I had six pairs of pants on. Thermal, thermal, thermal. Socks. You took your hand out of the glove, it was instantly almost frozen.

But I could see everything of New York. Central Park. Lights. You sit there and you're just amazed. But you had a time limit too. There was so much to do. They had to shut off RF before we went up there. It was one o'clock, you had to be up there ready. One a.m., ready. Everybody on the dome. Right on top of 104.

One a.m. At 1:45 they're shutting everything down. You've got to be down by four. It turns on at four. You only have that time frame to do the work. First, we decommed. Cut off existing power and started running aluminum. Everything's all galvanized. Actual feeders we'd be cutting and replacing. Cut and replacing sections into these boxes, and then from those boxes we would pipe out for the LEDs, so it's a new power source.

Everything's a new power source for the LED, and we would put obstruction lights. It would be so dark and as we're going, it's just lighting, lighting until we're done. At the end everything was lit. Every floor would have a work light, a blue LED . . . you know? Those are obstruction lights only. Just so you could see. It was cool.

Until the end, you're getting there and then we're at the top. It's all the red lights. Red obstruction lights for airplanes now. Underneath that metal tower they had these cones . . . like jelly jars, and the beacon up top. The beacon ain't small. That's when I froze. Wasn't cut out for it, man. I was like . . . I'm up *really* high.

I'm scared of heights.

Not scared, but . . . aware. I'm not the, "Oh, let me look over the edge." No, I'm like, *aggghhhh*. I did the obstruction lights right under the tower . . . the bridge before the pegs. Because you're just climbing pegs now. There's two people that went up there and they were the craziest ones. My partner was on the outside of the tower climbing. It's a metal thing with beams. Now you've gotta imagine ship ladders going floor to floor right there. It's very tight. You can't have harnesses. He changed the whole thing, yeah, to LED. It's a whole new fixture.

Your adrenaline's pumping so much up there. It's not like you're tired . . . it's like you're on a roller coaster, but are you going to get tired? Nah. Nah, not so much. You're so into what you're doing because you've got to be focused.

They say do not write your name, but everybody wrote their name. People that's been there, did tower work. It's a small group of people that have been up there. My name's up there. I'm sure the mustache guy was up there.

I see it now, the tower. When I was done with it, you look at that thing and like, I fuckin' did that shit, you know. And my son is like, "Daddy, that's the building you did." Yeah, damned right. It lasts for a while. But somebody is going to be ripping up my shit soon.

In the 1990s, the West Village was still partly industrial but the maritime trades were mostly gone, and the abandoned Hudson River piers and the Gansevoort meat market were frequented at night by sex workers and other people seeking, uh, companionship. And there were homeless encampments.

One Sunday morning I wandered over to Sixth Avenue and into a Mass at 16th Street. I knew the Jesuits from high school. I didn't know much about that parish, although I recognized it because it was a well-known place, sort of their lower Manhattan headquarters for 150 years.

I went into the Mass, which was very progressive and intelligent. Light on the bells and whistles. Maybe some whistles, but you know. It was consoling, and humane. After the Mass, the pastor said, "You know, they need help with the Welcome Table downstairs if anybody has any time." So I went downstairs and stuck my nose in and thought, "Oh, this is interesting. This is strangely familiar."

It had once been the old lower church, so its atmosphere somehow held a familiar way of being communal. It was the kind of Catholicism that was true to my experience. I mean I'm as familiar with rules and obligations as anybody, but that's not the essence of it. My sense of religion was always of a kind of culturally unified experience, ecumenical and charitable, or at least openhearted. Like when the Sacred Heart says, in a mystical encounter, "Don't love each other out of love for Me, do it out of love for each other!"

There's a tradition at Xavier of dedication to service, and the pursuit of social justice. For instance, the character Father Barry in *On the Waterfront* was inspired by a Jesuit from Xavier, who was active in the reform of labor unions. In fact, the story is that in the movie, Karl Malden is wearing Father Corridan's black fedora. Which is maybe why, if you notice, it doesn't really fit. There's other traditions there too, of course. You can find many ways of seeing things in the history of Catholic spirituality and Jesuit spirituality. There were some Jesuits who were vigorously left-wing. And there's also been some very right-wing Jesuits, you know. They'd tend to be at every corner of every controversy. It's a big order, and there's a lot of them, and they're mostly smart, and they all think they know what they're doing; and so, frequently, they're at opposite sides of the same issues.

One thing all three major Western religious traditions share when they're at their best is a sensitivity to social—I want to say—*harmony*. Social order? Taking care of one another, right?

So, as I say, I went down there and it was familiar for those reasons. There's a particular look in their eye that people get when they're having fun doing something slightly weird like that. An enthusiasm. The "How can I explain that this is more fun than watching the football game on television?" look that they get in their eye. Because it is.

That first day, I just picked up trays. I didn't get put over on the door for a while, and I don't know exactly how long, how many trips it took before that happened. I washed pots, which was the easiest job, because you only have to feel sorry for yourself, washing pots for two and a half hours.

One time, some nasty winter afternoon, the guys out on the door needed some help. The boss sent me out to help the guy who was running the gate, a good man who became a close friend named John Brady, a wonderful salt-of-the-earth Irishman from Queens. He'd been a noncom in U.S. Army intelligence on the Mexican border in the '50s, where he had developed a sensitivity to social inequalities. He was also an electrical mechanic and very active in his union, Elevator Constructors Local One, NYC; guess it was in working in that trade that he lost two of his fingers. It was in knowing John that I first developed the dictum that you can always trust what you are told by a man with fingers missing.

We fell right in. John and I just got to being very good pals pretty quickly. He was good-humored and he had that Queens kind of deadpan jolliness, you know. A certain skeptical amusement. He used to go to the track. Mostly to Aqueduct. We went with him once, and he made a two-dollar bet for us and won us fifty bucks. He used to enjoy going flounder fishing on party boats from Sheepshead Bay. That was really living. He was a wonderful man. I loved him. He used to run that gate, and it was a different scene in those days. It was kind of raucous and improvisatory, and there were fights, and the kitchen operation was less institutionalized, so there were a lot of ugly casseroles and canned vegetables. There was substantial business they did, though, because it was already a thousand or so people of a typical Sunday.

It was around 1982 that the Welcome Table was invented. It was around the time of the Reagan administration, when a lot of programs were shut down and a lot of mental health facilities were shut down. A lot of people who had psychiatric diagnoses ended up on the street. It was the beginning of the great inflation of the number of homeless people on the streets. There always were homeless people, except before then they were called bums. . . .

In the '80s, the numbers expanded, and that number came to include a lot of different kinds of people. It became a political issue. Some of the churches responded organically to it. Ours is downstairs, which is more, like, cavernous, although brightly lit, with side alcoves where the coffee station is, and a table for free loaves of day-old bread, some of it quite fancy, and a table where some very goodhearted ladies will give you encouragement and inspirational literature. One alcove is available for volunteer chiropractors, and nursing students doing blood-pressure screenings and all, and a table of law students counseling on housing issues, you know. Kind of a mercy mall around the perimeter, while the meal is buzzing along in the middle of the dining hall. And there's a room on the side for distributing donated clothing, which has to be done earlier or later so as not to start a stampede. Some of the guests are homeless, but many aren't. Many are working poor, or have health problems, or substance problems, or are elderly people who live alone and come to socialize. Some are crazy, like the poor fella who lives in Penn Station and insists on just wearing plastic bags on his feet, even in the snow. Although lately he's been given a pair of Crocs, so there's progress. And some who you'd take for crazy, like the man who always wears the thermal quilted hood over his head—without a parka—and sunglasses, summer, fall, winter, and spring.

We had an elderly man come in once at the end of the day, looking for a referral, who had just become homeless, and it turned out he was an international chess grand master. Go figure. Used to always be guys outside selling "loosies," but we had to curtail that because they were squabbling over the territory. And besides, smokin's no good for you.

To do this job, you have to know people. I don't mean you have to know the right people. In fact, you should know the wrong people. You have to listen. And remember, such as you're able to. You might learn something.

I heard that they did some kind of a survey of qualifications for success as a psychotherapist. What kind of aptitude did you need to be successful as a shrink? It turns out that the most essential aptitude was whether you were a good friend, right? Not meaning you have a soft heart, but that you have the capacity to do the practical tasks of being a friend. Listening, discerning, sympathizing, but being willing to express differences of opinion. You know, just like being a normal person rather than a disinterested party. A normal other. A thou, you know. Your aptitude for being a "thou" to someone's "I."

Working the door is much the same thing. It's like learning the skills of how to live in the city, how to walk down the sidewalk, stuff we don't even fucking know how to do anymore. How to walk down the sidewalk without bumping into each other. How to see the person when they're coming, rather than not see them.

Mitch Snyder, a political activist and advocate for homeless people who died a number of years ago, gave a talk once where he said something like, "If somebody's asking you for a dollar, you don't have to hand them a dollar, as long as you say something." If somebody asks you for a handout, don't feel constrained to give them a nickel. Your constraint is to acknowledge that they have just asked you for a nickel. You can say no, but just don't ignore that they just asked you for a nickel. People are hungry for acknowledgment of their being, their personhood.

So how do you keep the door? Well, you better know how to close it, how to open it. I mean, hey, you've got to know those essentials. I actually have kind of a talent for doing that ridiculous job, because I also know a little bit about what's going to happen next.

I have a pretty strong capacity for systems analysis, for—what's the word? For social dynamics, you know? So you have to keep that in your back pocket, because you work for a different boss every week. It's my little game that I play for twenty years that I never tell them what to do until they don't know what to do. And then I tell them what to do. Or I say, "No, but what if you do this?"

My claim to this talent is about quantitative stuff, right—time, space, you know. Father John Bucki, a good friend who used to run that joint, was great that way because he has a big heart, he's generous and good-humored and all, but he also has a really strong quantitative talent, like how many cans of tuna will it take. He could just do it off the top of his head. My quantitative capacity has more to do with stage management, right? How many in and how many out, what the rate of flow has to be in order to not slow things down, or when to stop, or "Cripes, don't do that now!"

And then there are the situations . . .

Like the time I went down the subway to get a MetroCard or something, and there was a guy down there being hassled by some undercover cops because they were accusing him of being about to jump the turnstile and they were kind of inviting him to get violent in his response so they could get him. He looked at me and he said, "Yeah, ask him, ask him. Ask him!" Me. "He's one of my peeps." You know? "Ask him. That's where I was. I was just over there." And I said, "Yeah. In fact, why don't you come back with me now? Let's go get another sandwich." Somehow, I rescued him from this encounter with the cops, and I didn't know the fucking guy, but I mean, you know . . . whatever. He was trying not to react and it was kind of devilish. The cops were trying to coax him into resisting so they could get a collar. He left with me and we went back and he came inside.

It's like sanctuary. People come in. We're on pretty good terms with the cops, and I respect the cops, and we need the cops and everything. This is who we are. From the cops to the felons, people to a large part respect where we're at and what we're doing and who we are.

There's a saying, "You have to do it with humor because it's only with laughter that the poor will forgive you the charity you show them." The idea is that good humor is an indispensable tool because there's always tension about it if you're giving somebody something. Most people would rather laugh if given the opportunity, and if they can relax for a minute, they find the way.

One of the greatest compliments I've ever received, and it was the first time that I ever really talked to him or even knew his name, was from Elliott Carter. Some years ago, something happened, some tussle on the line, you know, and afterwards, he said, "Can I tell you something? I don't think I've ever seen you lose your temper." I said, "Really? Well, I have, but I know what you mean." I know that it's on the back side of the Ten Commandments. On the back of the tablet there's a few other commandments, and one of them is "Never Lose Thy Temper." Remember that losing your temper never gets you closer to where you want to end up. In .05, .005 percent of the time, does losing your temper get you further toward where you're heading? 99 point whatever percent of the time, it doesn't.

Yes, it's an actual statistic. It's just the truth. If your trench is being invaded by a gang of storm troopers on a foggy night, then you might have to lose your temper in order to survive, although your chances aren't really good anyway. You always lose ground by losing your temper, so just don't do it. You can get pissed off as much as you want, but redirect it.

In the city there's people who don't give a damn, and other people who do. But everybody has to leave by the sidewalk, right? So that's where the real true human encounter happens. And so when you get acclimated to the atmosphere on the street, or, geez, in the subway . . . you begin to understand the city in a new way, and to see the people as they really are, each a kind of blossom. However fragrant.

Sometimes you do get wounded of course, get physically or maybe emotionally exhausted. Part of the job is to enter into, as some have put it, the chaos of another's person's life, even in this relatively circumscribed, civil way, and that energy does burn emotional fuel. There's a cost. And sometimes you can get hurt just by colliding with your own limits. Sometimes all you can do is witness and sympathize.

Most people don't see what's right in front of them at all. They don't. Especially now, lately. It used to be that crowds of people moving in the city were like schools of fish, in the coordination of their movements. But now it seems that, while fish I guess still know how to do it, we humans have lost the knack. Now we just walk around bumping into each other all the time. In all seriousness, I worry that the social fabric of the city has eroded, as it has changed from an organic social entity into some strange virtual-reality theme park. You can actually watch the people *not* seeing what's going on around them. They're in their own world.

I THINK THEY'VE COME to understand that the ticket is a good analog tool for managing the flow. It's a good way for everyone to see what's going on, rather than just come and go and "I'm the boss" and "You do what I tell you to do." If it's like, "Tickets, please, tickets," it's a good, kind of old-timey way of keeping a number but also keeping a rate. A connection. You have an orderly rate of flow and everybody can get on the merry-go-round.

It's a way of saying, "I see you. I welcome you back."

It's almost eucharistic in its gesture, you know. Communitarian, whatever. And that is a constant. That's always been the case. We used to joke about how fast you tear them. You could manage the rate of flow.

There's the little bits of song and dance that it takes to keep people willing to wait a little longer. We used to tear the tickets as if they were hard to tear. You can get ten whole seconds to tear one ticket off. "God damn this thing!" You know? Then people are moving slowly, but at least they know they're moving. They've not been forgotten about.

We don't have to do that so much anymore because people get to know you and then they trust. Some always complain, of course, but for the large part people know where you're coming from.

I do say "Peace be with you" when I give them the ticket. It's a sincere expression. In one sense it's just a figure of speech, but it's a good one. I can offer you at least this much. Here's an inch of peace. How big is a ticket? Five centimeters of peace.

We always try to be fair, but if you get back on line, or even just ask, you can usually have as many tickets as you want. . . . Certainly as long as the food lasts. In a world of "no" we try to cultivate a culture of "yes." It's compassion, right?

The only thing I respect in the world is compassion. The only thing that's of any interest to me in the world is love. It's the only thing that's interesting. The greatest, the most precious thing in the world is company—the company of those you love. So all you need to do is love everybody and then you can always have it.

BALEM CHOI A nurse

In New York, people come here to get treatment. They want cures. Most of the time it's impossible. According to Medicare, a patient is eligible for hospice when they have a prognosis of six months or less. No one ever knows definitively how long a patient has to live. Some doctors will refer patients too early and some patients will be referred to us days before they die.

Some patients aren't ready. They're still in a stage where their doctor's just told them, "There's nothing else I can do for you. You have to go into hospice." So they're still accepting that, coming to terms with their death, imminent death. Some patients come and they know exactly what they want.

The reality is, yes, when I come into the picture it means that there's nothing else they can do, but if I can somehow improve whatever time they have left, that's a win.

A lot of people in New York—either they live here or they come here for treatment. If you live here, you've got money. You know where to go for treatment. It's well known that the hospice referral rate in New York is the lowest in the country because of that.

This is a city of people who get what they want when they want it. It's stressful for the medical profession. People come from all over just for that. *Some* option. "There *must* be something you could do for me." They have to give them something. It's stressful to be in that position. Another surgery? You want chemotherapy?

People who should be in hospice will have to die in the hospital because they haven't been given this option. Doctors don't refer them in time or they just don't refer them at all.

I used to work at a cancer hospital, that's how I moved on to hospice. That's the reason why I left, because I saw people who shouldn't be in the hospital. People who should have been home, not getting treatment, enjoying their families. It was all because their team, their medical team, weren't up front with them. Of course, yeah, some people are not accepting and they're difficult, but a lot of that is the team working with them, walking them through.

I'M A NATIVE NEW YORKER, maybe I'm drawn to other tenacious New Yorkers.

One of my favorite patients, she loved the rugelach at Zabar's, and she got to a point where she couldn't walk there anymore, like she wasn't even strong enough to take the car there, so she'd want the rugelach from there, and she knew exactly where she wanted her bagels from, even when she could barely eat.

We went out to lunch once together. She took me to the Chinese restaurant across the street because they had really cheap lunch specials. On the Upper West, a hole-in-the-wall Chinese place, and she ordered the chicken wings. This tiny, emaciated cancer patient. That was also the only place she could walk to, so a block away.

We're very proud of the few things that we have.

Towards the end, she was still making pickled herring at home, which I had never had, apart from meeting her. She sent me home with some. I think I was pregnant with my first then, and I almost threw up, the smell of it. But she was making it and she couldn't eat it herself, she was just giving it away.

She is someone that I think about a lot. Like, what if I had done more. Those are the things that you have to disconnect from, because it'll haunt you.

SOME OF THE PATIENTS will get into conversations about New York. I get to know their stories, what New York was like years ago. They don't forget New York, but they aren't able to express it as well, or to be part of conversations, to participate in conversations at all.

Today I visited a dementia patient who is a poet, he's always singing. But he will never talk to me. He will just back me away if I want to do anything with him. Today he talked to me. He asked me where I went to nursing school, and he told me that he went to graduate school here in New York. He sings his poetry. He keeps everyone awake, including his wife, who is in the hospital bed next to him.

After doing this for five years, I don't think there are any situations that I'm nervous about walking into. I just feel like, most situations boil down to someone's afraid of reality. They just need to be listened to.

YESTERDAY I MET this amazing woman who has brain cancer, who was diagnosed just a few months ago, and was told that she had maybe five months to live. She decided that it was a good time for hospice. She kind of pursued it herself.

She just laid it all out, and said, "I want to be home, and I want the few months that I have left to be good. I know that when I'm no longer functional I'm going to need help." She just was like, "I've had a great life, I had a great job, I have a great support system." Every question I was about to ask her she answered before I even asked.

She opened up to me and said that she had a history of depression for over forty years. I'm assuming she'd spoken to counselors or therapists and processed all that already, so she was in a place where she came to accept her life.

I don't know what I'm walking into. Sometimes it's really fulfilling to meet a patient who hasn't come to grips with their end of life and to help them through that, in whatever way that I can. I can't say that I'm very comfortable talking to people about afterlife and death and what it's like and, spiritually, what they are going to go through. But often you just go and listen and have them talk about it.

THE WOMAN WHO loved Zabar's and took me to the restaurant, I was in her area last week, and it was pretty much a flood of memories. It was almost four years ago that I was taking care of her. I was back in the area and I was trying to piece it together. I couldn't exactly remember what street she lived on, but everything looked familiar.

I was even remembering the thoughts that I had while I was caring for her, while I was making my way to her house, leaving her house. I remember certain bus stops that I would wait at to catch the bus to leave. At that point it was just like a rewind, remembering all this.

In the end, I was just thankful that I had that experience to get to know her. She was one of those people who encouraged me to do a lot of things. She, I think, was a well-known social worker and a teacher. She taught a lot of social workers her trade. She was used to mentoring people.

She had a big dinner party at this place on the Upper West, a restaurant she loved. She planned out the menu, she knew exactly what she wanted. She had a quartet come, some Julliard students, and they played. There was some opera singers, all the music that she loved. She planned everything out.

I remember the last few weeks of her life. She sat down quite a bit with her lawyer, and with her nephew who was her health-care proxy and power of attorney. And I think that's what she was doing, she was planning the rest of her life.

She was a big traveler, she would collect little knickknacks from all over the place, and she would have them all over her apartment. At the memorial service, there were gift bags, and in each bag they had wrapped a few of her knickknacks, for people to take home. She probably planned that too.

THE POET I TOOK CARE OF, I've taken care of him for two admissions. This is his third. He got referred back. I haven't heard him singing recently, it's been a few years since I've heard him sing, but I hear that he does it at night.

When he used to sing, well, yeah, it was nonsensical, same words over and over, which I think, to him, is his poetry of New York now.

EDMÉE REIT On growing old in New York

I can't really imagine living in another American city. I have sixty-eight tickets for concerts and ballet between now and May. In February they're having this great bunch of things over at Carnegie Hall. It's eighteen days out of the month. Which is when it's cold and snowy and you can't ever get a bus over there, but I'll do as many as I can.

It's gold in the bank. That's how I think of it. Sixty-eight tickets is a gold mine. Because of the pleasure. It's wonderful. I've been to three concerts this week. I don't always do that, there's some times when you go much longer.

I adore the ballet. I was lucky, I started with the New York City Ballet in 1949. The top balcony. I saw ballets for years where I never saw the top part of the scenery. But I came across a ticket that was in a book in the library and it was $1.50 in the balcony. Somehow we felt it was affordable. So I've seen the New York City Ballet since 1949 and I adore them. I also give money to them and to the School of American Ballet. They're very big in my heart.

I don't go to SAB very much, because it's the old things. Some of them are really quite clunky, and it also troubles me in a sense that half of their stars are European. I don't mind one, but when you have six or seven . . . Well, we've got a lot of good ones here that I think should have a chance. I could see *Giselle* a lot, but I don't particularly want to see *Sleeping Beauty* all the time. What I love is these other companies and more avant-garde types of things. So you didn't have the endless *Nutcracker* syndrome.

Some of it I don't like, and then I don't clap. I once booed when the Russian ballet was here. I don't support bad art, but then I realized it was selfish of me to do that, because these people had worked hard and I know what they do. These kids give up everything for a short period of the work that they love and suddenly they're forty years old and they've got forty more years to live, if they're lucky, and they've got to find a whole new career.

Well, I only booed once. Now if I don't like something, I just sit.

My concert last night, it was all Bach, who is my lifetime favorite, but they did it terribly fast and I couldn't savor it. The encores were great because they were much slower, but they whizzed through everything else. Finally, after the third one, I thought, I'm not happy. But I don't boo anymore.

Look what we have. Look what we have every night. I mean, aren't you stunned by what there is available? I just gave away four tickets because they were the same night as other things I wanted to see more.

I'm lucky I have the money to buy these things, but I don't buy Arche shoes much anymore and I don't buy clothes anymore, 'cause I don't really need them now that I'm not in the public eye. But I do like my concerts.

There's so much in New York for beans, that if it's not free it's practically free. Just look in the back page of the *Times* on Friday on what's doing. You see so many things that there are available. And in many places . . . I hate to say it, I get in free now to all the museums with my pass, but you can pay minimal in certain places. You can figure out a way. And you don't have to sit in a bar every night and spend your money on drink. If you want something, you'll find a way to get it. Not easily, but you've got to give up something else.

It's just a matter of priorities, what's important to you. This is such a cornucopia. It's fantastic. I simply can't imagine living anywhere else.

I didn't have to sit in the orchestra, I was perfectly content to sit on the balcony because that meant I could either see more ballet, or if I sat in the balcony I could, you know, maybe see two or three ballets for one in the orchestra. To this day, I never sit in the orchestra.

Physically it's a big struggle for me at times, but I go out in rain or snow. The only time I didn't go out was the day we had the blizzard, unfortunately. I couldn't. I really thought, "Let's be smart about this." But otherwise I don't care if it's raining or if it's cold.

It's my dinner, it's my lunch, it's my breakfast. Seeing art, seeing music, seeing ballet. I love going to the Morgan. It's very comforting and it's just enough. The Frick always interests me.

I'd never take a cab. New Yorkers don't do that.

MICHAEL RODRIGUEZ A seeker

Throughout my whole life I've seen death so many times.

I mean Craig, my whole life, dude, I've been done. You know what I mean? I just can't say that I know why. You know what I mean? I'm just being led.

It's almost like a coffin for me sometimes, this is my resting place. This is where I wanna lie dead. In that river. And it seems like being in that river, if I'm dead, I can almost see all these souls, all these creatures, all these things approaching me, marveling at me.

Even these microbes and all these things around me, it's comforting in a way 'cause they there. I'm not dead by myself. So whatever I chuck myself into, I know I won't be there by myself. Either there's gonna be spirits or there gonna be microorganisms, there gonna be some form of life there. The afterlife is there and the present is there, the past is there. We're carrying all this weight.

In the water all that weight dissipates. You might go down, but somewhere it'll start slowing down it seems like. That's the biggest fear, reaching the bottom of that river and being sucked into the bottom. Almost like if your soul reaches the bottom of that, it's a big chance you're not getting out.

NEW YORK CITY being mystical, the water is even more so. The water here in that river, it's nothing like, let's say, the Mississippi.

The Hudson and the East River are different. There's definitely a difference. I can say it like this: one is a negative and one is a positive. Because in nature you gotta have a negative. In order to make the two you need positive and negative. Even in nature in order to have children you need a woman and a man, right? So you need the two. There's more to New York City than people are freaking aware of, man. There's something substantial here. The East River's the negative and that's the positive over that side.

In New York, I think that the energy that we're referrin' to, ideally to me, are souls. I know that they're souls.

So there's all these souls that are tryin' to reach out. And not for anyone in particular, but mostly to grasp an understanding, almost like what I'm going through is stuff that they're goin' through. You know what I mean? It's like why, why, why, why, you know?

And there's gotta be an answer, 'cause we're here, so there's gotta be a reason to that why.

I can almost see somebody waitin' for me, and probably has been waiting for me . . . to say somethin' to me, like mention somethin' to me, like, "Oh, Mike, it's okay." Like, yo, you wasn't all zany.

ONE TIME I JUMPED off the roof, it was in South Bronx on Wales Avenue. Another time it was on the Grand Concourse. Another time was on Marcy Place. And another time was on 171st Street.

I did it. I jumped.

What I feel is time diminishing, you know what I mean. This was my technique: just go, bend my legs. And my tush hits the ground too. My feet be in pain, though, like throbbing, pulsing, *boom, boom, boom, boom.*

I thought the first time I did it: it's a wrap, it's a done deal, you know what I mean? I hit the ground and I'm lookin' around. I hit the ground and thought I was dead and shit. I was like, *Is this what hell looks like?* This is no fuckin' different from what I just left.

It's the Bronx.

I had to really pay attention. I'm hearing people talkin'. This guy's, "Are you alright?" I was like, "What are you talkin' about, dude? Isn't this, like, the spiritual world and shit?"

This was Wales Avenue in the South Bronx. Where the old Lincoln Hospital used to be, like three blocks away from there. I was leaning like *this* off the roof, I had got half my feet out, and I said, *That's it. I'm going down.*

There's no way in the world you're going to go straight down like that and not wobble. I was wobbling, that's for sure. Maybe two or three moments prior to hitting the ground, I was like, "I better straighten out because I'm not going to look too good if I hit the ground with all this wobbling and shit, you know? I'm going to look really fucked up." So that's when I tried to pull myself, keep myself together. And something told me, as soon as I hit that floor, it said, "Bend your knees, go down, because if not, your bones' going to shoot right out your knee-caps." So when I hit the ground, I'm going down, and my butt hits the ground.

But when I did that, that shit is like, *boom,* and my butt hit the floor. Wales Avenue.

It didn't even seem like my organs were necessary, you know what I mean? Well, if you're not going to be on this earth, what the hell do you need that for? That was the kind of thought that went through my mind. I won't need a brain maybe. I won't need a heart, lungs and stuff, bones or anything. So what am I going to be? Like Jell-O or some shit?

I don't think anybody in his right mind is going to be trying to analyze what the fuck he's feeling on the way down from the roof.

At my last point, I'm trying to analyze the last of my moments here on earth, I'm just like, what am I? Am I mashed potatoes and shit at the end?

I was like, "Is this heaven or hell?" I'm thinking it's heaven because I'm hearing people and they seem concerned and shit. Wow, people are this uptight here in heaven? This is a bummer, man.

I saw somebody standing there and he's singing something and it's like, you know, my reasoning is not all there yet, you know? I didn't even think I was alive. So my thought process wasn't all clear, you know? And I was like, "Wow, the transition was so quick too." Because I thought, damn, there's a transitional state that you're dead, you're in a box, and then you go to some other thing. But this shit was so instantaneous.

It was like a flash. I wanted some time off, you know what I mean? I wanted a break.

I wanted to go up and examine this guy. Where's your feathers and your wings and stuff, you know? I'm like really freaking out. Like damn, I said, "Hopefully, I'm not in the other spot where I'm thinking I *should* be." So I don't see the wings and I'm like, "Oh, shit, could this be hell?"

But I'm seeing angels walking into the store and buying groceries. And I'm like, "What the hell? What kind of currency do they use?" That's what's going on in my head. And I'm trying to figure out am I alive? In my mind, I was dead. I was a dead dude.

I was thinking, *Heaven looks like the South Bronx.* Yeah, I swear to

God that's what I thought. I'm stamping the concrete. I was like, "Wow, this is heaven? They got concrete on the ground in heaven?"

Everything I'm seeing is freaking heaven to me, you know what I mean?

This *could* be freaking heaven. I'm almost dead set on the idea, you know what I mean? We're here. There's no getting out of this. And if you're thinking you're going to go to fucking Coney Island and get on some merry-go-round and be off this mortal coil, good luck, dude, you know? Because I don't think that shit is going to happen.

Everybody's around me and I'm like, "This is heaven? Holy shit. This look like my fucking neighborhood."

MICHAEL DOS SANTOS A singer

I've been singing since I was fourteen. I was in school and I won a talent contest. I was in India at that time and this big band asked me if I would sing. So I started singing. I've been singing since. But then when I came to New York, things are not really as you expect them to be. So I stopped singing for a really long time.

And then when I settled and I was back on my feet again, I decided maybe I should sing at least in the nursing homes. That's how I started singing in New York. Now I've been in the nursing homes for fifteen years. Then, you know, people come to the nursing home and then they say, "Oh, you know, we go to this restaurant, they have entertainment, why don't you come?" And that's how it started.

My mother's a singer. She used to be the Ella Fitzgerald of India once upon a time. She's got that deep, husky kind of voice. When I was a little boy I used to go and see her singing, so I know all the songs from then. You know, "The Man I Love," "Embraceable You," this kind of stuff she would do. At that time, in Bombay, Western music was a big thing in hotels. Every hotel had a band. But now I think it's changed. I haven't been back in . . . too long.

Anyway, that's how I started.

I used to work in this bagel place, sixteen hours, sleep eight hours, sixteen hours, sleep eight hours, sixteen hours, sleep eight hours. So there was no such thing as entertainment or anything because I was trying to save up. Just work-sleep, work-sleep, work-sleep, work-sleep, work-sleep . . . I used to bake all night and then I used to work at the register in the day then go home, sleep eight hours, and come back again.

Everybody kept saying, you know you should buy, you should buy, don't rent, don't rent, don't rent, so I was set on buying an apartment. You meet a lot of people in New York that are willing to tell you what to do and how to do it, you know.

My mother made friends with this Italian woman that lived in Flushing, and her father was in a nursing home. She said, "You know we have entertainers coming to the nursing home, you can at least sing in the nursing home." That's how it started.

I wore a suit, just a regular suit. It was in the afternoon and I was accepted almost instantly. It's kind of nice because for Grandparents' Day and for Father's Day and for Mother's Day they ask the patients, who do you want? And all the time it's "We want Michael."

I was there last night. I am there the last Sunday of every month. I just take them back in time, I am sure they must remember where they were when the song played, what they did.

A lot of people say I sound a lot like Elvis Presley. If I sang an Elvis song, they would say, "Wow, you sound just like him," but I don't think so. I've never tried to imitate. I won't even sing the arrangement they sing. I will just try to do it the way I want to sing it.

My mother still comes and sings with me. She still comes and always pulls the house down. She has an exceptional voice. She's eighty but you would never say she's a day past fifty. She's got this energy and drive that I hope I have when I'm her age.

At the restaurant most of the people that come back are regulars. They tell them and they tell them, and they tell. That's why I'm not on the internet, I'm nowhere. It's all word of mouth, my whole crowd is word of mouth. I can call people and say, "Oh, I'm gonna be at this place," and I know sixty to a hundred people will show up, which is cool.

Now I sing at this hospice at Roosevelt Island. Nobody comes to see them, some of them are one hundred years old. Nobody. I go and I sing "Happy Birthday," and you know, it's sad. Can you imagine, you live your whole life and end up with nothing? In fact, when I first sang at this hospice in Roosevelt Island, for three days I was just so depressed. I couldn't stop thinking of it. Because they were all in there, they couldn't even get up, they were all wheeled in their beds, into the room. The hospice is very depressing.

Then I was singing, and I could see them, while they were laying down and listening, their fingers would move and they would smile, so there was a connection, I made a connection. But I was so depressed when I saw them. I said, "I can't do this." But then I thought to myself, maybe I could bring them some joy.

You're told when to eat, you're told when to go down, you're told when to go up, you're told when to sleep. And nobody really has time for them.

I have so many friends who think I'm crazy. If it's a beautiful Sunday afternoon, they'll say, "What's wrong with you? Let's go here, or let's go there." But I know I'd rather go to the nursing home. I like to make people happy.

I go there at two o'clock, but at nine-thirty, ten o'clock in the morning, I'm told they're all dressed and waiting downstairs. Someone tells them, "Michael's coming today, Michael's coming today, Michael's coming today."

No money could buy that.

I SAW FRANK SINATRA LIVE. Oh, he was great. I mean, he wasn't up to par, 'cause it was his last concert at Madison Square Garden, and he was drunk, he was forgetting the words, he was just like muttering stuff, but it was Frank Sinatra.

Madison Square Garden, his last concert. You know, he was singing "New York, New York," and he was like, *blah blah blah*. That's what he was doing. You could see the teleprompter with the words, going up, the words of the song. It was disappointing, but he was with his cigarette and his glass, and it was Frank Sinatra. And sold out. $250 a ticket. That was the last time he ever sang "New York, New York." That was it. "My Way," he was mumbling. Losing it, between that and the whiskey.

I like Liza Minnelli's version the best of all. I love her singing "New York, New York." She puts so much emotion into New York. But I think I do a pretty good job. Because I love New York. It's like I'm singing about her. I sing it at the nursing homes. Everybody wakes up, everybody wakes up. And then when I'm leaving it's like a garden and I've just sprayed water and all the flowers have come up.

And they love to sing along to "My Way." Even though I don't really like to sing that song in the nursing home, because it's like, "the end is near." But they love it. What can you do?

I almost feel guilty, you know, just singing "the end is near" to a bunch of people for whom . . . the end is near. Some of them are bedridden. Some of them are hooked up to IV. Some of them are in wheelchairs. Some of them are just lost, but when "My Way" comes, they all remember.

And I keep saying, "I must not sing this in a nursing home, I must not sing this." But they'll ask for it. It's like, they know that that's gonna be the last song. If I don't sing that song, they don't know I'm done. My last song is always "My Way." And you know, they put all their energy in. Yeah, it's sad. "We're in a wheelchair. But we still did it our way."

They're feisty, some of them. Even at this age. That's the one thing, I don't think they say die 'till they're dead. In New York, they keep on going.

The End of the Journey

CODA

A Last Sunday
on the Street

A FEW YEARS HAD PASSED. My visa was coming up. As much as I wanted to keep riding the subway, I knew I'd have to leave New York. I'd met hundreds of people in the city. Most had said their piece and continued with their lives. But I was implicated in the lives of others. Joe still came to stay with me most Sundays, and on one of them I asked him how it would feel to finally say goodbye to New York.

"Like a breath of air," he said, "or unloading a pack. Taking your pack off like you're finally where you're gonna be for about a week, or at least a couple days."

He reconsidered his answer.

"Look, when I get off that bus, when I go home, in Pittsburgh, it's like . . . I breathe in. I do all that crazy stuff like in the movies. Every time."

I asked him, "Are there moments in New York when it's okay? When you kind of enjoy it here?"

"No."

"Not even when you're swimming in the river or something?"

"I would go back to Pittsburgh when I was in the East River."

"What do you mean?"

"I'd think, *Man, remember this?* I would liken it to when I'd be in the Allegheny. You know?"

"Where were you?"

"There's a bridge that goes across the FDR. You're coming from Avenue D out to the FDR, you walk up the steps, over the bridge. You come down, there's a couple ballparks there, go through the ballpark. There's a road where they bicycle and walk and picnic," he said. "They thought I was an oddity. *What's he doing?* I guess some of them thought I was committing suicide. I didn't care what they thought. I was having fun."

"You're out in the East River," I said. "But it feels like . . ."

"No. It didn't feel like . . . *in here* it felt like it," he said. "I'm thinking, *Man, remember when you was a kid, all the fun you had?* I look at the shore. I don't know no one."

"I feel like this city is a magnifier of the problem, you know?" I said.

"Yeah, agreed," he replied. "I don't live. I *exist*."

"Then when is it time for both of us to leave New York?"

"When is it time? Craig, listen to what you just asked me. I don't call those shots. You have to go to your mountains."

"I know when the time is for me to leave, but I have a love-hate relationship with this city. I think you have a hate-hate relationship with this city."

"Okay, I'll go for that."

"So, why am I the one who is going to leave?"

"Because you're living your life, Craig. My life's over. Every time I say that you say, *ahh*. You don't want to believe anything I say."

"I believe it all but I just don't believe that one thing."

AND THEN ONE DAY he finally broke. I saw Joe's anger. I stood at the front door of my apartment. Joe was taking forever. Since I was going to give up the place soon, I'd already escorted one of his bags down to the basement, and now I was trying to get him out the door. The negotiation continued. I told him he could keep one stack of clothes at the apartment.

"It's 11:30," I said, again and again. And I hoisted one of his other bags, the Wilson bag, onto the top of his cart, and then I started clicking my fingers. That was all it took. Anger *is* like a blossom. When it rose in him, it brought him up to standing posture. It straightened his spine. Mine too. I'd been worn down by those bags, but now my generosity was gone. I was so tired of being the steward of the bags—and maybe I was the one who first said *fuck*, maybe I broke the barrier. We hadn't ever sworn around each other, but soon Joe was looking straight at me.

"Don't you fucking snap at me," he said. "Don't you fucking invite me into your place to treat me like an animal."

His lip curled, and I saw the anger was finally pure and unadulterated, it was survival anger. He finally got his luggage through the door, with the Wilson bag slung around him, some other bag hanging off the cart, and even though he was angry, I had to hold the door of the elevator. When we walked out onto the sidewalk, he wanted me to go ahead.

"I thought you had somewhere to *be* at 11:30," he said.

So I walked ahead, pretended to hustle to my appointment, crossed the snow-covered scrap of a park, and then I waited to see if he'd walk away. I doubled back, crossed over Grand Street. Joe was in the distance, bent over, walking the other way, toward the Williamsburg Bridge, toward the underpass, pushing his cart, but when I returned to the building I saw he'd stashed his bags by the door. I let out a groan—a year's worth of frustration. I would never be free of these bags. I couldn't leave them in the lobby. I picked them up and threw them into the elevator and brought them back into the apartment, plus the ground sheet and his sleeping bag. Snow was expected for Saturday, but I couldn't care any longer. It had to end.

I thought of our anger, finally let loose, two tempers we'd kept hidden for so long, me in the doorway, petty, waspish, snapping my fingers, my patience and empathy drained, my bag on my back, packed for no good reason, a prop to get him out. And Joe exuding some of this volcanic anger against authority because finally I'd become the authority. At the very least it would give him something to draw on, wherever he'd be tonight. I wished myself home, out of New York, walking home along unpaved roads, I wanted to breathe fresh air. I wanted to admit to this place that I knew nothing of it. I wanted quiet. I wanted to get away from those who lined up their cars along Willett, anxious to get to Grand, anxious to get to Clinton, anxious to get on the Williamsburg Bridge, always anxious.

I kept his bags. New York is a city of implication. The essence of New York is that most people here will pass you on a sidewalk, like Sixth Avenue, without acknowledgment. Others remain linked to you. I remembered how once, one Sunday soon after meeting Joe, he had said he had something to give to me. He'd gone digging into his bag and retrieved a big packet of egg noodles, which he held out to me, and

New Yorkers

smiled. I thanked him. I took the noodles and put them, carefully, in my bag. I wondered what I could give him in return. "Maybe I could tell you about what I've been getting up to as I listen to people talk about their own New Yorks," I said.

"I'd like that," Joe said.

So I had told Joe about walking out onto the Panorama of New York City, a floating consciousness over the city, and watching the curator shuffle in her paper booties up the river; how I had to gently step over the Williamsburg and the Queensboro bridges. I'd told him about stepping onto the top of an elevator car with a repairman and ascending a dark elevator shaft in the heart of a building near Madison Square Park, clutching a cable, aware of the dropping counterweight nearby, before coming to rest behind one of the unopened doors where I could hear the conversation of office workers on the other side, like I was inside a secret New York. I'd told him about visiting the quiet Upper East Side apartment of an elderly woman who didn't have a computer, or a TV, and instead gently spread the *New York Times* open on her dining room table and read it cover to cover each morning, like an ancient ritual. I'd told Joe about the subway dancer who'd stood on Clinton Street and performed shoe tricks, forcing his Adidas to bounce up off the sidewalk.

Joe had asked what some of these people looked like, and often it wasn't their faces but their gestures I remembered: the way a medical student waved her hands in the air when she described Staten Island pizza, or the way a Statue of Liberty security guard pointed at the statue from his bench in Battery Park as he described seeing it from all angles. He told me about the light dusting of snow on her shoulders in the winter.

I'd told him how I wanted to set down the words of New Yorkers who'd become important to me over the years, the thumbprints of those who'd made a mark on my own New York. We agreed that they'd soon be smeared, covered, gone—we'd all disappear, the city would flow on. *The speed of the river is the speed of the river.* But I wanted something at the end of my time, just as every New Yorker wanted something, like the Broadway stagehand at the Playwright Tavern who told me about his life as a cabbie as the music got louder and he was interrupted by other stagehands wishing him well in his new life in Florida. They reached out to clasp his hand. He turned back to me and said, "Let me tell you what you're going to need to know."

I had told Joe about my New York to prove I was alive here, that I wasn't lost, and that something could emerge from all this. I'd told him about when I'd doubted myself, or felt that maybe these people weren't extraordinary. Joe was proof they were—he'd laugh or say, "Can you believe that?" Or even just shake his head. "Weird people," Joe said to me, "try to talk to me on the street."

"I think I am one of those people," I replied.

New York burned and stung. It was a paint stripper; it was the great revealer with a complex cell structure. It dominated conversation. It was the power. It was the stage. It was a contained world. There might be territory outside its limits, but what lay beyond the panorama looked so dusty and unappealing. All of life was here. All pleasures. Even the afterlife, Michael Rodriguez had told me, might look like the Bronx.

Over the course of our Sundays together, I'd told Joe what I loved about this place; I pleaded New York's case. I wanted him to see what I saw: the connection. Both he and New York survived. They both showed an unexplainable resilience. Despite his own feelings for the place, his suspicions, his pain, Joe had sat across from me at the little table in my kitchen as I said all this. He might not have agreed. He might not have bought what I was selling.

But he had listened to me.

ABOUT A YEAR LATER I was back in New York. I came back to the Welcome Table on an afternoon when the Pride parade had taken over the streets. My usual route was blocked, and I had to take a winding path through crowds and streamers to get to 16th Street. I had to push past people in novelty sunglasses. The air smelled of sunscreen. At one point, I felt the brush of feather wings against my cheek as a costumed figure passed. When I descended into the basement to the Welcome Table the scene was the same: the clatter, the lineup, the roar, the loaves of day-old bread, and even someone pounding tunelessly on the piano. Elliott stood outside with a bag full of cans. Ralph dispensed tickets.

I spotted Joe from a distance. He was sitting at his usual table. He stuck his fork into a scoop of mashed potatoes and when he lifted his head he noticed me and nearly smiled. He jabbed a thumb my way and shook his head. Either he couldn't believe it, or my return was inevitable. His hair was Parris Island short.

"I was told," he said as I approached, "you'd be here. Do you believe that?"

"I believe that."

After the meal, we sat on a bench in front of the café on Sixth Avenue. Trumpets sounded from somewhere, amplified beats drifted in. I'd failed to stay objective, but I'd also failed to get involved enough. You can't lift someone out of New York. You can't save someone from New York, shield someone from its force. I couldn't even rent that car to get him to Pittsburgh. Any attempt to shield a person from the forces here was laughable.

"It's good to see you, buddy," Joe said.

"It's good to see you."

He turned to me and opened his eyes wide.

"I had my eyes looked at," he said.

"You did?'

"Yes, I can read again. I got that done," he said. "Do you believe that?"

"I don't have to believe that if it's what happened. The proof is you can read. You can see."

He nodded.

"You read at night?"

"I read at night."

It was a good day to be out there in the midst of Pride. We leased some of the passing joy, the vitality, and felt the sunshine, and after a while we didn't have to say much. We were in the noise, under the roar of New York. I wasn't recording anything for posterity. I reached over and, for a moment, rested my hand on Joe's tanned and wrinkled neck. He patted my knee.

Acknowledgments

Thank you to each of the interviewees who took the time to tell me about their own New York.

Thanks also to:

Sarah Larson, Liz Clayton, Estee Pierce, Marc Gilman, Deirdre Dolan, Roger Burlingame, Saoirse Burlingame, Remony Burlingame, Jamie Brisick, Maxyne Franklin, Jon Elek, Jenny Lord, Anna Orchard, Daniel Tatarsky, Lauren Wool, Chris Lochery, Molly Murray, Jakob von Baeyer, Phillip Oltermann, Muriel Fox, Jess Kim, Eleanor Birne, Logan Werschky, Lottie Moggach, Deborah Moggach, Leanne Shapton, Richard McGuire, Paul Ewen, Zainab Juma, Nathan Schneider, Claire Kelley, Thuy Nguyen, Tamara Lecker, Lindsey Crecco, Megan Wakely, Matt Anderson, Erin Hallett, Jana Prikryl, Emily Campbell, Angela Hyland, Michael Kissinger, Paul Bangah, Leslie Day, Flora Biddle, Hephzibah Anderson, Damian Bradfield, Joel Lovell, Paul Tough, Adam Sternbergh, Hattie Crisell, Trina Hamlin, Ann Fleuchaus, Amity Paye, Mohammad Khan, Marci DeLozier Haas, Jennifer Kabat, Liz Jurey, Eugenia Bell, Anna Kelly, Brendan Dolan, Ashley Thomas, Gordon Cameron, DJ Alperowitz, Sasha Koren, Chris Garrecht-Williams, Jessica Johnson, Marianne LeNabat, Jimmy Jacobson, Samantha Majic, John Rasmussen, Vince Caro, David Essig, Chloe Pantazi, Tasleema Mohamed, Joan Dolan, Andrea Kremer, Roberta Leone, Sara Neufeld, Lisa Fernandes, Sheila Heti, Jessica Jackson, Efrat Kussell, Malcolm Addey, Sara Batmanglich, Pat Addiss, Margaux Williamson, Anna Polonsky, Julia Dault, Brian Sholis, Eduardo Gil, Erik Hinton, Beverly Joel, Des Yankson, Danielle Mattoon, Joanna Prior, Josephine Greywoode, Fred Hutchins, Fred Street, Sandra Contreras, Thora Howell, Louise Hamilton, John K Samson, Alice Twemlow, Molly Heintz, Eric Schwartau, Kathryn Tucker, Kevin Baker, Marla Joel, Lynn Nunes,

Meredith Kolodner, Peter Krashes, Rachel Cohen, Jimmy Roussounis, Sukhdev Sandhu, Gail Armstrong, Elizabeth Greenwood, Corey Brothers, Aaron Linn, Tony Moran, Harry Smolin, Alison Smolin, Wai Wong, Frances Dodds, Veronica Nizama, Fadila Diaz, Yurany Arboleda, Kathy Pappas, Sylvie Barthelemy, Beverly Torres, Jesus Andaluz, Walter Walker, Paul Woolmington, Sarah Deutsch, Dragan Jovanovic, Jessica Ramos, Mario Gooden, Eon John, Jess Gibson, Rosalind Porter, Tyree Browning, Hugo Aleman, Stacey Sutton, Elena Goldstein, Albert Cruz, Krink, Ed DeFreitas, Karley Sciortino, Elianny Salcedo, Brett Saarela, Kerry Carnahan, Freddy Molano, Hermann Mendez, Nena Mendez, Natalia Mendez, Leah Kelly, Maria Helena Aleman, Dennis Mykytyn, Maria Brinkmann, Michael Costello, Donna Chiu, Peter Gee, Jessica Key, Samuel Colbert, Michael Schmelling, Shaira Kunhardt-Valerio, Coss Marte, Ronald Richter, Danielle Cunningham, Chance Krempasky, Estee Levitt, Una Perkins, Bobbie Sackman, Chloe Kernaghan, Heather Gregory, Sally Mara Sturman, Alex Villani, Kate Porterfield, Liliam Barrios-Paoli, Gail Armstrong, Helen Rosenthal, Josh Brown, Jeffrey Lewis, Jim Meehan, David Giffen, Key Key Foster, Sarah Corsie, Bailey Huguley and Jadrien Ellison at The Door, Ashok Kondabalu, Bronwyn Fleming-Jones, Carol Lim, Chris Marte, Josh Rubin, Mike McCann, David Selig, JoJo Annobil, Deborah Stewart, Carol Matthews, Devorah Nivitsky, Jennifer Diaz, Skott Taylor, Alexandra Taylor, Ellen Baxter, Josh Scannell, Khalid Latif, Kamal Manilla, Emily Skeggs, Evin Robinson, Frank Wainwright, Steven Polan, Klara Klinyanskava, Mark Katz, Rich Derby, Sabrina Husband, Shabazz Ali, Steven Maglio, Tickets, Tony Canolino, Tyrone Curry, Vicky Virgin, Meredith Urben, Paul Bardo, Gavin Covey, Ginger Williams, Willie Rashbaum, Michael Korosty, Greg Green, Jamie Saltsman, Joanna Andreasson, Merle Lister, Amber Gregory, Mike Treglia, Jay Mitchell, Marlena Fontes, Lewanne Jones, Robbie Roth, Kim Temple, Lado Pochkhua, Javier Castaño, and Sarah Lyall, for the countless leads and the wise advice.

Acknowledgments

In memory of Lorena Borjas, Lee Gelber, Dean Allen, and Jacqueline Pettie-Lucas.

Portions of this book have previously appeared in the *Guardian*. Thanks to Ruth Spencer, Lee Glendinning, and Kath Viner.

Thanks to Simon Prosser, Hermione Thompson, Hannah Chukwu, Amandeep Singh, Remi Graves, and Jay Bernard.

At the Wylie Agency, thanks to Tracy Bohan, Sarah Chalfant, Andrew Wylie, Rebecca Nagel, Jennifer Bernstein, and Dorothy Janick.

Thank you to Joe Zigmond, Caroline Westmore, and the rest of the John Murray team, including David Marshall, and also Melanie Tutino and Amy Black at Doubleday.

Thanks to Rebecca Homiski, Don Rifkin, Beth Steidle, Ingsu Liu, Elisabeth Kerr, Zarina Patwa, Lily Gellman, and the rest of the Norton staff. This book exists only because of the patience of my editor, Matt Weiland, who saw this project through from conception to publication and once again faced down more than a million words of recorded voice with good humor, compassion, and miraculous editorial skill.

Thanks to my mother and father, who both made cameos, and to Mayita Mendez. *Gracias por compartir Nueva York conmigo.*

Index